From the Holocaust
to *Hogan's Heroes*

From the Holocaust to *Hogan's Heroes*

The Autobiography of Robert Clary

Robert Clary

TAYLOR TRADE PUBLISHING
Lanham • New York • Boulder • Toronto • Plymouth, UK

Published by Taylor Trade Publishing
An imprint of The Rowman & Littlefield Publishing Group, Inc.
4501 Forbes Boulevard, Suite 200, Lanham, Maryland 20706
www.rlpgtrade.com

Estover Road, Plymouth PL6 7PY, United Kingdom
Distributed by NATIONAL BOOK NETWORK

**The hardback edition of this book was previously cataloged by the Library of
Congress as follows:**

Clary, Robert
   From the Holocaust to Hogan's Heroes : the autobiography of Robert Clary /
Robert Clary.
      p.   cm.
   1. Clary, Robert.   2. Actors—United States—Biography.   I. Title.

PN2287.C5447 A3   2001
792'028'092—dc21   2001049206

ISBN-13: 978-1-58979-345-3 (pbk : alk. paper)
ISBN-10: 1-58979-345-5 (pbk : alk. paper)

♾ ™ The paper used in this publication meets the minimum requirements of
American National Standard for Information Sciences—Permanence of Paper for
Printed Library Materials, ANSI/NISO Z39.48-1992.

Manufactured in the United States of America.

Contents

Acknowledgments

I want to thank the following:

- The late Ronny Graham, without whom this book would never have been written. He kept asking me questions—as early as 1952, when we appeared together in *New Faces of 1952*—about my youth, my years in concentration camps, my surviving that dark period, and urged me to write it down.
- My friend Robert Bassing, who helped me tremendously to put this book together and corrected all my grammatical errors.
- My nephew, Brian Gari, who read the finished script and told me he would find me a publisher, and, thanks to his tenacity, did.
- And last, but far from least, my wife Natalie, who always encouraged me with every enterprise I tackled.

This book is dedicated to my parents, who brought me into this wonderful imperfect world.

From the Holocaust
to *Hogan's Heroes*

CHAPTER ONE

GEFILTE FISH ON THE RUE DES DEUX PONTS

I have a photograph of my parents taken in 1929 when I was three years old. In that picture, they appeared to be absolutely mad at the world, when actually they were furious with me. Not wanting to be photographed, all I did was cry my eyes out. I didn't want to face that frightening man with the piece of black velvet draped over his head. My, how I have changed. Mention picture call to me and I'm the first one ready with a big smile. Moishe and Baila look quite handsome, he standing straight with his right hand holding the back of the chair where my mother was sitting. Her brown hair simply coiffed, her eyes clear and blue, projecting tenderness. I have inherited her nose, which is short but wide at the base, and her full lips. My father at that time had a trim Vandyke beard. He always managed to be well dressed. He was slim and of medium height, with straight dark hair, getting grey at the temples, deep brown eyes that could make you tremble with fear when he was cross, and a slightly aquiline nose.

My father was an orthodox Jew. On Friday evening before sundown, he would stop working, bathe, put on clean clothes, and go to the synagogue on the Rue de Pavée, very close by. My mother would prepare the dinner—gefilte fish, chicken soup, and all the marvelous foods orthodox Jews have on the Sabbath. Nobody in our household would work on Saturday or touch the electricity or gas. It was a day of rest. My parents would walk, because they couldn't use transporta-

1

tion, to visit my brothers and sisters who were married. That was their Saturday. Then my father would go back to work on Sunday.

We lived in Paris on l'Ile St. Louis, in a small apartment on 10 Rue des Deux Ponts. It looked immense when I was a kid, but it was ridiculously tiny. There was a small narrow entry hall, a kitchen, a dining room, two bedrooms, and a toilet. Three sewing machines were in our kitchen near the window where the sunlight came through in the afternoon. We had a large armoire, painted ivory, with a top glassed-in cupboard that held the plates and eating utensils; in the bottom cupboard, we kept fresh, delicious bread and all the canned goods and produce. Next to the big stove, which was fed with black charcoal and small pieces of wood and was used in winter, we had a two-burner gas plate on the sink counter. We washed up at the kitchen sink. On Friday evening before sundown, my mother, against my will, would bathe me there. Later on I was sent once a week to the Bains-Douches, a public bathhouse on the first floor right under our apartment.

There were five girls living at home. Ida and Aimée, the two oldest, shared a couch in the dining room. Hélene, Cécile, Madeleine, and I slept in one of the two bedrooms, except in the winter when my folded bed was moved into the kitchen near the stove. Hanging in our bedroom was an enlarged photograph of my grandparents on my father's side. They looked directly into the camera when the picture was taken, so no matter which part of the room you were in, their eyes stared at you. Having your picture taken in those days was a serious business. That's probably why they looked so severe. My grandmother was wearing a terrible wig under a flowered hat. It was required by orthodox law that, when she got married, she shave her head so as not to entice other men. She had a glass eye, and the real eye was glaring at me.

That photograph scared me to death. Because I was the youngest, I would always be the first one to go to bed, and there I would be alone in the dark room, knowing my grandmother was staring at me with her one good eye, and fearing that she was going to come out of the photograph, suddenly alive, grab me and take me with her to wherever she was. I used to sleep with the covers completely over me, except for my nose and my mouth, so I could breathe. I slept like that for quite a few years, even when I wasn't sleeping in that room any-more. My grandfather didn't look too bad, with a *yarmulke* on his head, and a greyish beard. He looked rather nice, but not smiling.

For years I didn't know where my grandparents were born. My real name is Widerman (pronounced Veederman). It sounded very German to me, and I had always assumed that my ancestors came from Germany. But my half-brother Henri straightened me out. He said, "Your grandparents were born in Poland, and so were your great grandparents." My mother also had a German-sounding name, Stul-man. She was born in 1886, either in Radom, Przyszk, or Pizytyh. None of my family knows for sure. Her father was a wine merchant in Warsaw. Her mother, who sold eggs in a market in the suburbs of Warsaw, was mean and stingy and would never give her anything. My mother became engaged to a man who went to the United States with-out marrying her. Feeling rejected by her family, she married my father when she was eighteen, fifteen years his junior, and suddenly found herself the mother of his many children, some of them only a few years younger than she.

Until 1978, I always thought I was the thirteenth and last of my father's children. That year, when I was in Paris, I talked to my father's only sister, Aunt Saresta, who was eighty-eight years old but still sharp and lucid. I asked her, "How many children did my father have? Didn't he have five with his first wife and eight with my mother?"

"No," she said. "He had *eight* children with his first wife, who died giving birth to the last child, a girl, who shortly thereafter died of typhus. Two others had died, two stayed in Poland, and three went to live in Paris. With your mother, he had another eight children. Between your sister Aimée and your sister Hélène, there was a boy, Bernard, who died when he was very young." So according to my aunt, I am the sixteenth instead of the thirteenth child. Eventually I was told the truth. I am the fourteenth child, not the thirteenth or the sixteenth.

My father was the second oldest of five children and was born in 1870 in Nadzhin, Poland. In 1913, already married to my mother and with a big family to support, he found out he was no longer able to make a living. He decided to go to Argentina with his younger brother Yankef, in the hope he could have a better life there. In those days, it was customary for men to go by themselves, leaving their wives with all the children. Goodbye, take care—I'll send for you. They stayed in Argentina for only a few months. Unable to find work, they returned to Poland.

In Paris in 1918, the last year of World War I, my father's oldest brother had been electrocuted with his whole family in the subway during an air raid. Three years later the French government contacted my grandfather to notify him of his son's death. Bureaucracy is the same everywhere: slow and incompetent. My grandfather, thinking his son might have left a will, sent my father to investigate. Again, uncle Yankef went with him. They found no will, but they stayed with an old friend from Poland who had his own restaurant in Paris, on the corner of the Rue des Ecouffes and the Rue des Rosiers, in the Jewish ghetto. It took my father two years to make up his mind that the family should live in Paris. In 1923, he sent for my mother, who schlepped Ida, Aimée, Hélène, and one-year-old Cécile all the way from Warsaw. Jacques and my father's children by his first marriage, Henri, Adèle, and Fanny, stayed in Warsaw a while longer before joining the rest of the family. Sarah and Régine never emigrated to France.

In Poland, my father for a while had run a butcher shop (selling tripe) that my half-brother Henri brought back from the *abbatoires* (slaughterhouse). But for as long as I knew him, the first sixteen years of my life, he was a tailor. He made pants. For some time, when I was very young, on Sundays he would go with my mother to sell suits at the *marché aux puces* (the flea market). I was the best-dressed kid in the whole apartment house. He would make me at least three suits a year. I have inherited his neatness. He had an armoire in our little bedroom. *His* armoire in *our* bedroom, along with the terrifying picture of his parents, and when you opened the armoire, there were suits, always very clean and lined up precisely the same way each time. And his ties were put exactly the way I have mine in my closet today— *exactly!* Only recently have I identified strongly with him. I had very little rapport with him when I was a child. My sisters and I always found him to be strict, often short of patience, and at times very cold. He had behind his sewing machine a *martinet,* a cat o' nine tails. He never hit us with it; it was just there to threaten and scare us and make us behave. We were devils. We would cut the strips off, until nothing was left except the wooden handle. He never replaced that *martinet.*

In his later years, my father developed a sweet tooth. He had to have his little candies, at least three or four times a day, and *we* could not have any—they were *his* candies. Imagine when you're a child not to share candies! He kept them in his bedroom, and we all knew where they were. Every day I would steal one candy and put the tin box back where it was hidden, thinking, "He's not counting them; I'm sure he'll never miss that candy." But suddenly there were a lot of candies missing. He exploded. "Who's the thief? Come on, who did it? Who took my candies?" Nobody answered. Everybody knew I was the guilty one. Even my father knew that. Still, he accused all of us, and I never confessed.

My father couldn't stand noise at mealtime. There was a huge rectangular wooden table in the middle of the kitchen where we all sat, eating, talking, and laughing loudly. I was always the first one to finish, gulping my food, getting scolded by my mother telling me to "take it easy, the house is not on fire." I would be drenched with perspiration after swallowing the hot chicken soup with homemade noodles. I couldn't wait to get the fresh fruit for dessert. In late spring, we always counted the cherries we were given. My mother would manage to slip a few more onto my plate without starting a revolution. Sometimes the commotion during meals bothered my father so much, he would reprimand us and take his plate to his sewing machine, just two steps away from the table. It was his way of telling us to shut up.

But he was proud of us. Whenever I sang and danced, greatly encouraged by my family, by their applause and kisses, I would say, "Kalla, kalla," my word for orange. I was only three. My father was the one who always gave me my "kalla."

I was very good at drawing, and though my father never let me know it, he would take my drawings and show them to everybody—family, friends, even complete strangers. "My son, the *artiste,* did this—how about that! And he's only six." I wasn't aware of this, but people would tell me later. He would never say directly to me, "Reevela, that's great what you did, that's marvelous, don't stop."

Never. In school, at promotion, the pupil with the highest mark would get, along with his diploma, a big red, beautifully bound book. Each time my sister Madeleine and I received this honor (which was rather often), my father would take us with the books to our married sisters and brothers, to let them see our prizes. That was how we found out he cared. It never occured to us to take our books around.

My father would speak to us only in Yiddish, except when he didn't want us to know what he was saying. Then he would speak to my mother in Polish. We would, naturally, object—in French. There was a rabbi who used to come to our apartment twice a week, like a psychiatrist, to give counsel. He was a short, portly man, with a long black beard and *payis,* who always wore a black shiny overcoat. He had the sweetness and patience of an angel. He would stay in our apartment from noon until six in the evening, and people in the neighborhood would come to him for advice. I liked his being there, and when I came home from school, I would rush in to the dining room to see him. He would put his hand on my head, asking me if I had been a good boy today, bless me, and then give me five *sous.* The moment I got the money, I was out the door and on my way to the candy store. He never had a chance to give me advice.

When I was about ten, my father was taken to the hospital for hemorrhoid surgery. There was a huge void at home. He wasn't there, and he was missed. My sisters Hélène and Cécile, who worked with him, continued to make pants. My father stayed in the hospital for what seemed a long time. I went to visit him in a big ward with lots of beds. The hospital, l'Hôtel Dieu on l'Ile de la Cité, was very close to where we lived, a step away from the Cathedral Nôtre Dame. It felt strange to see him lying helpless in a hospital bed. I had never seen him sick before. After saying hello and asking how he was, I had nothing else to say to him and couldn't wait to leave and go and play with my friends.

My father loved classical music. When we had our first and only radio in the mid-1930s, when we let him, he would listen to operas. We would scream at him, "Come on! Change the station!" All we wanted was popular music. Opera bored us. Sometimes, he would take me to the Theatre du Chatelet, where they put on big spectacular operettas. We would go up to the last balcony, the cheapest seats he could buy. I was in awe. The songs, the dances, the costumes, the scenery, the glamour of it all enthralled me, and the first time we went I knew at that moment it was what I wanted to do for the rest of my life. My father never took any of my sisters to the theater. I was the only one who ever went with him.

In 1937, when the World's Fair had opened in Paris, my father one day said, "Reevela, get dressed, you and I are going to visit the world's fair today!" I was delighted. For days people had been talking about it, how *formidable* it was, the best fair ever! I was eleven, and the trip alone was a great treat. I even washed my face and ears before going. We took the subway and got out at the Trocadero Station, near the Eiffel Tower, where it was all happening. It was a section of Paris where I had never been. My mouth never closed all day. I had never seen so many beautiful sights, except in movies. Among the pavilions from different nations, I was most impressed by the ones from Russia and Germany. They were enormous, with marble statues in front of them, depicting strong, healthy men and women, proud to be citizens of their countries. The buildings were opposite each other. They were awesome in their imposing stature, and in a way frightening. Their flags flapped in the wind, one with the huge swastika, and the other with the sickle and hammer, both dominated by the color red. I was attracted by the small but beautiful Asiatic pavilions with their delicate art work. After we ate the sandwiches my mother had packed for us in a paper bag, my father treated me that day to ice cream. Riding home on the metro, I was exhilarated and exhausted. I felt special that my father had taken me to the fair, and I talked about it for days, making my sisters envious.

One day my father came home with a used violin and put it in my lap. "All right, Reevela," he said, "open the case, and play the instrument." Just like that! I opened the case, took out the violin that looked too big for me, grabbed the bow in my other hand, looked at the instrument for a few seconds, then put it under my chin as if I knew what I was doing and proceeded to scratch at it. The violin responded as if it were in pain. I don't know what my father expected from me. A boy genius I was not. Precocious, yes. Cocky, yes. Adorable, yes. A violinist, never. Despite the help of a neighbor who tried to teach me to play, after a few weeks of cacophony my father

returned the violin. He must have dreamed that I would pick up the
instrument and instantly play it like Heifetz. I wish I could have done
that for him. It would have been thrilling for my father and revealing
to me to discover I was a genius.

My mother had love in her for everybody. Nothing was too difficult for her. She was always the first one to get up in the morning.
She would wake up, give us hot coffee and hot milk and a piece of
bread with butter, then send us to school. She would go marketing on
the Rue St. Antoine—where twice a week merchants with carts sold
fresh vegetables and fruits a bit cheaper than in the stores—cook the
meals, clean the apartment, help my father sew the pants. Once a
week she would go to the *quais,* to a barge on the river Seine near
our apartment house, and spend the whole day washing our clothes.
She never stopped and was the last one to go to bed. She was a simple,
uneducated woman who was loving, devoted, and completely
unselfish.

I can remember only once when she lost control. It was terrible.
I don't know what precipitated it, but there she was banging her head
against the wall, screaming, "I can't stand it anymore! I'm leaving!
From now on, you all run your lives without me!" I cried, pleading
with her, "Please, Mama, don't hurt yourself. Please don't die!" I had
never seen her like this. My mother always smiled, never screamed at
anyone. My God, I thought, what's happening? She's going crazy,
banging her head against the wall like that! She just didn't care. She
took her coat, walked out, and disappeared. Where was she going?
Nobody rushed after her. We were all paralyzed, not moving, not
talking. I felt deserted and desperate. Hours later she came back, saying not a word, hanging up her coat and resuming her life as if nothing
had happened.

My mother was very short and overweight—that's a graceful way
of saying it—and she became an old woman before her time. When
you bear eight kids, and raise most of your stepchildren, you don't
wind up looking like a fashion model. It bothered me a lot that her
stepchildren were not nice to her. My half-sister Adèle had a *boulangerie* (a bakery). When we would go to visit her, she would cater to my
father, give *him* some pastries, but never ask my mother, "Do you
want anything?" It was the same with my half-sister Fanny, who was

the last one we would visit before heading home. She would ask my father, "Would you like a glass of tea, some cake?" and completely ignore my mother, a woman who had devoted years of her life to raising them.

It's hard to say if my mother was ever happy. I guess in her simple way she was. She adored movies. Later on in life, her big treat was to go by herself in the afternoon to a neighborhood movie house. She would always come back with her eyes glowing, as if she had seen the Taj Mahal.

CHAPTER TWO

MADAME HALPHEN

I loved our apartment house. The smell of Jewish cooking meant to me security, stability, warmth, comfort. Entering our building to be greeted by the intoxicating aromas from all the kitchens of fried onions, gefilte fish, and chicken soup made you feel that all was well with the world.

Winter was my favorite season, because it was then that my parents would take my folding bed from the bedroom and put it in the kitchen near the stove, the only heating system we had in the whole apartment. That's where everybody would gather for the evening.

My father's younger brother, Uncle Yankef, lived in the annex of our apartment house, and every evening after dinner he and his wife Chave Lea would come over for a few hours. Uncle Yankef was big and fat. He drank water with huge gulps. Everything about him was big—his tone of voice, his gestures, his belches. His laughter could be heard all over the building. After eating cookies and drinking his fourth glass of tea, while people talked he would fall asleep in his chair and immediately begin to snore. His snore was a roar. We would all tease him about it and sometimes scream "Fire!" to wake him up. Chave Lea was my Uncle Yankef's first cousin. She was a small person, like most people in my family, with dark auburn hair, and her eyes twinkled when she looked at you over her reading glasses. Her smile displayed a few gold teeth. She was also a Widerman and therefore, when she married Uncle Yankef, didn't have to change her name. My father became her brother-in-law as well as her cousin.

My mother would sit in the kitchen, calmly sewing pants, doing her work, while the neighbors and family all talked at once. The Wnouks, who lived on the first floor of the building, visited our place regularly. They were dear people, Rumanians by birth. Monsieur Wnouk was a shoe repairman who had a stall on the Rue St. Louis en l'Ile. Madame Wnouk was a very good baker and very often would open her cookie jar to give me some of the delicious chocolate squares she had just baked. I never saw her in a foul mood. She was always sweet and soft-spoken and spotless in her appearance. In her apartment you could eat off the floor. Madame Zilberberg, a widow with five children, was rather on the nervous side. Her eyes never stopped blinking. She talked very fast and would stutter when excited. But she would give you the shirt off her back if you needed it. One of her daughters, Zelda, was a darling, feisty little girl whom I cared about a lot. Madame Tarnegul, our next door neighbor, would often join us without her husband, but mostly her intention was to borrow things, which we had a hard time getting back. All these people sipped glasses of tea with lemon and red wine and ate homemade cookies.

Chave Lea was a good storyteller as well as a knitter. She would make sweaters, shawls, socks, and booties for new grandchildren; her hands were never idle. Above all, there was the tremendous rumble of Uncle Yankef's snores. All that noise and warmth was very relaxing to me; it was my lullaby. In the thirty-one months I spent in concentration camps, the memory of those evenings helped to sustain me, reminding me in the midst of terrible cruelty how life could be and that not everybody was bad.

We were less than middle class. I don't remember if there was a depression. We were never richer or poorer at one time than another. We didn't think of ourselves as poor, because we didn't know any differently. My mother always managed to have food on the table, and not only for us. I remember complete strangers coming from Poland or Palestine, stopping by to bring news of mutual friends, and my mother immediately inviting them to stay and eat with us, offering whatever we had.

Our island, l'Ile St. Louis, was like a village, but what a village! Cut into quarters, with the Rue des Deux Ponts running horizontally, it is still the widest street, going from the Pont Marie to the Pont des

Tournelles, where a stone statue of Sainte Geneviève, who saved Paris in the fifth century, is erected. The Rue St. Louis en l'Ile, a long narrow street, cuts the island vertically, and numerous streets, all short and narrow, make this small island a very warm village. Practically everybody knew each other. L'Ile St. Louis and l'Ile de la Cité are the oldest sections of Paris, two of the most picturesque sites of this beautiful city.

There were in my childhood what seemed to me to be thousands of little shops—grocery stores, bakeries, jewelers, wineries, hardware stores, pharmacies, repair stalls, barber shops, cafés—everything was there, an old church, even antique shops. One didn't have to leave this island, ever.

I knew most of the store owners, and they called me by my first name when I went to buy food. I remember a small bakery where, for a few *sous,* you could get all the French pastries you could eat. They were two days old, but who cared? We never got sick or had indigestion. We always bought our bread—*baguettes, biscottes, petits pains, croissants*—at Madame Goutron's *boulangerie.* What a delightful, warm person she was, always a smile on her bright scrubbed face.

My favorite shop was owned by Monsieur Verdier, a small man with a brush moustache. He sold lots of small items, but mostly magazines and newspapers. He had a son my age whom I envied because he had free access to all the magazines. I was an avid reader of comic books. I could not get enough of Flash Gordon, Mandrake the Magician, and all the others. I devoured movie magazines and clipped out the pictures of my favorite movie stars, which I pasted neatly into scrapbooks. I would look at those books for hours on end. When I was sent to the concentration camps, I took my scrapbooks with me and kept them for the first nineteen months, until I was moved to my second camp, Blechhammer, and all our private belongings were taken away.

Directly across the street from the apartment house, Monsieur Hourtoule, who looked like a teddy bear, ran a pharmacy. And next door, Monsieur Bosselut—a roly-poly bald headed man who was very businesslike and not friendly, the only one who didn't call us by our names—sold all kinds of kitchen utensils, hardware, and paint. He was called un *Marchant de Couleurs,* a merchant of colors.

On our island, there was an elementary school for boys and another for girls, as well as kindergarten. Surrounding were the quais, the Bourbon, de Béthune, d'Anjou, and d'Orléans, where the elite lived in luxurious apartments with magnificent views. One could see such landmarks as Nôtre Dame, the Panthéon, and the Eiffel Tower.

A rich widow, Madame Halphen, who was an aunt of the Rothschilds, had built the seven-story apartment house where we lived on the Rue des Deux Ponts. It was completed in 1926, and my family moved in from a one-room rat-infested apartment on the Rue de l'Hôtel de Ville. Madame Halphen's purpose was to provide apartments for underprivileged Jewish families with children, the more children the better. There were only five non-Jewish families among the forty-five tenants, including that of the concierge, Madame Froment. Madame Halphen asked for very little rent. I suspect some didn't pay any. For families who had lived in only one room, this was paradise. An actual *apartment,* with three or four rooms! Today there is a plaque on the front of the building, over the entrance, which reads "A la mémoire des 112 habitants de cette maison dont 40 petits enfants déportés et morts dans les camps Allemands en 1942." "In memory of the 112 inhabitants of this house, including 40 young children, deported and dead in German camps in 1942."

Madame Halphen was a remarkable person. Not only did she have this apartment house built for poor Jewish families, she also hired a staff of social workers, young women in their early twenties, to take care of us children when we came home from school while our parents were still at work. At four o'clock, five days a week, we would meet in the *Locale,* a three-room gathering place, on the ground floor of the annex building, where we would do our homework. The first room had round tables where, in addition to doing our studies, we would draw and paint. Our best drawings and paintings were tacked to the white walls. The second room, partitioned by glass doors that could be opened to make those two rooms one, was sparsely furnished with an upright piano, shelves of books, and straight chairs set against the walls. In this room, the social workers would read us children's stories and passages from the Bible. Madame Halphen's secretary, Madame Jacob, would play the piano and teach us songs. We would perform in plays about Hanukka, Purim, and other holidays. I was always chosen to be one of the stars, and I reveled in it. The third room was empty except for a sink and was used mostly for small meetings, rehearsing plays, painting scenery, and making our own costumes out of crepe paper.

We would stay at the *Locale* until it was time for us to go to our apartments for dinner. The social workers were remarkable. I will remember them as long as I live . . . Lili, Mathia, Yette, Lou. In the late 1930s, most of them emigrated to Palestine. One of them, Lou Kaddar, was, until Golda Meier died, her private secretary and companion. Thanks to these wonderful young women, who devoted so much of their time to make us feel loved, not one of us became delinquent. When the weather was nice, after we did our homework they would take us to the nearby Nôtre Dame Gardens to play games in the fresh air. On weekends they would take us on picnics to the outskirts of Paris to one of the *Bois*. Sometimes we would go to the Tuileries and Luxembourg Gardens. There we would watch puppet shows that intrigued me so much, I decided to build my own theater creating my own puppets. The star puppet was always my hand, my voice. The puppets became a part of the live show that my friends Roger, Zaza, Georges, and I put on in our kitchen. I would design costumes for my puppets, cutting patterns out of paper, and use one of the sewing machines to make them. We would turn the kitchen into a theater by moving the big table out of the way to make room for rows of chairs and hanging a white sheet for the curtain. We would then improvise plays and musical numbers to the delight of the other kids from the building, who paid admission fees to watch us.

Madame Halphen had a big house in Colleville sur Mer, at the seashore in Normandie near Deauville, and during the summer, fifty children a month would vacation there, under the guidance of Lili, Lou, and Mathia. I went there only once. Other summers I was sent to camps run by charitable organizations. I loved the one at St. Ouen le Mône, not too far south of Paris, because they showed us Charlie Chaplin movies. We called him "Charlot," and absolutely idolized him. We looked forward to his movies, relishing his adventures while sucking on sugar cane candies. We talked about them for days, imitating Charlot.

Every evening before we went to bed, they would give us cold *coco* in a big tin cup, which we had to finish. It was difficult for me because I didn't like the bitter taste of it. One night, when the others had finished and were getting up from the tables, I tried to drink the rest of my *coco* in one big gulp. I got out of breath and started to choke. It was a terrible sensation, like drowning. I began to panic. But my greater fear was that I would make a spectacle of myself. I told myself that death was not knocking at my door just yet, took a deep breath and then another, and somehow emptied the cup.

Drinking *coco* before going to bed did not help me with the other problem I had at summer camp. Though it didn't happen every night, there were times when I peed in bed while I was asleep. I didn't know what to do about it. I was afraid of being reprimanded by the counselors in front of all the kids and being nicknamed "pisher." In the morning I would try to hide the yellow spot on the sheet by making my bed as soon as I woke up. Maybe it was too much *coco,* or maybe it was my fear of going to the bathroom in the middle of the night because of the darkness.

At camp that summer, I was examined by the doctor for a sore throat. The next morning I was taken to a ward in the Rothschild Hospital in Paris. Nobody told me that I was there to have my tonsils and adenoids removed. A nurse grabbed my hand, we took an elevator down to the basement through dark corridors, and suddenly I was in a room, sitting on a stool. On my left was a table, full of shiny, spotless instruments. In came the doctor, wearing on his head what seemed like a gigantic round mirror with a little light in it. Then, without putting me to sleep, he placed a clamp in my mouth to keep my jaws open. I thought, I'm going to die. I stared at that table with all those instruments, all kinds of knives, scissors, gauze, everything neatly lined up, and at the doctor who, with the mirror on his head, looked like a monster. Holding my tongue with gauze, he probed down into my throat. The pain was excruciating. My terror was even worse, as I watched those instruments coming up from my throat all covered with blood. All I could do was cry. The operation went on for what felt an eternity. Afterwards my throat was on fire. My family visited me every day, bringing me ice cream. The cool vanilla, strawberry, and chocolate cream melted in my mouth and soothed my misery. A week later I was taken home as if nothing had happened to me.

The only thing I missed was the ice cream. How I had always looked forward to summer when, just before dinner time, the ice cream vendor would stop in front of our apartment house! The moment I saw him I would scream for my mother, until she would open the window and throw down a *sou* or two. I didn't care where she got the money. I would yell, "Ma! Ma!" until she gave it to me. Much of the time my selfishness blinded me to the realities of life. My father worked very hard to give us what little we had. But I never thought about that.

Until I was twelve years old, I attended school in the Jewish ghetto, on the Rue des Hospitalières St. Gervais. We were taught in French by French teachers, none of them Jewish. We went to school from Monday through Friday. In the regular French school system, the students attended school Monday through Wednesday; Thursday was a day off, then it was back to school on Friday and Saturday. But Saturday was the Jewish Sabbath, so we were sent to a school that took Saturdays off. We had more vacations than any other children in Paris, because school was closed on both Christian and Jewish holidays. In 1981, when my wife Natalie and I were in Paris, I took her to the ghetto to show her my school and the synagogue where I had my Bar Mitzvah. Like the apartment house on l'Ile St. Louis, there is a plaque on the front wall of the school which reads "165 enfants Juifs de cette école, déportés durant la seconde guerre mondiale, furent exterminés dans les camps Nazis. *N'oubliez pas.*" "165 Jewish children from this school, deported to Germany during World War II, were exterminated in Nazi camps. Do not forget."

CHAPTER THREE

Toy Soldiers

The only one of my mother's children who wasn't living with us was my brother Jacques, eighteen years older than I and already married. He would come and visit us often, sometimes with his wife Golda, sometimes alone. When we were eating and didn't like certain dishes, he would take off his belt and fake threatening us with it. We were not fooled by his threats and his belt and would remind him that he had not set such a good example. We had been told stories about what a devil he was and how difficult he could be about food, demanding steaks when my parents couldn't afford to buy bread.

I was absolutely adored by everyone in my family. I could do nothing wrong. My sister Aimée loved to take care of me. Because we were such a big family and couldn't afford a comb for everyone, we shared an iron comb that was durable and never had to be replaced. Aimée liked to comb my hair and make a curl, a la Clara Bow, right on my forehead to make me look cute. She would scrape my forehead until, unable to stand it anymore, I would scream at her, "I'm cute enough! Stop it!"

We also had a fine-tooth comb that my mother would use when she saw us scratching our heads. She knew that was the sign. She would wash our hair with hot water and vinegar and then use the fine tooth comb to catch the lice, cracking them with her thumbnail.

In her teens, Aimée worked in a department store, Au Magasin de France, on the Rue de Turennes. On holidays she would bring us great toys. One year, she gave me soldiers. They were beautiful in their

Napoleonic uniforms—shiny blues and reds and yellows. I played with them for years on the kitchen floor, inventing battles, strategies, and retreats and singing background music to the movements of my troops. Unfortunately, the soldiers were made of clay and were very fragile. It literally pained me if an arm got broken. I was very orderly and always arranged them back into their original boxes. Nobody dared to touch my soldiers.

My sister Ida, a tiny woman with wild, kinky hair and huge, dark-brown eyes, was the first of the girls to get married. She had two sons, and often I would go to her apartment and play with the oldest, Bernard, who was six years younger than I. I would travel alone, taking the metro. It was a long trip; she lived in the twentieth *arrondissement,* and the train made many stops. I was never able to travel well, and, by the time I arrived at Ida's apartment, I would be sick to my stomach. She would greet me with a big kiss, then sit me at the kitchen table and give me a large dish of chocolate pudding. It was the best cure.

When I stayed overnight, she would make a bed for me by setting five straight chairs in a row with pillows for a mattress. I loved being there, away from the others at home. Being with Ida, Bernard, and his younger brother, Edmond, and spending the afternoon in the *Jardin d'Acclimatation* and riding the carousel, was sheer joy. My brother-in-law Jacques Pankenfeld was a quiet man. Small but well fed by my sister, he was beginning to show a pot belly. I was fascinated watching him work at his machine in the living room, stitching intricate designs on ladies' shoes. In the bedroom, there was a banjo hanging on the wall. I never saw or heard anybody play it. I never knew if it was there just for decoration or if Jacques, in moments of passion, serenaded my sister.

I was always aware of my religious background but took it for granted, without particularly being interested in it. Passover was a special holiday. Just before it began, we would spring-clean the apartment, even wash the walls and ceilings, preparing for the total change—Passover dishes, matzohs instead of regular bread, and special foods for this time of the year only. My father stopped working for the entire eight days. The whole family—in-laws, children, and grandchildren—would gather in our apartment for the first seder. Some of them even stayed overnight and slept on the floor to be there for the second seder. My father would go through the seemingly end-less formal ceremony that bored us children to death. We had to pay attention and pretend to be serious. There was no fooling around. We had to control our laughter, which was especially difficult when, as part of the ritual, we had to put our little pinkies in a small glass of sweet wine and say "Zemedala" ten times while removing drops of wine from the glass each time. It was supposed to be the enunciation of the ten plagues, but the word "Zemedala," rather than instilling us with awe, struck us as being hilarious.

Traditionally, next to the head of the family there is placed on his left an empty chair with a pillow on it, and an empty plate and a glass of wine is set on the table for the prophet Eliyahu Hanavai. The youngest child of the family has a very important part to play during the seder. He asks his father the four questions: "Why is this day different from all the other days?" and so forth. It is also his duty to go and open the door of the house to welcome Eliyahu. The first and only time I did it, when I was seven, I was so frightened that I refused to do it ever again. I had to walk down the entry hall, open the door, and then stand there for what seemed an eternity, looking down the long, dark corridor, waiting for the invisible angel to brush past me. As my imagination took over, I shivered and shook with terror. I was sure he was going to grab me and take me away and not enter our apartment at all. Finally, Hélène called, "You may close the door! He's in." During the whole evening I stared at the empty chair and the glass of wine, fearing that it would get empty by itself. I kept my feet off the floor in case the prophet decided to drag me under the table and take me God knows where. From the next year on, the duty fell to one of my sisters who, after making fun of me, would go and open the door for Eliyahu.

We kids in the apartment building were always together, racing up and down the stairs, playing hide and seek, and running in and out of apartments, corridors, and toilets that were not locked. The noise, the laughter, and the shrieking were constant. The concierge, Madame Froment, a tiny wisp of a woman, would chase us with a broom. "Stop that racket all of you. Stop dirtying my stairs. Go away. Go back to your apartments!" We would laugh at her, dodging her broom, and go right on with what we were doing. She seemed funny to us then, but not so funny a few years later when, after we were arrested and sent to Drancy, she looted our apartments, secretly thrilled to be finally rid of the Jews.

The family who lived above us, the Smilianskys, were always fighting among themselves at the top of their voices. My father used to take a stick with a tin can connected to the end and hit the ceiling with it to tell the Smilianskys to quiet down. One of their sons, Pava, whom we nicknamed "Pava Schtinker," could not control his bowels. You could always tell when Pava was near. Most of the time we avoided him. Poor Pava Schtinker. He was sent to concentration camps with his whole family, and none of them came back. The family under us were called the Schwimmers. The father, a violinist, had a vile temper. The walls were paper-thin, and the whole house shook when he yelled at his wife and kids.

There were times when I was six or seven that I didn't feel like getting up in the morning, especially in winter, and going to school. I would have given all my clay soldiers and comic books to be able to stay lounging at home and not have to solve arithmetic problems. Sometimes I would fake sickness, which never fooled my mother. She always told me it was imperative that I go to school. "What do you want to be? A *schlumpack* like Salomon Schwimmer? Or a *gonif* like Albert Smiliansky?" At such times, she always mentioned her two least favorite kids in the apartment house. I had to get an education even if I didn't like it. Otherwise, she would say, the policeman on the corner would come and arrest me and take me to jail. The choice was unbearable. But school tasted better than jail.

My earliest memory is of being sent to kindergarten when I was three years old. It was in the Jewish ghetto, not far from where we lived. I would go with my sisters. They never took me by the hand, but always grabbed me by the back of my coat collar as if I were a dog on a leash. On our way, we would stop at the candy store and spend a few minutes looking in the window. If we had one or two *sous,* we would buy some candy and eat it instantly. There was an elementary school for boys, a separate one for girls, and a mixed kindergarten, where I went for the next three years. That first day, I cried and didn't want to leave my sister Madeleine, who was a year-and-a-half my senior and two classes above me. I cried and cried until they let me stay with her. That same year, we were given shots for diphtheria. They gave me a lollipop to appease me, while the nurse was saying, "It won't hurt, little boy." It did hurt. By the time I was five, I looked forward to going to that kindergarten.

Our elementary school was not a large one. There were seven grades with maybe thirty pupils in each class. I had the same teacher for the fourth and second grade. (In France, elementary school begins at grade six, then proceeds up to grade one.) His name was Monsieur Chapdeleine. A tall, blond, athletic, and handsome man, he was always kind, never impatient, and he inspired us to want to study. Chapdeleine was the direct opposite of our third grade teacher, whom we nicknamed "Pigeon" because a pigeon had once entered his classroom, and the poor man had gone into hysterics. He was a scrawny man with a beaked nose; ironically, he looked like a bird. He was sadistic and enjoyed striking our finger tips with his ruler if we didn't behave or do our homework. In the assembly hall, where we had lunch, Pigeon would always eat overripe bananas, which he would put on a hot stove to warm up—yecchh!

None of the teachers were anti-Semitic. As a matter of fact, one of them, Monsieur Mineret, who later became the principal, was marvelous to the Jewish people during World War II. He gave false I.D. cards to a number of the Jewish kids and hid others with their parents in the school. Those of us who have survived regard him as a hero.

During recess we played cops and robbers. I was a cop, never a robber, except when I was Robin Hood. When we played soldiers, I was always a captain. I discovered that I could get away with murder because of my size. I was never picked on because I was protected by my pals who were much bigger than I. In gym, I could climb ropes faster than most of the other kids. I was very competitive. Impatient to give the right answer, I was always the first one to raise my hand.

My least favorite subjects were geometry, algebra, and chemistry. The teachers, even Chapdeleine, failed to make me interested in them. I loved things that came easily to me—French, singing, and painting. Geography and history bored me a little, but I didn't mind them too much.

I was nine years old when I completed my fourth grade, and I was sorry that Chapdeleine wouldn't be my teacher the following year.

At the promotion ceremony, when I went up on the platform to pick up my big red book (one of the years I won it), the woman who presented it to me patted my back and discovered that one of my shoulder blades stuck out more than the other. After the ceremony she took me to the school infirmary where, although I felt perfectly well, I was given ultraviolet lamp treatments. The following school year, she had me sent to a special summer camp in *Die, Drôme,* a beautiful section of the French Alps. She thought the fresh air would do my shoulder blades good. As a result, I missed two months of the third grade. I was thrilled to get away from Pigeon, his ruler, and his rotten bananas.

My first day at camp I got very homesick and cried all over the Alps. By the third day, I started to entertain everybody. It was a wonderful place. We were maybe two hundred kids in the camp with shoulder blade problems, sleeping in wooden barracks, fifty to a dormitory. We did a lot of hiking, played outdoor games, and practiced all kinds of sports. We had plenty of fresh air, the food was hearty, and the counselors were friendly and helpful with any problems we had. I don't know whether all this helped my shoulder blades, but I loved being there. It was the first time that I performed in front of a large audience. We did sketches and musical numbers. In one number, we were all Chinese and doing a dance. Wanting to be different than the other twelve kids so people would notice me, I decided to stare without blinking during the whole sequence. I became a star performer at that camp.

When I was eleven years old, I entered an amateur radio contest for children that emanated from the *Théatre Empire* every Thursday. I auditioned for it by doing imitations of French singing stars like Maurice Chevalier, Mistinguett, Charles Trenet, Jean Sablon, and others. Josephine Baker, appearing at the Casino de Paris at that time, was the toast of the city, and I imitated her singing her famous song, "J'Ai Deux Amours" ("Two Loves Have I"). The ladies holding the audition loved me. They thought I was outrageously bold. Could I do something else? In school, we were just learning an aria from the opera *Thaïs,* called "Il Etait Un Roi De Thulé" ("There Was a King of Thule"), so I sang that aria for them in my little boy soprano voice, and they agreed that's what I should sing at the contest.

We were ten contestants that day, and we each had to rehearse with the house pianist. I looked at my competition and felt I had a pretty good chance of winning. The show was sponsored by *Zébraline* and *Zébracier,* products for cleaning pots and pans. Each week a sister and brother team opened the show singing the sponsor's jingle. I envied their regular job—their being professionals, their heavy makeup, and their costumes. They wore top hats—she was all in gold, he all in silver—and they were fitted into papier-mache horses made to look as if they were on horseback. I pictured myself doing both parts better than they.

I sang my aria with passion and gusto. I came in second. The winner of the contest was a tiny girl, smaller than I, with a huge voice and the drive of an Ethel Merman. One felt that she was destined to stardom, but she was never heard from again.

In spite of my not winning, a year later, when I was twelve, the two ladies signed me to appear with five other children as a background singing chorus on a radio show every Thursday at the *Poste Parisien,* on the Champs Elysées. The show catered to young audiences. It starred Jean Nohain, who was very well known in France as "Jaboune," and featured his brother Claude Dauphin.

It was a great satisfaction being a professional. I was no longer Robert Max Widerman. I was Max Robert, the stage name I chose by switching the order of my first two names. I called myself Max Robert because I was ashamed of my last name. I was aware of anti-Semitism, and I didn't want to be different. I was afraid of being rejected, of being called a "dirty Jew."

During my last year at elementary school, my radio "career" caused me to miss a lot of classes, and I was getting low grades. Before the final exam, I stayed up all night studying, and I passed everything with flying colors. In fact, I had the highest marks in the whole school. By luck I knew the answer to every question. *Et ça, c'est la verité.* And that is the truth.

CHAPTER FOUR

CHARLES TRENET:
LE FOU CHANTANT

I learned to dance at the movies. I would go to the Saturday matinées with my sisters Hélène, Cécile, and Madeleine. As soon as I
came home after seeing Fred Astaire and Ginger Rogers perform, I
would say, "Mama, look what we've just seen!" Then I'd dance
around the whole apartment, tapping my little feet off. I was in love
with the enchanted land on the screen.

One of my idols was Tom Mix. If I could have been on his horse,
I would have been in heaven. I wanted to be all of them—Charlie
Chan, the Marx Brothers, the Ritz Brothers, or to be as brave as Errol
Flynn was in *The Charge of the Light Brigade* or *Captain Blood.* My
friends, Schmil Adoner, Yossi Grinfeld, Zaza Galowsky, Bernard
Wioreck, and Roger Helwasser, and I would go on the Quai de
Béthune, beside the Seine—a step away from where we lived—and
reenact all the movies. I saw a French movie about the Foreign Legion
with an actor called Jean Servais. To me, that was it. That's what I
wanted to be. We played soldiers in the Foreign Legion for hours,
dying from thirst and killing Arabs. For France! We thought the reen-
actment was even better than the original.

Victor Francen, who was one of the biggest French movie stars
before World War II, lived on the Quai de Béthune, in a new building
owned by Hélèna Rubenstein. We all knew where the windows to his
apartment were. We would stand under them and scream, "Victor!
Victor! Victor! Show your face! We know you're home! Please!"

until he would come out on his balcony and talk to us. We were thrilled that he never told us to go away.

Ray Ventura had a big orchestra. I never missed the movies he made. What a glorious orchestra! One of my dreams was to be part of it. I envied the musicians with their white uniforms and black ties. They seemed to have so much fun, and I adored the sound they were producing, the songs they were singing. Maybe that's why later on I became a band singer, in a way fulfilling my dream.

On Sunday mornings, the radio disc jockeys played all our favorite records, and we listened to singers like Damia, Frehel, Marie Dubas, Jean Sablon, Edith Piaf, Leo Marjane, Maurice Chevalier, Charles Trenet, Pills and Tabet, Lys Gauty, Jean Lumiere, and Jean Tranchant. We stayed glued to the radio from ten to noon, singing along with them. Charles Trenet was my all-time idol. I memorized all the songs he composed and couldn't think of doing anything else but imitate him. He was nicknamed *Le Fou Chantant,* the singing fool, because of the energetic style he innovated, singing mostly jazz-oriented, up-tempo songs.

But I lived for the Saturday afternoons at the movies. I would sit at Le Cinema de l'Hôtel de Ville, in that neighborhood theater in the dark, longing to jump into the picture myself. I would have given my right arm to be Eleanor Powell's partner! When we saw those American movies, they were dubbed, but they were still effective. Sometimes too effective. Once I saw a Boris Karloff movie, *The Walking Dead,* where he is sent to the electric chair. Then they find out he's not guilty and somehow revive him. Karloff is going to get revenge and kill the ones who sent him to the chair. Well, it scared the *merde* out of me, especially the scene when one of the men responsible for his death is shaving and sees in the mirror Karloff alive and ready to murder him. After I saw that movie, I was afraid for months to walk down the hallway to the toilet by myself.

My sisters always took advantage of my being afraid of so many things. They were as afraid of the dark as I, but I was the youngest, so they teased me, pretending they weren't scared at all. "Frankenstein's monster is in the toilet waiting for you," they would say. Any monsters they could think of were in the entry hall. When they knew I was on my way to the toilet, they would switch off the hall light and scream, "Grandma Chaya is coming to grab you!" I would run to my mother shrieking, "Ma, they're scaring me. Tell them to stop!"

When I was a child everything scared me. I was terrified of birds, even chickens, and the live carps my mother brought home on Fridays. If a dog didn't wag his tail, I would cross the street. I was afraid of anything I could not sit down and talk to.

What terrified me most was death. My family always talked about my brother Bernard, who had died when he was eighteen months old—cursed, they said, by an "evil eye." One of my father's brothers, *Fettuh* Schmil, was married to *Meemuh* Sheindle, one of the rare people my mother did not care for. My mother was convinced that Sheindle gave the "evil eye" to everybody. When my aunt would come to visit us, she would look at me, smiling with approval, and comment how darling and bright I was. As soon as she left, my mother would lick my face to wash the evil curse away. I would scream, "Oh, Ma, stop doing that. Leave me alone!" But she went on and on, like a cat cleaning her litter. "Why? Why the licking!" I would ask. She would say, "Sheindle put an evil eye on you. She's no good." It worked magic, because I was never sick after my aunt's visits.

My *Fettuh* Schmil died from a heart attack on a Christmas Eve, right in the middle of an all-night party. Somebody at the party came to tell my father that his brother had just died. My parents spared me by not making me go to the funeral, knowing that I would never go near a coffin or look at a dead person. At funerals in my neighborhood the casket was put into a horse drawn carriage and people walked behind it to the church. I would fear that the dead body would arise and take me with it to the grave. In concentration camps I had to be on guard duty in the middle of the night in complete darkness. I was only sixteen years old, but I knew I had to overcome my fears. There was no running to my mother for protection, no more pampering. When I had to go to the latrines at night, there were no lights and no voices to reassure me that all was well. If Boris Karloff was there, it was too bad.

In my early teens, the chore I hated most was to take down the garbage, because the cans were in the courtyard that was infested with rats. Oh, were they big! And fat! And my sisters would always shove this chore onto me, because they were as frightened as I. "It's a man's job," they would say. If everybody in that apartment house had been as neat as my father and I, I don't think we would have had a rat problem. Our garbage was practically gift wrapped.

One of my other chores was to iron the laundry for the whole family. My father didn't trust any of my sisters to do his shirts. Somehow I didn't mind ironing. As a matter of fact, I was proud to be able to satisfy my father. We had two small irons that were heated by being placed on the stove, and I never burned a garment. One day, while I had a hot iron in my hand, Hélène ordered me to do one of her shirts. She had to have it right that minute. I wasn't in the mood to comply with her command. We started an argument that became a fight. I threw her clothes on the floor and told her that if she was in such a hurry, she could iron her own *shmattas*. We didn't talk to each other for days and behaved as though we were strangers in our small quarters. Cécile and Madeleine, knowing how much Hélène and I cared for each other, thought we were idiotic. Then one day I saw Hélène on the Place de l'Hôtel de Ville walking with her best friend, Paulette Novak. I couldn't stand it anymore. I rushed up to her and embraced her. We made up on the spot, to the relief of everybody in the family. I loved her, and the whole incident had been foolish. I had missed not giving her the cues to the scenes she was practicing for her acting class. Though she never asked me again to iron her things, I gladly did it. She was always good to me, and later it was she who paid to send me to art school.

My sister Cécile was the Cinderella of the family. Whatever chores Hélène, Madeleine, or I didn't want to do fell into her lap. Nice, lovable Cécile would do it: wash the dishes, go with my mother to do the marketing, or help her scrub the kitchen floor. Cécile always looked sad even when she was happy. She had the cutest face with wide greenish-blue eyes and thick, unruly brown hair. Unfortunately, she had my mother's nose, and her mouth happened to be in a pout even when she smiled. She rarely complained, even when she felt trapped into doing things she didn't want to do. She was extremely friendly with everybody and made friendships last. She was a marvelous dancer, and I loved to jitterbug with her.

Madeleine, on the other hand, was the family princess. Because my father needed help making pants, he took Hélène and Cécile out of elementary school before they could graduate and installed them in front of the sewing machines. Madeleine felt superior because she was allowed to finish elementary school, go to junior high, and even go on to business school. She had beautiful penmanship. She felt, like me, that everything was her due. She was the only blonde in the family, with bright blue eyes and a personality to match. She took command of her life at a very early age. She had a good sense of humor—like most members of my family—was extremely smart, and she was the apple of my father's eye.

Gaston Zelonka had been courting my sister Aimée in 1931 for a year. He was rather timid by nature, but thoughtful and always extremely polite to everybody—the epitome of a gentleman. They were both very romantic. A tiny woman with a cute figure, Aimée had black straight hair and huge brown eyes. She was famous in our family because she didn't start walking until she was three years old. She was very much like my mother; she had her sweetness and a heart of gold. Gaston and Aimée would often go to the Jardin de Nôtre Dame where they would rent chairs, take them to a secluded corner, hold hands, and kiss by the hour. I would see them there when I went with the *Locale* group to play.

In 1932, Gaston's parents asked for a meeting with my parents to discuss their engagement. A cloth was put on the dining room table. My mother had baked cakes. My father put out the schnapps, Gaston and Aimée were also there, and he formally asked my parents for Aimée's hand. Everybody was satisfied that it would be a good marriage. The engagement became official when Gaston put a ring on Aimée's finger, and they were married a year later.

I recall two weddings very distinctly. First was my sister Ida's wedding to Jacques. I was only four, but I can remember myself singing and dancing on top of a chair, getting all the attention I wanted. Aimée's wedding in 1934, because I was older, is more vivid. She looked darling in her white wedding gown and long train. I loved any excuse to get dressed up, and, for the occasion, my father made me a dark blue double-breasted suit. I thought I looked sensational with a white handkerchief in my breast pocket. I felt cheated that I wasn't the main focus that day and sulked at the synagogue. But at the wedding reception, which was held in a *salon,* I felt a lot better after I was asked to sing.

Two months after the wedding, Gaston had to begin his eighteen-month service in the army. Aimée continued working and living with us. When Gaston came home on furlough, Hélène, Cécile, Madeleine, and I had to sleep in the dining room so the newlyweds could have our bedroom.

My friends and I enjoyed life in simple ways. We didn't need cars or luxury items. We would take wooden boards and any kind of wheels we could find and make scooters out of them. We called them *patinèttes.* I remember how noisy the metal wheels with ball bearings were. We managed to make our own toys with whatever scraps were available—*sabres,* pistols, and little boats carved in wood that we would race in the gutters when the street cleaners opened the water valves.

In the late spring and summer when it was hot, because we could not afford public swimming pools, we would go a few blocks away from our apartment house to the Quai d'Orléans and down a wide ramp leading to the Seine where the first few meters were shallow water. We called the place *La Baigne Des Chiens,* the dogs' bath. It was against the law to swim there, but we were never caught. Most of the kids were much braver than I. I would venture into the water only up to my knees. I never loved sharing the river with the dogs who were there and always managed to avoid them. Very few of us owned bathing suits. We would take off our shoes and socks and roll up our pant legs as far as they would go and splash each other until we were drenched. Some of the boldest kids would even take off their pants and shirts and swim in their underwear. We often took with us make-shift fishing rods—long sticks with pieces of string attached—and little hooks improvised out of hairpins. I never touched the worm or the fish I caught. I was repulsed by slimy things. Fishing did not excite me. I got bored quickly and would talk Yossi, Zaza, and the others into drying themselves off so that we could play cops and robbers or Foreign Legion—games in which I excelled and where I was the boss.

Robert Birenbaum, my cousin once removed and Aunt Chave Lea's grandson, would come and spend the holidays at his grandparents. He was my age, and when he was there we were constantly together. I looked forward to those times because I had a holiday pal I could take advantage of. Since he was in my territory I was the law, and he would do exactly what I wanted. His Uncle Maurice was an eagle scout and had a hat that reminded us of the kind worn by the Canadian Mounties. We used that hat to play different characters. When we played cowboys and Indians, most of the time he would be the Indian so that I could wear the hat. We would take small wooden kitchen chairs as horses, saddle up in my aunt's long entry hall, and have a ball galloping from one end to the other for hours. Once in a while I would go to visit Robert in his neighborhood, where his parents owned a grocery store. He and his sister Cécile were happy children, never temperamental, and easy to be with. When I would introduce him to my friends, he would retreat into shyness and not really participate in our games. He only liked to play when the two of us were alone in his grandparents' apartment.

I always looked forward to spring, when on Saturday mornings the bells from the church on the Rue St. Louis en l'Ile would toll. There was a happy sound to them, and we knew it meant somebody was getting married. My sisters and I and the other kids from our building would rush down the stairs and go stand across the street from the church to get the best vantage point from which to view the arrival of the groom and especially the bride. All the brides looked beautiful— even the ugly ones. Their long white gowns elicited "oohs" and "aahs" from my sisters and the other girls. It was like a fairy tale. We thought everything was enchanting, and that the bride and groom would live happily ever after. It was even more fun when we knew who they were. We adored watching the guests arrive in all their splendor. When finally the limousine with the bride and her father stopped in front of the church, we all screamed, *"Vive la Mariée! Vive la Mariée!"* What a treat it was! Practically the whole l'Ile St. Louis showed up with everyone screaming and applauding. I used to imagine what the interior of the church looked like. We had never, of course, been inside. It was forbidden territory. Intrigued, I pictured the great ceilings, the opulent altar, and everywhere the statues of the saints and Christ on the cross. Years later, after the war, I finally had the nerve to go in. It looked small and quite ordinary—nothing at all like what I had envisioned.

The fourteenth of July, Bastille day, was probably the most exciting day of the year for us kids. The celebration was organized by the city council. In the afternoon, there were games, races, and contests for which we won prizes such as roller skates, watercolor paint boxes, yo-yos, dolls—toys that our parents couldn't afford to buy us. Candies, chocolates, and pastries were distributed to everybody. There were no losers that day. Of all the events, the one I looked forward to all year was the *grimace* contest. One year it was held at the Jardin de Nôtre Dame in the kiosk where band concerts were usually given. I entered that kiosk with great confidence, positive that I was going to make the world's ugliest face. I had practiced for weeks. My eyes went right up into my upper lids until only the whites were showing. My mouth was a contortion of unbelievable elasticity, with my upper lip drawn into my mouth and my lower teeth reaching up to my nose. It was painful, because you had to stay in the frozen state for a full minute in order to give the jury time to pick out the best ugly face. I didn't give in to my pain—didn't move a muscle in my whole body. How could I lose? I was astounded when I came in only second. After that year, I was determined to work out better and better contortions, and I always won.

At the end of the day when the contests were over, all the kids in our apartment house would get together to display and exchange prizes and toys. Then after dinner, we would go out into the streets to dance. A combo composed of a drummer, a bassist, and an accordion player supplied the music, which was mostly waltzes. We would dance for hours. I loved it. I would dance on and on until I was so dizzy I thought I would die from happiness. During the intermissions, we watched fireworks coming from Nôtre Dame. Our parents would let us stay in the streets until eleven or midnight. The holiday celebration would go on for four days, and we would talk about it for months afterwards.

A lot of kids in our apartment house were very talented. When I was about fourteen, Georges Goldstein, Roger Helwasser, Henri Adoner, and I formed an orchestra. Georges was the drummer, and the rest of us were the kazooists. We imitated different instruments—

trombone, trumpet, and saxophone. Henri was only ten and he could instinctively harmonize anything. We would gather at my apartment every day and rehearse like professionals. Being a show business trouper, I was the leader. I decided what numbers we should play and sing, in what tempos, and I was a tough taskmaster. We saved money to get some kind of uniforms. I very badly wanted us to have white suits like the men in the Ray Ventura orchestra, but we settled for dark blue sweat shirts worn over open collared white shirts with dark blue trousers. Part of our repertoire consisted of songs that Ray Ventura and his band had made famous like "Tiens, Tiens, Tiens," "Qu'est-ce qu'on Attend Pour Etre Heureux," and "Le Petit Bateau de Pêche."

In 1941 we entered an amateur jazz contest at *La Salle Pleyel* in Paris against real musicians playing real instruments. The effrontery. Technically, we were *hors concourt,* out of competition, because we didn't play real instruments. But the jury gave us a consolation prize, and our names and picture appeared in the newspapers and jazz magazines!

I still see Roger Helwasser when I go to Paris. He's an art dealer, is married to a marvelous woman, Lucienne, has three children, and still can charm the pants off you with his singing voice. I once saw Georges (the drummer) Goldstein, who looks old and fat, and resembles his father. Henri, the harmonizer, died in Auschwitz.

I have always wished there were a way to do a film about the happiness and the marvelous childhood we had, and the sudden terrible thing that happened to our families and to us while we were in our teens—just when we had started to blossom.

CHAPTER FIVE

BAR MITZVAH

During puberty we were preoccupied with sex. All the boys masturbated a lot—bragging about how often we did it. We got together in a circle and masturbated while we talked about girls. "Oh, those boobs on Simone! How about that tight ass on Nenette!" We made bets to see who could get it hard first and who would come the fastest. Whoever came first got a package of bubble gum with a sports card. Our parents had never told us anything about sex. They said we were born in a field: the boys in cabbages and the girls in roses.

I was at a high school in the 80s, giving a talk on the Holocaust, and during the question and answer period one of the female students asked me, "Did you have sex in camps? You know, while you were in concentration camps, did you have sex?"

I said, "Me, are you kidding? I was still a virgin when I was sixteen! It was not like today when you have to lose your virginity by the time you're twelve or your friends won't talk to you." Then in all seriousness I said, "I never thought about sex. Getting a piece of bread, that was my sex in camps."

Before my internment I fantasized about sex. But I didn't know much about it. The subject was taboo. You got married, you automatically knew where to put it, you had children, and that was about it. I was a virgin until I was nineteen. After I came back to Paris from Germany, my friend Georges Goldstein, who escaped deportation by being hidden at a farm, took me to a whorehouse. I couldn't do it. The fact that the girl was dirty and uncooperative didn't help. She sat on her bed like a stick, naked, expecting me to go to work, never helping me, and I didn't tell her that it was the first time I was going to have intercourse. After a few minutes of agony and embarrassment I put on my clothes and left.

Before I turned thirteen I went to a little synagogue on the Rue des Ecouffes, not far from my elementary school. After school at four o-clock, I would go and study for my Bar Mitzvah with the rabbi for at least an hour every day. The rabbi was a big man with a white beard, and he smelled of schmaltz herring, onions, and garlic. His odor was overwhelming. Nobody I knew bathed every day. There was a sign on the wall of the men's room in the synagogue that said, "Please wash your hands before leaving." I wondered why. What could there be about this bathroom that would make it necessary?

Even though my parents were religious, they were never strict with us. All they wanted from me was that I have my Bar Mitzvah and gain the knowledge of my Jewish ancestry. It always bored me to go to the synagogue and to learn Hebrew, and studying for my Bar Mitzvah was a chore. My mind was always wandering. I can remember one hot day in the synagogue when the windows were wide open and the radio was playing in the courtyard. Rather than paying attention to the rabbi, I listened to the coronation of the Duke of York when he became King George VI. Still, I learned everything by heart though not really understanding what I was reading in the Torah but just faking it. When the day of confirmation arrived, I sang my heart out, coming through the whole thing with confidence and ease like a pro, knowing that I would get my first ring, my first watch, and my first fountain pen.

After my Bar Mitzvah, I stopped going to *shul.* My father never forced me to continue. It was the same with my sisters. They were all Bat Mitzvah, and like me never went to Hebrew school after that. Being Jewish did not make me happy, because I learned when I was very young that most people did not like Jews. We were aware of anti-Semitism in our neighborhood. We were "that Jewish apartment house." There were a lot of Italians who lived across the street from us, and some of our older boys got into fights with them because of their anti-Semitic remarks. I was never a fighter, even in school—except once at junior high during recess when a kid my size called me a dirty kike. Unlike elementary school, 90 percent of the kids in junior high were gentiles. I wanted to be part of them—more French than Jewish. When the kid called me a dirty kike, I saw red. To my great surprise I went for him and slugged him. He gave me a bloody nose, but it was worth it. For the first time I had stood up and it made me feel good.

Sometimes in the summer I was sent to spend a month or two with farmers in *Auvergne,* in the middle of France. Farm families were paid by charitable organizations to take care of children. In that environment I felt ashamed of being Jewish. When they asked me what my religion was, I answered without hesitation, "Same as yours." Therefore, with guilt, I had to go to church with them on Sundays because they were Catholic.

Apart from having to go to church, I really enjoyed my stay with the farmers. I would share a bed with two other boys who were sent, like me, to spend their summer there to get the benefit of fresh air. We would bathe in the brook naked, never going in too deep. We would take long hikes in the woods and invent all sorts of games. We picked fresh fruits from the trees and vines and ate them right on the spot without washing them. One year we caught lots of frogs and, for dinner that night, were served their little fried legs. I don't know which I hated most, catching the frogs or eating their legs.

Our summer foster parents were always very nice to us. They gave us great freedom as long as we behaved and arrived on time for meals. In the morning we would be served hot coffee with fresh hot goats' milk in large bowls and thick slices of homemade bread with lots of butter and jam. The food at lunch and dinner was always delicious and abundant. There were hearty soups, meats, vegetables (which I never craved), potatoes always prepared in different ways, and fresh summer fruits, which I liked most of all. There were some things I did not care for. Worse than vegetables were blood sausages, which, unfortunately, I saw being made. A chicken, after being chased and caught, was beheaded and its blood was collected to make those bloody sausages. I could not stand the sight of it.

We helped out on the farm. I did not relish feeding the animals, particularly the pigs, or milking the goats and the huge cows. One summer we worked for several days harvesting wheat. It was a big event and people came from surrounding farms to help gather it into sheaves, which then were assembled into haystacks. I enjoyed the excitement and festivities of the harvest, but the work was exhausting.

In the evening after dinner we would go to the village square where sometimes I would sing the latest hit songs for the people gathered there. When our summer parents took us to the train station to send us back to our families in Paris, they packed up boxes of food for us full of all kinds of vegetables, cheeses, and fresh fruits. We each took home enough to feed our families for a week. I always returned tanned and, to the delight of my mother, a few pounds heavier.

I never told my parents that I was ashamed of being a Jew. I never had the guts to say to the farmers, "I'm Jewish. I'm not a Catholic. I don't believe in Christ." I was frightened, because I knew that in their peasant ignorance, they believed that Jews were evil. I didn't know what they would do to me. Send me to the devil? Burn me? Crucify me?

In the late thirties, my folks must have known what was happening in the world. My father read the Yiddish newspaper every day. But he never told us, "There's a terrible man in Germany, a dictator who has taken over, who's doing horrible things to German Jews." We children never knew and never really cared what was going on in Germany. I once heard Hitler on the radio. It was the voice of a screaming maniac. "What is this lunatic yelling about?" I said, and left the room. I didn't realize that this man, with the aid of thousands of willing accomplices, was going to try to annihilate the Jewish people and almost succeed. I remember grownups in my apartment talking about what was happening in the world. Gradually, as war grew imminent, I would sometimes become scared. Am I going to be killed? Is it the end of us? The end of the world? But I listened with one ear, not really wanting to know what they were saying, and then escaping into my own safe little world while they were in deep discussion about the real one. They must have felt helpless. Where could they go with all those children and no money? Perhaps they felt safe in France—protected by the Maginot Line. Who could ever have imagined that the Nazis would go as far as they did?

Before, during, and after the war, I used to think my father and mother knew nothing of those matters, but now I'm convinced that they did. A picture of my father stands out vividly in my mind. We were in the cattle train for three days going from Drancy to Germany—to the camps. My father never moved from the corner of the boxcar where they had shoved him; he never said a word. Maybe he prayed in silence; I don't know. Or maybe he had a premonition of what was going to happen. I wish now that I had sat with him, talked to him, asked him questions, and found out what he knew. But he was not an easy man to talk to.

When you're a child there are so many things you should comprehend but don't. It is interesting how people blame their parents for their shortcomings. I could blame my father for so many things: for being too old, for not having spent more time with me, or for failing to develop any rapport with me. I never do that. I greatly respect my father. I blame him for nothing. In his way he was a marvelous father, who worked very hard all his life so his children would have a better life than his. I don't blame him for any of the terrible things that happened to me.

During my years in concentration camps, the last thing I did before falling asleep each night was pray to God to save my whole family. "God, keep them safe. Bring them back alive." Even though I was not especially interested in religion, I believed in God. By the time I was liberated, I had stopped believing. I could not accept a God who would sacrifice millions of innocent human beings—to prove what? I respect the rights and needs of people who are religious. What I object to are hypocrites—people who do terrible things, then go to church or synagogue and ask for forgiveness. I was put in camps by such hypocrites. I came out of the camps with a very realistic appraisal of people. I realized that they were capable of anything. I wonder sometimes how I ever survived, how I ever took the kinds of blows that came my way without becoming crazy or warped with bitterness. My wounds healed, but the scars are there. They just don't show. I did not suffer as much as some of the others. I was never tortured; I was never left hanging by my wrists with my hands tied behind me. I never worked as hard as the ones who labored in salt mines. Every survivor had to be lucky to escape even a little of the great brutality that was there.

In the 90s Ronny Graham said to me, "For years, I thought you didn't talk about your experiences in the camps because of some deeply buried feelings, and you didn't want them opened up to agonize you." It is quite true; my feelings were deeply buried. I wanted to live a normal life. I didn't want people to feel sorry for me. I never wanted to talk about my experiences in concentration camps. I did not want to live in *that* past. I had put a period there. In the late fifties, my friend Arthur Siegel and I were eating at the Colony Restaurant in New York. I had known Arthur since we were together in *New Faces of 1952*, and I had never talked about that part of my past to him. I don't know if it was the wine, but I started telling him about my parents and how they died, and it hit me as it never had before. I started to cry, and so did he. The customers probably thought, "What are those grown men crying about?" After that, he was the only one to whom, once in a while, I was able to open up and talk about the concentration camps. When people, seeing the tattooed number on my arm, would ask me, "You were in camps?" I would say, "Yes, I spent three years there." That's as far as I would go.

Now I talk freely about my experiences in concentration camps. I do it with a purpose. I feel it is my duty. It's still not for sympathy. It's because I want people to remember that the Holocaust existed and must never occur again.

CHAPTER SIX

MADAME ARON

I never heard anybody call Madame Aron by her first name—not even her husband. She was a portly woman; she was what we called *zaftig*. She had a fuzz of a moustache, slightly kinky grey hair coiffed very simply, thin lips from which a cigarette always dangled, and lovely, kind, light brown eyes. She was a Benoit-Levy by birth. Her husband worked as a manager in a movie theater. Her brother, Jean Benoit-Levy, was a famous French movie director. The Benoit-Levys were an old distinguished French family.

Every Thursday, Madame Aron would rent a theater and put on a show—Laurel and Hardy movies and Tom Mix westerns followed by variety acts performed by professional child actors. Lili, the head social worker at the *Locale,* knew Madame Aron and, aware that I had been appearing on the children's radio show, decided that I should audition for her. With my parents' permission, an appointment was made. I got dressed in my newest suit, shined my shoes, borrowed my father's best tie, and admired myself in the full-length mirror of his armoire. Until I was twelve, my hair had been very straight. Then overnight it became kinky. From that time on, I wore it in a pompadour with lots of brilliantine. I loved my pompadour; I loved to comb it. I would stay in front of the mirror for hours, making every little curl fall into its proper place. In my mind I would play all kinds of parts, I would reenact melodramas that I had just seen on the screen, and create fantasies such as one in which Fernand Gravet, who was a tremendous star, would discover me, then he and his wife would adopt me, and I would live with them and become a star like him.

Lili took me on the subway to a very chic section of Paris not far from l'Arc de Triomphe, where Madame Aron lived. I was very impressed as well as excited about taking my first elevator ride. Madame Aron lived on the fifth floor in an elegant building with carpeting on the staircase in an apartment that had the largest rooms I had ever seen. There were draperies on the windows going all the way to the ceiling and rich Oriental rugs on the highly polished floors. I was twelve years old, and for the first time in my young life, I was speechless, overwhelmed by such opulence.

We arrived after dinner, and I was introduced to Madame Aron, who was to be an important influence in my life. Sitting there with her were her husband, her daughter Nicole, her secretary Mathilde, and Martha, a German Jewish refugee who was her cook. I was asked to sing without an accompanist, which I did, and it must have impressed them because Madame Aron, smiling while she applauded, said, "I like your singing very much, Robert. I like your verve, the way you move, the way you use your hands." She puffed on her cigarette, sending up smoke signals only Indians could understand. "You are going to perform in my shows. I'm going to call my brother, who's ready to make a movie with children, and tell him that you would be perfect for it."

Leaving the apartment, I was walking on air. I was going to perform in real professional shows—maybe become a movie star! I wondered if she was going to pay me. Days later I met Jean Benoit-Levy at his office. Madame Aron had told him that I would be right for the lead in his movie. Obviously I wasn't, because I didn't get it. I did work on the movie as a favor to Madame Aron for three days as an extra and felt like a star.

Madame Aron liked me so much that she gave me the lead role in one of her productions, a musical for children, where I played three different parts. I opened the production as the *compère*, introducing the show that was about to unfold: "Here's another empty seat. Come on in and get ready for the parade. You will see appearing before your eyes puppets like the ones from your childhood where you pull the strings. They will enchant you . . ." My costume consisted of a white open collared silk shirt, pink satin knee britches, white stockings, and golden shoes—a sort of Little Lord Fauntleroy outfit. Near the end of the first act, I became an old witch, wearing a false nose, a cape covering everything to my shoes, and a shawl over my head. I used a gravelly voice for the role. In the second act, while wearing the first costume and adding a crown, I played the King.

One day, as the King, I experienced my first actor's nightmare. I had been rolling along beautifully when suddenly my mind went blank. I forgot everything. Fortunately, I was sitting at a table with pages of the script in front of me. Subconsciously I must have been worried that something like this might happen. I found the lines and went on with the play. It has never happened to me again, although, like most actors, I have nightmares about it.

I was thirteen years old and the star of this production. I loved the footlights, especially the spotlight on me. I loved putting on makeup. I thrived on all of it. I wanted more, more! When the musical closed I continued to work for Madame Aron in movie houses where I would sing three songs between the shorts and the main feature.

Madame Aron believed so thoroughly in my talent that she tried very hard to make me a star. She was aware of how much I adored Charles Trenet, *Le Fou Chantant*. She heard me sing over and over all his songs: "Boum," "Je Chante," "La Route Enchantée," "J'Ai Ta Main," and "La Polka Du Roi." She knew Raoul Breton, Trenet's song publisher, and through him arranged an audition for me. The afternoon of my appointment, Madame Aron took me to the publishing house, Les Editions Raoul Breton, and there to my surprise and great joy I was confronted by my idol. There he was in person, a big man with blond curly hair and the brightest smile I had ever seen. And shaking *my* hand! I was dreaming; it couldn't be true! There he was, talking to me. "What songs do you know?" he asked.

"All of yours by heart," I replied.

"All of them, by heart? Well! Let's hear some of them. Come sit down." He sat at the piano, and I sat on the bench next to him. My heart was making a marathon run. Monsieur Breton and Madame Aron sat facing us.

"How about singing 'Boum?' " Trenet asked.

Without shyness, I said, "Oh, yes, with pleasure." Trenet started to play the introduction, and I went into the first verse of the song. After the first chorus and the second verse, he changed key for the last chorus, and I followed him without faltering. When we finished, he gave me a huge smile and complimented me for my *joyeuse* way of singing and my natural rhythm. Then, playing and singing the same song, he gave me a few pointers on how to do it with more understanding and feeling. At that moment I knew what heaven was.

After a few more songs, Trenet left us, and Raoul Breton talked to Madame Aron and me. He told us he thought I was unusually talented, but—and it was a big *but*—in his opinion I should concentrate solely on my education, graduate, and if I still had the bug when I was twenty, come back to see him, and he would try to help me. I left the office completely elated by the experience. Though Breton's advice was very sound, Madame Aron and I didn't exactly follow it. I never stopped going to school, but I continued to work for her as a performer.

In the summer of 1939, I went with Madame Aron to Cabourg, a resort town on the Normandie coast near Deauville. She had the concession of a theater in the casino, and there, three times a week she would show movies, and I would perform with just a pianist. I would do four or five songs and my imitation of Maurice Chevalier, and I would tap dance like Eleanor Powell, whom I had seen in *Broadway Melody of 1937*. I would put my finger on my cheek like she did and ra-ta-ta-ta-ta-ta-ta-ta-ta. I was a natural mover. Charles, my pianist, was twenty-four, single, and quite a ladies' man. In spite of our age difference we became good friends. He still found time between ladies to teach me new songs and help me get the right tempos and feelings for them. I never saw him with the same woman twice, which was very intriguing.

For Bastille Day, Madame Aron staged a special patriotic show for which I opened the program singing the French national anthem, "La Marseillaise." Every child in France learns "La Marseillaise." Children everywhere sing anthems by rote, without feeling. The first time I sang "La Marseillaise" for Madame Aron, she stopped me cold after the first four bars and said, "That's not the way to sing it! This song has a profound message!" She made me start again, singing as if my life depended on it, as if France would win or lose a war because of my interpretation. Madame Aron made me understand every word of this beautiful anthem. "More volume and strength, Robert, when you sing *Aux armes citoyens, formez vos bataillons. Marchons, march-ons* [Take arms, citizens, form battalions. March, march]. You have to *feel* this sacred song, you should be *proud* to be a Frenchman and die for your country," she said, her cigarette moving rapidly up and down, smoke coming out furiously from her nostrils. "People should get *chills* when they hear you. Okay, sing it from your gut, I know you can." And by God, I sang "La Marseillaise" with everything I had, feeling I was stirring up and recruiting every Frenchman in the nation to fight for his country. Madame Aron did everything with great enthusiasm and passion.

The whole Aron family and a rabbi and his family lived with us in Cabourg in a large rented house not too far from the casino. I shared a bedroom with the secretary, Mathilde, on the top floor. One day Mathilde scolded me for having called Madame Aron by name when we were out shopping in a market. "Never call Madame by her last name—always and only 'Madame' in public places." I found that bizarre. What was she afraid of? Anti-Semitism? Mathilde was slightly retarded, and she had a speech impediment. I made her life miserable by continually and cruelly mimicking her: her walk, her speech, the way she was always arranging her hair net with a nervous jerk. She was extremely devoted to Madame Aron and was equally as religious. Monsieur Aron tolerated their beliefs with a shrug and a little smile.

That September, after the German Army invaded Poland and England and France declared war against Germany, I remained in Cabourg. Afraid that Paris might be bombed, my parents with Hélène, Cécile, and Madeleine joined me there. As refugees, they were given by requisition two rooms on top of a garage in a private home.

The Arons returned to Paris because Monsieur Aron, who had been a captain in the French army, was ordered to join his regiment at Versailles. I went along with them at the railroad station to say goodbye to everybody and kissed Madame Aron. "Keep well and in touch," she said.

I moved in with my parents and sisters into the two rooms over the garage. Life seemed empty at first. I felt lost. The casino was closed. I missed Madame Aron's schedules and activities and the excitement she generated. I had to go to a new junior high school several miles outside of Cabourg, where nothing was familiar. It took me a little while to get accustomed to my new surroundings. But as soon as I made a few friends, I stopped missing Madame Aron, and began to enjoy life again.

Though I was happy, sometimes I was ashamed of my parents. In Cabourg, my friends were non-Jewish. I had a girlfriend, whose father was an auto mechanic and owned his own garage. To me he was a rich man. One day, when a bunch of us were walking along the main street, joking and having a good time, I saw my parents across the street. I turned away, pretending I hadn't seen them. I'm sure they saw me, though they never mentioned it. I had felt ashamed of them because they seemed too old, because my father did not speak French, and because my mother, when she tried to speak it, had a heavy Jewish-Polish accent. At that moment I wanted parents who were youthful, sophisticated, beautiful, and rich. That experience in Cabourg is not one of my most cherished memories. The irony is that I was very proud to be one of their children. I *loved* my mother. But on that street, with my friends, it was as if a voice had said to me, "Who are these strangers? They're servants. She looks like a maid. He looks like a gardener." I wanted nothing to do with them.

I was the only one among my friends in Cabourg who did not have a bicycle. I saw a used bike I was dying to have. Though my father had not yet been able to find work, it never occured to me that there might not be money to pay for it. "I want a bike," I said. "Everybody I know has a bike. Why shouldn't I have a bike? What do you mean, you don't have the money? It's a used bike, a bargain, a steal. I need it!"

After I sulked and nagged a lot, my parents finally bought it for me. I painted it dark red and rode it all over Cabourg with great pride. At the end of June 1940, after the German troops occupied most of France, Cabourg was no safer than Paris, so we returned to our apartment on Rue des Deux Ponts. I was able to use my red bike to deliver the pants my father made. His investment was not wasted.

In the fall of 1940, the Arons rented a large villa south of Paris to be closer to Versailles, where Monsieur Aron was stationed. The Arons; their daughter Nicole; the secretary, Mathilde; and Martha, the cook lived in the villa with the rabbi, his wife, and their two young daughters. Madame Aron invited me to move in with them for a while, knowing it would be a relief for my mother to have one less mouth to feed. Again I shared a tiny bedroom with Mathilde, who snored a lot.

Nicole was a charming nineteen-year-old, who had developed polio as a child. She could hardly walk. Her legs were like two sticks. Yet, she was always smiling. She seemed to be without self pity. She adored children, and would take care of the rabbi's little girls. She was very kind to everybody. Only rarely, when she would erupt into a temper tantrum, would she reveal the frustration she must have suffered. Monsieur Aron would come home every evening from his duties. Though slightly bald and grey, he was a handsome man, with a neat trimmed moustache. He was not the warmest human being I ever met, but could be charming when he wanted to.

Madame Aron decided I should take piano lessons. At first I was absolutely delighted with the idea. The lessons lasted only for a short time because I became bored reading the notes and translating the clef on the left hand, and I was too lazy to do the scales. Seeing that she was wasting her money, Madame Aron, to my great relief, dismissed the piano teacher.

Madame Aron could never be idle. She had us make Alsatian dresses for little celluloid dolls that she would sell, giving the proceeds to Jewish charities. We all pitched in, whether we liked it or not, with sewing the dolls' dresses. My job was to make the big bow hats they wore.

Two months later I returned to my family in paris, and that was the last time I ever saw Madame Aron and her entourage. Eventually they went to Free France.

Before the Nazis imposed their restrictive laws, I was hired to appear in a night club on the Champs Elysées near *l'Etoile,* called *Le Tyrol.* It was a very big club, extremely successful, and was decorated like a Swiss village. They would have variety shows with all kinds of vaudeville acts. At fourteen, I was the youngest entertainer on the bill. I went on first, doing my imitation of Maurice Chevalier, with straw hat and protruding lower lip, singing one of his big hit songs, "On Est Comme on Est" ("We Are as We Are"). The audiences liked "the little boy with long pants" being sure of himself. The star of the show was a female singer, well known at that time, who had a strange habit. Just before she went on, she would ask me to guard her dressing room door to make sure that nobody came in. I wondered why she did that. What was she hiding? One day, near the end of my two-week engagement, I couldn't stand it anymore. I opened her door, as if by accident, and found her naked under a loose silk robe, inserting the needle of a syringe into her arm. I said, "I'm sorry, I thought you called me." I stood there staring at her breasts; hurriedly, she pushed me out. I had absolutely no idea what she was doing, why she was giving herself a shot. When she came out of the room, she put her arm around me and told me with a big smile not to say anything to anybody, that it was our little secret. I felt privileged to be entrusted with the privacy of the big star. That was my last job in show business until my return to France after World War II.

CHAPTER SEVEN

REAL SOLDIERS

For a while, things were close to normal except for the sight of German soldiers in their immaculate uniforms, riding in their cars and on the subways, and playing the conquerors at full tilt. The street signs were now in both French and German.

Also, we were issued gas masks and assigned shelters in case of air raids. Ours was on the Quai de Béthune, in the underground garage of Hélèna Rubenstein's building, where Victor Francen had lived. When the alarm for the first air raid sounded, we were frightened. We grabbed our gas masks and ran to the shelter. The garage was further underground than most shelters in the vicinity, and we felt safe there. I was excited about being in that building, hoping I might run into Victor Francen and the other celebrities who lived in the neighborhood. (Actually Francen, along with Claude Dauphin, Jean Pierre Aumont, Charles Boyer, Dalio, Jean Gabin, Michelle Morgan, and others, had already fled France for the United States.)

By the fourth air raid, because Paris was never bombed, we stopped going to the shelter. The gas masks were put way back in the armoire, and when the alarm sounded, we would turn off all the lights and open the windows and watch the skies for planes.

I had two girl friends that year, not counting Zelda Zilberberg who lived two floors above us and had been my official girl friend since childhood, just because I kissed her on the cheek once. My two girlfriends were physically poles apart. Fanny was voluptuous, with long auburn hair and beautiful, almond shaped green eyes. Her

breasts were already nicely developed. Henriette was more of a tom-
boy, with a perky personality. She was the smartest of the three of us.
I was infatuated with both of them. We were very often together, but
I managed to see them separately, taking Fanny down to the banks of
the Seine and vowing to love her forever while we kissed passionately.
At the same time, I was making plans for the future with Henriette.
And on the back burner, I was saving little Zelda for marriage. I
enjoyed sharing myself with Fanny and Henriette and giving some
crumbs to Zelda—the occasional kiss on the cheek. I felt like a true
Casanova. While Fanny knew about my feelings toward Henriette,
she never felt threatened, and often made funny remarks about the
whole situation. Henriette, on the other hand, took the matter very
seriously, was very jealous of my affection for Fanny, and expressed
her sentiments vehemently. Yet, when the three of us were together
we had a great time.

   It didn't hurt that they were both great dancers. I was a very good
jitterbugger, as were my sisters Cécile and Madeleine. I was also a jazz
fanatic. I adored American music and singers—Ella Fitzgerald, Louis
Armstrong, the Andrews Sisters, Benny Goodman, Jimmy and
Tommy Dorsey, Artie Shaw, Chick Webb, Jimmy Lunceford. A kid
in our building, whom we nicknamed "Bobus" because he had a huge
nose and was kind of sweetly dumb, had a marvelous collection of
American records. He also had a portable record player, which was a
luxury for us. I made a deal with him. He brought his records and his
record player to my apartment, and I taught him how to jitterbug.
The poor guy couldn't dance; he had two left feet. It was sheer torture, but I forced myself to teach him in order to be able to listen to
those wonderful records. I learned all the orchestrations to songs like
"A Tisket a Tasket," "Undecided," "Little White Lies," "On the
Sunny Side of the Street," and Ella's "My Heart Belongs to Daddy."

   To earn money I worked for Madame Laurent, a widow who
owned a store across the street from where we lived—a crêmerie selling cheeses, milk, eggs, vegetables, and fruits. Everything was
rationed, and all the merchants had to get up very early in the morning to go to Les Halles. They would stand in line for hours to be sure
to get the merchandise before supplies ran out. I would get up at
three-thirty, splash water on my face, gulp down some hot coffee

with milk and a piece of bread while I got dressed, then run to Les Halles to be the first in line. Madame Laurent would join me there around five-thirty or six. In the event she didn't arrive on time, she always gave me the money to buy the produce.

Charles Trenet was doing a one-man show in a theater off the Champs Elysées. The seats were very expensive, and I was broke, giving what little money I made to my parents. But I *had* to see Charles Trenet. One morning, instead of buying food at Les Halles, I hid the money in my shoe, then walked back to Madame Laurent's store with tears in my eyes. "Somebody on the queue stole the money," I said. "We were getting pushed. I didn't feel anything. I don't know how; I don't know when, but the money is gone! I feel terrible!" A few days later I went to see Charles Trenet, without a twinge of guilt. Whether she believed me or not, Madame Laurent was very nice about it. She never asked my parents to reimburse her. However, I never worked for her again.

That was the extent of my criminal career. Except for once when I was six and stole fruit from a stand on the Rue St. Louis en l'Ile and ran away, eating as I went. And once when I stole some photos. On my way to art school, I would pass by a stationery store on the Boulevard St. Michel that sold five-by-seven-inch photos of French movie stars. I would go in every day and head directly to the revolving racks that held the pictures of my idols. Turning the racks, I would study them, craving them, longing to be able to afford to buy them for my scrapbooks of pictures clipped from movie magazines. One day, finally unable to contain my frustration at not possessing them, and with my heart in my mouth, I stole a dozen of them. I walked fast up the Boulevard, in a state of such abject terror, fearing I was going to be apprehended at any moment, that I made up my mind never to steal again.

To this day, I cannot hear the beginning of Beethoven's Fifth Symphony without its bringing me back to the start of the German occupation of France, before all the restrictions, when we could still go to the movies. They would show us German propaganda newsreels with all those young, healthy, cocky, aggressively victorious Wehrmacht and SS soldiers, goose-stepping their way through foreign countries. These films were always accompanied by the first few bars of Beethoven's Fifth, "Pom, pom, pom, pom—Pom, pom, pom, pom." For a long time, I related that theme to the evil of mankind and closed my mind to Beethoven's music. Even today, that symphony brings me back to 1941.

In June of that year, everything started to change for us. We had to go to the police station to register and to get our identification papers stamped with the letter "J". Yellow Stars of David, with the word *Juif* printed in black, were issued to us to be sewn on our outer garments and worn in full view at all times. There were new laws for us. One of them required that we travel in a special compartment on the subway. Those who were caught in the other compartments, if they were not arrested, would be thrown out by the Aryans. "Get out of here, you dirty Jew bastard!" they would scream. We were barred from public places—parks, hotels, restaurants, theaters, and all places of entertainment. Jews could not work for the government or be in show business; most shops and businesses were taken away from them.

Because we Jews were not allowed to perform anymore, I was terribly frustrated. Since I had always loved to draw and paint, and showed some ability, my sister Hélène (and I don't know where she got the money) sent me to an art school called Arts et Métiers, on the Boulevard St. Michel, which specialized in poster advertising. It was the only activity I was allowed to pursue, and I enjoyed going there tremendously. I will never forget the first day I wore the yellow star. I was very apprehensive about how my friends in art school, who were not Jewish, would react. Would they now voice the anti-Semitism I always knew existed? Would they reject me? Spit at me? Worse? I arrived at school trembling, ashamed, as if I had done something very wrong. But to my surprise, they did just the opposite of what I had expected. They were all sympathetic, angry at the Germans, and showed their defiance by walking with me after school down the Boulevard St. Michel to the café *Chez Dupont* in the Latin Quarter, daring anyone to say anything. It heartened me to realize there were decent people who would stand up to the tyranny.

I attended classes for only half a day. Not to have to go to school for a whole day was paradise to me. I learned the craft of making poster-ads, how to use all media: pencil, charcoal, watercolor, gouache, and oil. We had homework which was never a bore. Somehow I didn't miss being out of show business.

Prosper Arous, who lived in our apartment house on the ground floor, was my sister Madeleine's boyfriend. Although his parents were Algerian Jews, he was Nordic looking, with blond wavy hair and pale green eyes. He was tall and very handsome, had a Parisian *débonnaire* attitude about him, and the women found him very attractive. He had great flair and dressed beautifully. To me he was perfection, everything I wanted to be when I grew up. He worked as a telegram delivery boy—the only thing about him I didn't want to emulate—using a five speed racing bike, which he kept spotless, like himself. We got along very well together. I loved being with him; he was like a twenty-year-old brother to me. Often Madeleine was annoyed by my hanging around and made me leave to go and play with friends my own age. Prosper was five years older than I. I liked to pretend he *was* my brother, and proudly would introduce him that way whenever he was in the neighborhood and would stop by the art school to walk home with me.

The French Government, under the supervision of the Nazis, saw to it that we all went to register as Jews at the police stations. There were lots of Polish, Hungarian, Rumanian, and Russian Jews living in France who were not French citizens—including most of my family. My father, who had arrived in Paris and lived there since 1921, had never been granted French citizenship. These foreign-born Jews were the first to receive the blow of the Nazi machinery. Everything was well planned, the final solution being around the corner. There began to be *rafles,* round-ups, in Paris by *Arrondissements.*

The first members of my family to be arrested were my nephews Adolphe and Henri, sons of my half-sister Fanny. They lived in the eleventh *Arrondissement.* Fanny and her husband, David, were not arrested that day because their daughters Raymonde and Adée were minors and born in Paris, and Nazi ruling at that time specified that they remain under the supervision of their parents. Adolphe and Henri, however, were sent to a transient camp in Beaune-La-Rolande, 120 kilometers south of Paris, near Orléans. They stayed there until 1942, working on a farm. One day they told their parents, who had come to visit them, that they intended to escape. Fearing reprisals, Fanny and David talked them out of it. Adolphe and Henri were deported to Germany in June 1942, and never came back. Fanny and David never forgave themselves. With their daughters, they were hidden by the concierge of their building on the Rue de l'Orillon in one small room. For more than eighteen months, they barely spoke a word to each other and did not leave the room for fear they would be caught. Because of the goodness of the concierge, they were never deported.

The round-ups always occurred in the same fashion. The French police would arrive with buses and a list of the names of people to be taken that day, who were given ten minutes to grab a few belongings before they were ordered into the buses. Their destination would be to one of the transient camps in France.

On August 20, 1941, I was working part time for my half-sister Adèle who owned a bakery in the twentieth *Arrondissement*. That morning we were all working in the back of the store—her husband Bernard, their sons Jean, Marcel, Georges, whom we all called Jojo, and I—when we heard the buses arrive. Jean's wife Mariette, who was at the front of the bakery, called to us to come out and look. We saw the policemen burst out of the buses and run in all directions to the surrounding buildings. It looked like an invasion of thousands of dark blue uniforms swarming on the Boulevard de Menilmontant. Some of them formed a human *barrage* to be sure that no one would escape. We didn't know what to do. It was the first time that I had been involved in a *rafle*. We didn't know if we were on the list and would be arrested. My heart was pounding so hard I thought it was going to leave my chest. I also had instant diarrhea, something I would often have in the concentration camps.

Bernard, Jean, and Marcel ran up the stairway behind the bakery to their apartment. But they didn't have the time to hide. They were pursued by the police, apprehended, and told to be ready in ten minutes. Adèle, Jojo, and Mariette were not on the list. Mariette and Jojo were French citizens, and Jojo was a minor. Although he was Jojo's father, Bernard somehow had gotten on the list. My name was not there because I did not live in that *Arrondissement*. The short ten minutes were petrifying—policemen screaming orders, people running in panic, some trying to escape and being grabbed and then dragged and shoved into the buses. Their cries are etched in my memory forever. I stared at this brutal treatment in shock, numb with fear and unable to grasp the reality of what was happening.

I was spared this time, as were Adèle, Mariette, and Jojo. Adèle sobbed uncontrollably, as she watched her husband and two of her sons being taken. At the same time she knew she had to be strong for the sake of her younger son. She hoped that the others would not be kept prisoners in Drancy too long.

"It is all a mistake," she kept saying. "It can't be happening to us."

In the meantime, on the Boulevard, non-Jews were witnessing the arrests, some simply out of curiosity, others baiting the police to take all the dirty Jews away. "France to the French!" they shouted. "Good riddance! At last, justice is being done! Now we can breathe clean Aryan air!"

Jean and Marcel were released a few months later, on November 4, from Drancy, because they had lost so much weight and because the camp was so overcrowded. The Nazis had not yet begun mass deportations to concentration camps in Germany and Poland. Jean with his wife, Mariette, went immediately to Free France. Marcel, on August 4, 1942, a year after his arrest at the bakery, fled to Pau, in Free France, where, with my half-brother Henri, he joined the *Maquis* as an underground fighter. Henri, after the war, received a medal for bravery and became a French citizen. Adèle's husband, my brother-in-law Bernard, was deported from Drancy in April 1942 to concentration camps and never came back. In July 1942, Adèle and Jojo were arrested, then deported from Drancy in September. They both died in Auschwitz.

My sister Aimée, after sending her six-year-old daughter Sylviane to live with a family of farmers who were protective and sympathetic, stayed in Melun, a city south of Paris, until the end of 1942. She was told that a woman had denounced her to the Germans, and that they were waiting for her at her hotel to arrest her. Being forewarned, she stayed away from the hotel. She obtained some false I.D. papers from a woman who worked as a nurse in a hospital in Melun. Her name became Aimée Rigault, and she was able to work and stay in France. Her husband, Gaston, who had fought the short war with the French army, was captured and taken prisoner. He stayed in a stalag in Germany for five years, put in a special Kommando for Jews, and came back to Paris on May 5, 1945, after being liberated by the Allies. He came back a day after my return from Germany to Paris. It was a double celebration for Aimée.

My sister Hélène was a very independent person. She had a strong character, stubborn at times. I am sure she would have become a successful actress. She went to the Solange Sicard acting school in Paris, the equivalent at that time of Lee Strasberg's school in America. She was extremely talented. She took every acting job she could find, playing minor roles in local Yiddish theater and working as an extra in movies. She looked like a combination of Anna Magnani and Sophia Loren. She had Magnani's fierceness, her nose and jet black hair, and Loren's elegance and green eyes. She was very intense, very dedicated, full of energy, extremely sweet, and had a deep passion for life.

During the occupation, Hélène would ignore the curfew. She would arrive home at the last second, sometimes even after eight, causing my mother great anxiety. My parents feared for her, knowing she could be arrested.

"Nothing is going to happen to me," she would say. "Why would they arrest me? I'm Hélène Widerman!" She never got caught arriving late. But she was arrested in the first round-up at our building.

The now-dreaded buses with policemen arrived on July 16, 1942, to arrest non-French Jews. Cécile and Hélène were on the list, but my parents were not because Madeleine and I were French citizens. Cécile, fortunately, was working for a Dr. Etienne Albert who had heard rumors that there would be arrests the next day in the fourth *Arrondissement,* and had told her to stay at his apartment overnight.

From Dr. Albert's apartment, Cécile telephoned the bistro across the street from our apartment house. Le Bougnat, as we called the man who owned the café, yelled, "Madame Widerman! Telephone for you." I ran downstairs to take the call for my mother, always expecting bad news. Cécile explained what was happening and told me to have Hélène join her before curfew. Hélène was out with friends taking her acting lesson. She arrived that night a few minutes before eight, too late to go to the doctor's apartment, which was a good fifteen minute walk.

"If for once," my mother said, "you got home early, you could have gone and hid. Now you have to stay here. The risk of being arrested on the street is too great if you go."

The next morning, very early before anybody could leave the apartment house because of the curfew, it happened as the doctor had said. The buses arrived. One of the policemen knocked on our door and asked if Cécile Widerman was here.

My mother answered, "No, she doesn't live here anymore."

He never questioned my mother's lie. He then asked, "Is Hélène Widerman here?"

Hélène immediately said, "Yes, here I am."

He told her to pack a bag and come downstairs with him. She asked for permission to buy some magazines at Monsieur Verdier's store around the corner.

"Yes, you can go, but don't be too long," the cop said. She could have escaped easily. But she came back, as she promised, afraid if she didn't they would arrest my parents, Madeleine, and me. She was put on a bus with the others and taken to Drancy, where she spent three months before being deported on September 18, 1942, to Auschwitz. I have two cousins who survived Auschwitz who saw her there. They said she had become terribly ill. We don't know how she died—whether it was from typhus or some other disease, or if she was gassed. But she did die in Auschwitz at the age of twenty-two.

At the same time as my sister Hélène's arrest, we lost our very close friends, Madame Zilberberg, her two daughters—Zelda, my "girl friend" upon whose cheeks I bestowed kisses and Paulette, who was Madeleine's closest friend—and one of her sons, David, with whom my sister Cécile was in love. Henri, Madame Zilberberg's oldest son, had moved out of the apartment. The youngest child, Bernard, who was born in Paris and was not on the list, became my mother's responsibility. Before being taken away, Madame Zilberberg gave my mother the keys to her apartment and the W.C. which, because of the smallness of her apartment, was situated down the corridor.

The day after Hélène's arrest, Dr. Albert gave Cécile some money, bought her a train ticket, took her to the Gâre de Lyon, and saw to it that she was on her way to join my sister Aimée in Melun. Dr. Albert was one of the non-Jews outraged by the way we were being treated and the gross injustice inflicted upon us. He had taken over the practice of an old Jewish doctor who had fled to Switzerland and, understanding the situation, did everything in his power to help as many Jews as he could.

After being in Melun for a few weeks, hoping the police had by then forgotten that she existed, Cécile returned to Paris. To be on the safe side she did not sleep in our apartment but went to Madame Shuster's on the sixth floor. Through my nephew Jean's wife, Mariette, she got a false birth certificate and became Pierrette Nicodème. On August 4, she fled to Free France, aided by two farmers who were paid to sneak her through the demarcation line at five in the morning. She then went to a small-town *gendarmerie,* police barracks, and told the *gendarme* in charge that she had lost all her identification papers except for her birth certificate, and that she had to go to Pau to work there. The *gendarme,* without questioning her, gave her temporary papers. "When you arrive in Pau," he said, "go to the police station to get your I.D. card." Once in Pau she became officially Pierrette Nicodème. She worked for a while as a babysitter for a Jewish family. A few months later she was joined by Madeleine, and they both went to Marseilles where they had friends—among them Madame Zilberberg's son Henri—and where, because it was a bigger city, they would be less conspicuous.

Eventually Cécile and Madeleine went their separate ways. After the Germans occupied all of France in November 1942, Cécile joined some of her friends in the underground movement. She became a member of the *Maquis* in early 1943 and was a courier, delivering messages, guns, rifles, and machine guns to the fighters. She stayed in Marseilles leading this dangerous life for a year-and-a-half. She returned to liberated Paris in October 1944, joining an auxiliary group of women who had all been connected in one way or another with the underground. The group took care of prisoners of war and concentration camp survivors, lodging them temporarily in hotels, furnishing them with identification papers, and helping them to start a new life.

Because she didn't like to be called Pierrette, Cécile was known by the underground people as Nic, short for Nicodème. After the war, she adopted the nickname Nic, and became Nicole, dropping forever the Cécile of her youth. We all call her Nicky.

CHAPTER EIGHT

DESCENT INTO THE FIRES OF HELL: DRANCY

On September 23, 1942, they came to round us up at nine-thirty in the evening, when everybody was home. They came only to our apartment house, not in the usual manner to arrest the entire *Arrondissement*, which ordinarily took place in the daytime. They really took us by surprise. Nobody in the house had heard rumors that we were going to be arrested that day. There had always been anti-Semites on l'Ile St. Louis. After the war I learned that some of them had gone to the police and said, "Why don't you arrest this house full of Jews at 10 Rue des Deux Ponts? Let's get rid of them. Since some of them were arrested in July; get rid of the others."

The buses arrived unloading French policemen and two Gestapo agents in civilian clothes. They went from one apartment to another, banging on all the doors, and shouting, "You've got ten minutes to get your belongings and meet us downstairs!"

As soon as Prosper, who lived on the ground floor, saw the buses, he ran up to our apartment and told my mother he wanted to take Madeleine with him to one of his sister's who lived not too far away. They would escape from a bedroom window onto the side street. My mother refused to let Madeleine go with him. Prosper went back to his apartment and let himself be arrested with all the others, thinking he would be with Madeleine. Three days later he was deported from Drancy and never came back.

The apartment house was in a state of chaos. All you could hear was yelling and screaming. People rushed around like trapped animals, hysterical. Children cried in terror.

My mother took Madame Zilberberg's key and said to Madeleine, "Go up and hide in the toilet." My sister, without hesitating one second, took the key and ran upstairs.

"Reevela," my mother said to me, "you go with Madeleine."

"No, I'm staying with you," I said.

My mother begged me to go, but finally gave up. Twice I was sent upstairs to give Madeleine some money, clothing, and to tell her what to do. Somehow I managed to evade the police and the Gestapo who were swarming all over the place.

Madeleine stayed overnight in that tiny toilet, frozen with fear, listening to the pounding rain hitting the small window. Before the buses left, she heard two policemen pass by the door. One of them said, "We didn't look in there." The other answered, "We don't have time, let's go." The next morning, the concierge, Madame Froment, refused to give her the key to our apartment. Madeleine went to see my brother Jacques and stayed with him, and eventually, with false papers, went to free France, where she met her future husband, Jean Wegier.

My sister Ida, her husband, Jacques, and my two nephews, Bernard and Edmond, had moved in with us. Because they had escaped being arrested in their *Arrondissement* on July 16th, they thought they would be safe with us. Ida begged her two sons, who were very young, to go and hide with Madeleine. Like me, they refused. We wanted to be with our parents.

Uncle Yankef, who lived in the annex, where people were not being rounded up, had heard the tremendous noise that was going on in our building. "Chave Lea," he said to my aunt, "I'll be right back. I'm going to say goodbye to Moishe and Baila." He never did go back. He was apprehended and was taken away with everyone from our building. He died in Auschwitz. Chave Lea, who had always had moments of instability, went berserk. Her daughters had to put her into a sanitarium where she spent the rest of the war, thus escaping being arrested and sent to the gas chambers. She lived alone to the age of 95, climbing every day the six flights to her small apartment. She occasionally had relapses and would have to return to the sanitarium.

We were assembled downstairs, with suitcases and bundles. I had no suitcase, so I took my possessions—my scrapbooks and some of my drawings, fan magazines, comic books I had collected, and a few pieces of clothing—and wrapped them in a blanket.

We were shoved into buses and taken in the pouring rain to the local police station, where we stayed overnight. We were well guarded by the French police who saw that nobody left the room. People moaned and cried. Mothers, rocking back and forth, held dozing children on their laps. We sat on hard wooden benches, waiting.

The next morning we were shoved into buses again. I knew there was a place called Drancy, on the outskirts of Paris. I didn't know that people were transferred out of Drancy to slave labor and concentration or extermination camps. Nobody was told, nor could they have imagined, that they were going to be put into gas chambers. So we went like cattle to the slaughterhouse.

When we arrived in Drancy, we saw a huge camp enclosed by barbed wire. We were taken out of the buses, pushed and screamed at, and ordered into lines to be registered. Then we were led by groups to assigned rooms. Fifty of us were crowded into a small empty room with not even a bench to sit on and nothing but straw on the floor.

What has stayed vividly in my memory of the first day is the constant crying of children, the drone of moaning, and the desperation on the faces of people trying not to be separated from their families. Some looked for relatives who were arrested before them. We were doing the same thing, asking questions about Adèle, Bernard, and their son Jojo. We found out that they had all been deported. We also learned that Hélène had left on a convoy a few days before. Nobody knew the destination of the convoys.

My parents, my sister Ida, her husband and two children, uncle Yankef, Bernard Zilberberg, and I kept tightly together.

The following morning, they woke us up at three o'clock to call off the names of the people to be deported that day. Our names were on the list. We were lined up at the gates with our few belongings and registered for the second time. Vital statistics were recorded: first and last name, place and date of birth, profession, time and place of arrest, and date of deportation. We were put back on buses and taken to a railroad depot station where we were herded into a cattle train, one hundred people to each car. There was straw on the floor, and the only ventilation came from a few slatted air vents on both sides of the car. Before locking the doors, they gave us food: some bread, margarine, and slices of sausage. There were two small wooden buckets for toilet facilities for a hundred people.

We traveled in darkness with only a bit of light flickering through the slats for a long three days and two nights, not knowing where we were going. I could see my father sitting in the corner of the car with uncle Yankef. They never moved for three days. My sister Ida and her husband, Jacques, tried to console their two sons, promising them that everything would be all right. Bernard Zilberberg, who stuttered like his mother, kept asking, "Madame Widerman, wh-wh-where are we g-g-going? Wh-wh-what's g-going to happen t-t-to us?" Calmly, my mother told him that very soon he would be with his mother, sisters, and brother.

The moaning and crying never stopped. Old people, suffering in pain, fainted from the heat. Mothers holding their babies in their arms tried to quiet them. More than anything, I remember the unbearable stench. The buckets had no lids. They filled up very quickly, and there was no way to get rid of the defecation. The car was locked tight. Nobody could possibly have escaped. We were well guarded by German soldiers stationed on the platforms between the cars.

The first day on the train, my mother asked me to write a letter to my brother Jacques. Jacques, Gaby, and their daughter were still in Paris. Protected by their neighbors—especially Jacques' closest friend, Monsieur Masson, who worked as a postman—until the liberation of Paris, they never moved from their apartment. I found paper and pencil among the things I had thrown into my blanket, and huddling close to my mother with barely enough room to move, I wrote:

September 25, 1942

Dear Jacques,

We are writing to you, to tell you that we are on a train, traveling toward Hélène, in the east. We will surely rejoin Adèle and her husband. I am asking you, in Mama's name, that you take good care of yourself and Madeleine. We are a hundred in sealed cattle cars, and frightful things are happening in them, that I hope you will never see. We have lots of courage and hope to come back alive amongst you. Go up to see Mr. Bernard, and ask him to do everything he can to get us out, even if we go to Metz,* because you can't imagine what it is like. I have only one wish, it is to be able to see all of you again one day soon. Take good care of all of you and Madeleine. Excuse my handwriting, but I am writing while the train is in motion. Mama kisses you and Golda** and everybody. Papa, Ida, Jacques, their children and I, Robert, think about all of you.

Robert

P.S. Tell Madeleine, or you, to go up to see Mr. Zelichevsky, to take back what we left with him, rings, earrings. Madeleine should go to Adèle's concierge, give her 1000 francs, and the concierge will give her something. We are thinking of all of you. What is Liba*** doing? Take care of her and tell her to take out the ten sheets that are at the laundry. Uncle is with us. Tell his daughter.

I put the letter in an envelope, then dropped it out one of the slats. (I didn't learn until 1981 that Jacques had received my letter. He had kept the original and had given copies to Aimée, Nicky, and Madeleine. Because after the liberation, like most survivors, I did not want to talk about my experiences, they respected my silence and never mentioned the letter.)

Sometimes the train would stop for a few hours, then start again; often it would stop briefly, then go in reverse, then forward, back and forth. At stops, we would hear people talking. When they were no longer speaking French, but only German, we knew we had crossed the border, and we became even more apprehensive.

On the third day, in the late afternoon, the train stopped in a town called Kosel, in the upper Silesia region of Germany, near the borders of Poland and Czechoslovakia. They unlocked the doors. Dazed and blinded by the daylight, we were greeted by the barking of ferocious German shepherds held on leashes by the SS men who

---

*Metz is a city in France in the Moselle *departement* near the German border. Rumors on the train had it that there were camps there, large centers where Jews would be kept for the duration of the war.

**Jacques' wife Gaby.

***My sister Aimée.

were shouting orders at us. Most of us did not understand. "Raus, Raus! Schnell, Schnell!" they screamed. Fortunately, some of the people on the train understood German and translated for the rest of us. The SS guards, in their spotless grey uniforms and highly polished boots, wanted all the men between the ages of sixteen and fifty to get out of the cars. Hitting them with rifle butts, they ordered the men to sit on the ground. I grabbed my blanket and jumped off the train with my brother-in-law and sat where they pushed us. Before I left the car, my mother kissed me quickly on the forehead and gave me her last words of advice. "Reevela, do exactly what they tell you to do. Obey them. Tantrums won't work anymore. I won't be there to protect you."

We sat on the ground huddled together, wondering what was going to happen to us. The huge police dogs were barking at us, growling, and showing their teeth. You knew that it would take only one little word and they would tear you to shreds. I was always afraid of dogs, and I sat rigid with terror.

The SS guards looked us over and weeded out the men they decided were too young or too old and ordered them back to the cars. One of them stopped in front of me. "You!" he screamed. "Back on the train!" Although I was sixteen-and-a-half, I looked twelve. I did not understand what he said, but I understood his gesture. I took my bundle and climbed back into the car.

I stayed at the open door helping to pass cans of water to the elderly men, the women, and children. We were dying of thirst; we hadn't had anything to drink for three days. Another guard passed the car, looked at me and asked, "How old are you?" Paralyzed with fright by his screaming, and unable to understand him, I couldn't answer. The man standing next to me answered for me and, as it turned out, saved my life. "Sixteen," he said. The guard yelled to me, "Down on the ground, *schnell, schnell!*" So once again I grabbed my bundle and jumped off the car, pushed by the butt of the guard's rifle. I rejoined my brother-in-law Jacques, who kept staring at the open door, hoping to catch a last glimpse of his family. If the man had not answered for me and the guard had not ordered me off the train, I would have stayed with my parents. And I would have gone to Auschwitz and been gassed.

In the extraordinary book *Le Memorial de la Deportation des Juifs de France,* Serge and Beate Klarsfeld, after the war, assembled the names and dates of deportation of 80,000 Jews arrested and deported only from France. It shows that in my convoy there were 729 Rumanians, 111 Poles, 99 Frenchmen, 28 Germans; 446 were men, 431 women, and 12 were under the age of 17. At Kosel, 175 out of 1,004 people were selected to go to a slave labor camp. At Auschwitz, 91 women and 40 men were also selected, by Dr. Mengele, to go to work. The other 698—women, children, and older men—were sent directly to the gas chambers that day. Out of the 306 people who were selected and escaped the gas chambers, I am one of 15 men who came out alive. None of the women survived.

I sat on the ground with my brother-in-law Jacques, the only family I had now. As I watched the doors of the cars sliding closed and saw the train leave, I heard the loud cries coming from inside of women and children separated from their husbands, fathers, and sons, not knowing where they were going or what would happen to them. The lamentation lingered in the air long afterward. Jacques, who suddenly had lost his wife and two sons, said absolutely nothing. Most of the men were in a state of shock and extremely quiet. Those who could not control themselves were hit with rifle butts. None of us knew that the train was on its way to Auschwitz-Birkenau. For a long time, I thought that my parents and the rest of my family had gone to other camps and would have a chance to survive as I was trying to do.

After the train left, the 175 of us were ordered onto open trucks. We then traveled for an hour to our first camp. En route, kids lined along the streets laughed and screamed at us, pelting us with stones. To the amusement of the German soldiers guarding us on the trucks, they shouted, "Dirty Jews! Dirty Jews! Dirty Jew bastards!"

CHAPTER NINE

OTTMUTH:
"BEI MIR BIST DU SCHOEN"

We arrived at Ottmuth, a small transient slave labor camp. Ottmuth was not guarded by the SS, but by the Wehrmacht
troops, older soldiers who could not fight at the front, and younger
ones who had been wounded. We were ordered into a large barrack
containing approximately two hundred upper and lower bunks. Each
had a straw mattress, a straw pillow, and a blanket. A small pipe stove
stood in the center of the large room.

We listened, dazed, as we were told in screaming voices, in German and Yiddish, where we were and what was going to happen to
us. Some of us would be selected to work at a shoe factory, which was
called "OTA." Others, in a few days, would be sent to different
camps. We were then asked to file into the barracks, which housed the
washroom and showers. We were told to strip and then were shaved
like sheep from head to toe, disinfected in big vats containing a strong
solution that made our skin sting and our eyes burn. Then we took
showers, which, after three days of close confinement in cattle cars,
made us feel at least clean. We were then issued clothing, which more
or less fited us and had Stars of David cut out of the cloth in the front
and the back of the jackets and on each leg of the trousers above the
knee. We were each given a tin cup, a bowl, a fork, and a spoon and
were told we had better not lose them because they would not be
replaced.

The Nazis had delegated to Jews the work of overseeing the

inmates. Halberstock, the *Judenaelterster,* (Jewish Kommandant of the camp) was assigned by the SS to see that the camp ran smoothly. He was a short, stout man with gray hair, steel-rimmed eyeglasses, and a voice like a roaring lion. Under Halberstock were two *Kapos,* lieutenants, responsible for us at work and in the camp. *Stubenaelters-ters,* one in each room, were in charge of the barracks. The two *Kapos* came from Poland and had been in camps since 1941. One, a stocky man, uneducated and peasant-looking with a weather-beaten face and dark, mean eyes, abused his authority. He was the screamer and hitter of the two. We called him "the Schmuck." The other one, a tall, dark, good looking man named Burstein, was younger than the Schmuck and, unlike him, was not on our backs every minute. He was strict, but not cruel.

There were about ten Polish Jewish women who worked in the kitchen and the laundry. Some of them were girlfriends of the *Jude-naelterster,* the *Kapos,* the camp cook, and the dentist.

Compared with other concentration camps, Ottmuth was small. There were four barracks, one of which was used for new arrivals. Each of the other three contained twelve rooms with ten upper and lower bunks. A table and benches were the only furniture, and a small pipe stove sat next to the door. The *Judenaelterster* and the *Kapos* had private rooms with single beds. The latrine was a shack and consisted of two wooden planks set over an open trench. You learned how to function without privacy. In the middle of the camp was the *Appell Platz* where we would assemble for roll call at least twice a day, standing on our feet for hours in rows of five. Very quickly we learned how to count in German.

We were in the new arrivals barracks for a week without working. Nobody had as yet been selected to stay or leave the camp. We were on edge, fearing the worst. One day, while we waited, Jacques asked me to sing. We were outdoors on the *Appell Platz,* for once not at roll call. A few of the girls, who were hanging the wash, came over to listen. They especially liked the way I was singing "Bei Mir Bist Du Schoen" and asked me to sing it again. One of the girls, Miriam, who was the size of a football player with kinky hair and a broad smile, was the *Judenaelterster*'s girlfriend. She ran to his office and in a few minutes returned with him.

"Sing that French Jewish song again," she said. "Go ahead, sing it for the *Judenaelterster*."

After that I was always asked to sing for everybody in the camp, and I became a favorite of the *Judenaelterster* and the *Kapos*. They loved everything I sang but always requested "Bei Mir Bist Du Schoen."

At the end of the week, a Gestapo agent named "Hausschild," a frail man in his forties with a pronounced limp, came to the camp to make the selection. We stood at roll call while he pointed at us with his whip, indicating the ones he wanted to step out of line. These would be sent to other camps. Only a hundred and fifty of us would remain in Ottmuth to work at the nearby factory. In the nineteen months I stayed in Ottmuth, I saw that same Gestapo agent at least once a week, when he came to make the selections. At roll call, the *Kapos* would always put me—along with Jacques, as a favor to me—in a special column to make sure that we would not be selected to be shipped to other camps. Except for those of us who worked at the factory, and the fifty who worked in the camp, all the others—new arrivals who came weekly from Holland, Belgium and France—were sent to different concentration camps.

I was one of the youngest and the smallest men in the camp. Not only my singing, but my height helped me tremendously all through my ordeal. I used my smallness to my advantage. Later, at the Gross-Rosen camp, where I stayed for only three days, they used to hit us as we went in and out of the barracks. I would protect myself from the blows by staying in the middle of the group as we were herded and prodded along. At Ottmuth, when the weather was freezing I would keep myself in the middle, surrounded by inmates; the wind would not be so biting when it reached me.

At Ottmuth, one day when we were marching back to the camp after work, I was pulled out of line and slapped hard on the face by, of all people, the good *Kapo* Burstein, who liked me. Imagine if he hadn't! My immediate reaction was to hit him back. I thought, how dare he hit me! I don't remember what I had done to anger him, but as he yelled at me I yelled back, "You big peasant, why don't you pick on somebody your size!" He laughed and pushed me back in line.

That was one of the very few times in my thirty-one months of captivity that I received blows from the *Kapos.*

Each evening when we returned from work, we would stand in line to receive a small piece of brownish bread with a tiny square of margarine and sometimes a slice of sausage.

The shoe factory was a half-hour walk from the camp. Every morning we would rise at four o'clock. Two of us would go to the kitchen and bring back a vat of ersatz coffee. That was our breakfast. We made our beds and took turns sweeping the floors of the rooms and corridors of the barracks with primitive brooms made of twigs. Everything had to be spotless. Otherwise, when we returned from work in the evening, we would find the beds torn apart and the room in shambles, and we would be severely punished—beaten and given extra duty; whoever had been responsible for sweeping that day was made to sweep for a whole week.

By four-thirty we had to be dressed and washed, our chores done, and ready for roll call on the *Appell Platz.* Roll call usually took at least an hour. We always had to be counted more than once. Often, because of the hard labor, the few hours sleep, and the starvation diet, some inmates would arrive late at roll call. The *Kapos,* especially the Schmuck, would scream at them, beat them, and push them into lines, and roll call would have to start all over again from the beginning. Other times, roll calls were interrupted by announcements and lengthy speeches from the *Judenaelterster* warning us to shape up or be shipped out to other camps he assured us were far worse than this one.

While this went on I would watch the sunrise. It was always so beautiful—at times breathtaking. And with the start of the day there was always the crowing of the roosters. Along with the hens, they belonged to the German soldiers. And no matter what was going on, no matter what the *Judenaelterster* was saying, the roosters chased the hens through the *Appell Platz* and jumped on them, rushing from one to another. It amused me greatly and allowed my mind to escape for a few moments from the nightmare we were living.

After roll call, in the sweltering heat of summer or in winter when the snow was up to our knees and the wind was freezing cold, we would walk for a half-hour to OTA, the shoe factory. It was a large plant employing hundreds of German civilians—mostly females whose husbands and sons were fighting on both fronts—and Aryan Poles and Czechoslovakians. We were always kept separated from Aryans and well guarded.

Inside, we stood at roll call for another half-hour, to be counted again to make sure no one had escaped. Then we went to work. We started work at six A.M. At ten, we were given a ten-minute rest period. Some of us would save a small piece of bread from our ration of the night before and eat it then. But most of us did not save it. Because it could be stolen, we ate it as soon as it was given to us when we returned to the camp in the evening.

At first I worked outdoors digging trenches with a pick and a shovel. The tools were too big for me and terribly heavy. It was extremely hard work, especially for one who was not used to manual labor. My brother-in-law Jacques was lucky. A shoemaker by trade, he was selected to work inside, sewing the tops of shoes. After working a week digging trenches, I was transferred by Burstein to a job cutting specific patterns out of pieces of leather for the shoes. Although I was relieved to be rid of the pick and shovel, I was still working outside and was not looking forward to the harsh winter upper Silesia was known to have.

Finally I was moved inside a building of the factory, assigned to work in an assembly line making wooden heels. Nathan, the Jewish supervisor, was in his fifties and looked like a walrus without a moustache, with a W. C. Fields nose, a fair complexion, and white hair. German born, he was able to translate orders to us. He was extremely understanding and always kind. I had been given exactly one half-hour to learn how to operate my machine.

"Don't worry," Nathan said, "you're young and smart, you'll get the hang of it, and I'm here if you need me."

At the top of the machine there was a huge roll of thin wire that would be cut into nails. My job was to hold together in my two hands the wooden heel with a piece of rubber or leather and nail them by operating the machine with a foot pedal. My orders were to nail four thousand pairs of heels a day. They would go from me to the next machine to be trimmed.

The pieces of rubber and leather were brought to me in boxes.

Sometimes when the pieces were not cut properly, I would throw them away. Several times I came across a whole box of defective pieces. Not knowing how to cope with the problem, and not caring, I just went ahead and nailed them to the heels. All that mattered to me was that I had to process my four thousand pairs of heels.

The noise of all the machines was deafening, and the sawdust flew all over us like snowflakes. While I worked, I sang. I sang all day long and at the top of my voice, because nobody could hear me, to keep my mind off the fact that I was always hungry and frightened and that I was a slave.

We were separated by a glass panel from the non-Jews who worked in the same department. At the ten o'clock rest period we would watch them eat large pieces of bread with lots of margarine, jam, and sausages. At noon, we would go down to a wooden barrack assigned to us, where we would be given some soup. It was water with some rutabaga thrown in, and, if we were lucky, there would be a few pieces of potato. Sometimes, luckier still, there would be a piece of fat. By the time the soup was served, it was lukewarm or cold. We had a half-hour for lunch. We would gulp down our soup, then lie on the floor and sleep for the rest of the break.

The German foreman, a tall, skinny, string bean of a man, very often screamed at us to work faster, faster, but there was a twinkle in his eye that refuted his threats. It was a game he played for the benefit of the Nazi supervisor. At times he would joke with us, but stopped instantly when the supervisor appeared. Then he became all business and acted mean.

The supervisor was a Gestapo man. Slim and neatly dressed in civilian clothes, he spoke French like a native and frequently would stop at my machine and talk about how much he loved Paris. It always made me homesick. He was otherwise strictly business-like, interested only in seeing that we fulfilled our quotas. He hated Jews, but somehow never spoke harshly to me—except for one day when he and the foreman rushed to my machine carrying wooden boxes full of heels, yelling "sabotage" and showing me all those defective heels I had put together. They threatened to have me shipped to another camp where the work would be much harder. I stood my ground, explaining in French to the Gestapo man that I wasn't the one who had cut the pieces of leather and rubber. "What do you want from me?" I said. "I'm doing the best I can. Don't blame me." But they both kept yelling, repeating, "Sabotage, sabotage! We can't have that kind of work done here!" On and on they went. Fed up with all the screaming, I walked out and went downstairs to the barrack we used at lunchtime. I must have stayed there for half an hour, not caring what might happen to me. When I returned, the Gestapo man was gone. The foreman pointed in the direction of my machine. "Get your dirty Jewish ass over there and get to work," he yelled. "You have heels waiting for you, *los, los, arbeit!* (Fast, fast, back to work!)" I had risked my life that day, walking off the job. I could have been killed on the spot by the Gestapo supervisor.

The youngest member in the camp was a thirteen-year-old Polish boy named Josef, who was there with his father. He looked much older than his age and, passing for sixteen, had escaped the extermination camps. He was taller than I, had buck teeth, big lips, and wild sparkly eyes. He was street wise, always up, always laughing, as if this whole nightmare was a vacation for him. We worked together in the wooden heels section. His machine cut grooves at the end of the heel where I would then place the piece of rubber or leather. The machines were all dangerous, and you had to be very aware and alert at all times. One day, Josef's machine chopped off two of his fingers. Blood spurted in all directions and over the machine and the heels. Josef was taken to a nearby hospital run by nuns, who took good care of him and fed him well. The miracle was that he was allowed to stay at the hospital until he completely recuperated. People who were injured and too ill to work were usually sent to extermination camps. I will always remember his father's joy when Josef came back to the camp looking quite healthy. They both stayed in Ottmuth until we were all sent to Blechhammer.

During all the months I worked at OTA I had an accident only once, when my left index finger got in the way and received the nails intended for the heel. Nathan removed the nails with pliers and bandaged my finger. I was fortunate that the finger healed without getting infected.

Twice each day, once at noon before going down the four flights of back stairs for our watery soup, and again in the evening, we air-hosed ourselves to get rid of the sawdust that was clinging to our clothing and skin. Before leaving the factory, at roll call we would be searched by the *Kapos*. Sometimes they were thorough, but most of the time it was cursory. Some of the inmates, in order to survive, would take great risks and steal whatever they could to use in exchange for food. Very often they would take their lives in their hands, talking to Aryans, bartering for a loaf of bread or a piece of meat. One day, my brother-in-law stole a swatch of leather. At roll call that evening, the Schmuck found it on him. He struck him with his cane, knocking him to the ground, continuing to hit him and screaming at him, "You idiot, I should kill you right now! If I ever catch you doing it again, I will!" My poor brother-in-law limped all the way back to the camp, with blood running from a gash in his head. I helped him, supporting him as best I could. We didn't know it then, but we were lucky at Ottmuth. I saw later, at Blechhammer, that people were hanged for lesser crimes than stealing.

In the entire thirty-one months I was in concentration camps, I saw only two people trying to escape, both from Ottmuth. In the first room to which I was assigned, the *Stubenaelterster* was a burly, jovial man, who spoke fluent French and German. He was always very optimistic and positive about everything and talked on all kinds of subjects with great authority. Two months after my arrival he escaped. He had managed to let his hair grow into a crew cut, bribed a worker at the factory to get him civilian clothes and false I.D. papers, and one day during lunchtime disappeared, giving himself enough time to go to the railroad station and hop on a train going west. He is the only one I know who escaped successfully. I heard rumors, after the war, that he had been working for the Germans. He was suspect because he had gone from upper Silesia to Brittany, a long trip to make without being caught.

The other one, Max, was a short, husky man who worked inside the camp in the washroom barracks. For all his outgoing toughness he had a very sweet quality about him, always smiling and showing a row of gold teeth. He was afraid of no one. One day when we came back from the factory, we heard that Max had escaped. We all hoped that he would be successful, but a few days later we heard that he had been captured and shot.

The camp had a small barrack with a shower room and sinks where we could wash and shave. We were allowed to take a shower only once a week. When we came back from work, absolutely exhausted, most of us didn't have the strength to wash our faces and hands. Lice crawled all over the place. I tried to keep myself clean, but the lice reached me, and every night, like a monkey, I would search for them under my arms and around my genitals and kill them. We also had cockroaches, bed bugs, and all kinds of vermin. During the summer, on Sundays when we didn't go to the factory, we would take our bunks outside on the *Appell Platz* and kill the bed bugs. On those Sundays I would entertain in the afternoon. I would sing accompanied by a violinist or an accordionist. We were allowed to keep our personal belongings. I had my drawings and movie magazines that made me painfully aware of better times.

The cooks, the *Kapos*, Halbertstock the *Judenaelterster*, the few women who helped in the kitchen and the laundry, all had their hair. It was a status symbol. After a year, Halbertstock permitted me to let mine grow. I guess, as the singing star of the camp, I had won the privilege of keeping my hair. My morale was very high. I always thought, "If the Nazis do not shoot me, I will survive." That became the maxim that kept me alive. But there were times when I felt I was born, raised, and probably would finish my days in camps. Fortunately for me, those thoughts did not come into my head too often or stay too long. We heard rumors about extermination camps, but it was hard for us to believe that such monstrosities could exist until several inmates from Auschwitz, experts in shoe making, were transferred to our camp. They told us what was happening in Auschwitz.

When I was arrested in 1942, Hitler had already mapped "the final solution." The gas chambers were working with Zyklon B gas, the ovens were burning the bodies night and day. The reason the few of us survived is because they needed people to work in the factories and mines while their men were fighting. Lots of non-Jews were forced to go to Germany to work. But the Jews would only be kept alive as long as they could stay on their feet and do a hard, long day's work, with a minimum of food.

When we talk about the Holocaust, we talk about the six million Jews who died. But millions of non-Jews died during Hitler's regime.

The reason for the emphasis on Jewish deaths is because it was geno-cide. With the exception of Gypsies and some Russian soldiers, only the Jews were sent to the gas chambers by hundreds at a time. The non-Jews died mostly from typhus, torture, hanging, or malnutrition, but they were never sent to the gas chambers. By the time I knew about extermination camps, gas chambers, and ovens, I was so hard-ened by the way I was existing that it really did not affect me.

You always heard rumors about how the Allies were progressing in the war, about how, for example, they were gaining ground in North Africa. Most of the inmates were elated by the good news. But to me North Africa seemed a million miles away. And, following the rumors, my situation didn't change. I still had to get up at four in the morning, I still had to nail four thousand pairs of wooden heels every day, I still was hungry most of the time, and I still was a slave of the Nazis. I used to pray every night before I fell asleep. I would ask God to save my family, never missing a name. When I knew about the gas chambers, I did not want to make the connection; I knew what was being done to children and elderly people, and I knew it was futile to hope, but nonetheless I prayed every night that my family would be spared.

My brother-in-law and I were together in the same barrack for the first six months, Jacques sleeping in a lower bunk while I had the upper. We looked out for each other and shared extra food when we could get it. We got along without getting along. He was my brother-in-law and not my father, but he behaved like a parent, perhaps because he felt a responsibility toward me because of my sister Ida. Or maybe I became a substitute for the children he had lost. He became more and more possessive and strict with me, until I felt I couldn't breathe.

I asked the *Judenaelterster* to be moved into another barrack. There, I became very friendly with two boys my age. One was Georges, from Paris, who had a long, sad face and deer-like brown eyes. He was always cold, and wore a beret even in summer. We slept in the upper bunks next to each other. He was very bright and a joy to be with, always seeing the good side of everybody. He opened my mind about many things. The other was Shimon Shipper, who was born in Belgium, and now lives in Israel. Shimon, when excited, would stutter, but like Georges, he was levelheaded. Together they had a good effect on me.

They both worked in the same leather section as Jacques at the factory, making the tops of shoes. I would visit Jacques in his barrack frequently, and because we were not on top of each other, we got along better.

Georges and Shimon and I shared everything. When I had an extra piece of bread or a few potatoes, we would divide it, and they would do the same with theirs. Sometimes at night, never fully aware that I could have been shot for what I was doing, I would pretend to go to the latrine, sneak into the pigsty, which was close by, and steal some rotting rutabagas and potatoes, cut out the bad parts, and share what was left. We always talked about Paris, telling each other how marvelous our lives had been, keeping ourselves optimistically high.

With Shimon, who knew a lot of Jewish songs and had a knack for rhyming, I wrote a new lyric to a Jewish song. We called it, "Vie Is Mein Schteteluh?" ("Where Is My Village?") The song told the story of a young boy leaving his little village to try to make a life for himself. While he is away he misses his parents and his home desperately. Years later he returns to the village and finds nothing—no home, no mother, and no father. Both are dead and buried in the little village cemetery. The song brought tears to the eyes of everyone who heard me sing it, and I added it to my repertoire along with "Bei Mir Bist Du Schoen."

In December of 1943, during the holidays, we put on a show. We improvised a small stage out of tables in the corridor of one of the barracks. One of the inmates played a few schmaltzy numbers on the violin; others recited poetry and sang songs. I did a dance number, which I improvised, to the music of "In an India Market," barefoot and wearing a turban. I also sang some Charles Trenet songs: "Menilmontant" and "La Polka du Roi." But the inmates favorites were "Bei Mir Bist Du Schoen," "Joseph, Joseph," and "Vie Is Mein Schteteluh?"

For most of us in camp, sex was very unimportant, a memory tucked away in the backs of our minds. When you get out of bed at four in the morning, and you don't go to sleep before nine or ten, and three times a week you have guard duty in the middle of the night and get only two hours of sleep that night, who thinks of sex? This is especially true when you are always starving. The better part of my youth was on hold. From sixteen to nineteen, the important years when your life takes shape, my energies were focused on getting extra food, entertaining the inmates, and surviving. Nothing else.

Who was a survivor and who was not a survivor? I saw people who were older than I, who had families, decent jobs, good lives, and who could not cope with the nightmare of life in the camps. It was even harder for people who, in civilian life, had had luxury, who were well off financially. Their will to survive disappeared because they had lost everything that was dear to them. I was a survivor. Somehow I instinctively did the right things. My life was yet to be lived. Even though my first sixteen years on earth had been sweet and happy, I had not left a formidable background behind me.

Among the inmates there were people who were so hooked on smoking that they would sell their piece of bread in exchange for a few cigarettes. Smoking was more vital to them than food. Like my father, I had never smoked and had never liked it. Therefore, I could not understand these people. I would think, "What are these idiots doing, exchanging their precious rationed bread for a smoke?" We had barely enough food. They were killing themselves.

If you became sick, you were in danger of being shipped out. The sickest I got in Ottmuth, or for that matter in all my internment, was when I had a fever that lasted for two days. There was no hospital ward in Ottmuth, or even an infirmary, so they let me stay for those two days in my room. I was very fortunate never to have been seriously ill with something like typhus or TB. Later, when we were in Blechhammer, Zaza, one of my pals from the apartment house, developed TB. I went to visit him in the hospital barrack in Blechhammer shortly before he was sent to an extermination camp.

There was a marvelous Polish Jewish dentist in Ottmuth. He had a kind disposition, and he reminded me physically of my half-brother Henri. He was the camp doctor and dentist. When I had an abscess in one of my molars, he lanced it and filled my tooth—not with gold or silver, of course. I don't know what material he used, but he did such a good job that the filling lasted for six years. I liked this gentle man who never treated anybody badly. I don't know what happened to him, but I hope he survived. There are some people who stay engraved in one's memory.

There was a man from Vienna, Martin; he was tall and lanky, with a beaked nose. He was the intellectual of the camp. He spoke French, with a slight accent, quite well. He wore a dark brown corduroy suit, a woolen scarf, and a beret. Like my friend Georges, he was always cold. In the winter the poor man's nose was always running. He would lend me his books, French novels, trying to educate me. I had never read a novel before, and I was fascinated. I would ask Martin questions about certain passages I didn't understand. Because he was a teacher, he had a way of explaining that not only answered my questions, but made me aware that there was a world I had not known existed.

It was in Ottmuth that I was given my nickname. The Polish cook, who liked my singing and dancing, and who once a week gave me an extra bowl of soup, would call "Didi!" He meant to say *"Dit Donc,"* which in French roughly means "Hey you." But "Didi" was as close as he could master his French, and it became my nickname. Not only in Ottmuth, but later in Blechhammer, I was known as Didi (pronounced Dee-Dee). Today, I will sometimes get a phone call and the voice will say, "Didi!" and I will know that it is someone who was in camps with me. It is always a thrill to hear that nickname because I know another human being survived.

CHAPTER TEN

BLECHHAMMER: NUMBER A-5714

On April 2, 1944, the Germans decided not to keep us in Ottmuth anymore. They needed the camp as a stalag for British
prisoners of war. On that day, we gathered whatever few belongings
we still had and climbed up onto the open trucks that took us to
Blechhammer, an hour's ride from Ottmuth.

Blechhammer was a large concentration camp, surrounded by
guard towers, high brick walls, and electrified barbed-wire fences. In
place of the Wehrmacht that Ottmuth had, it was supervised by the
SS. We had become so used to that small camp in Ottmuth, Blechhammer was a shock to us. Over the entrance gate in huge letters was
written, *"Arbeit Macht Frei"* ("Work Makes Free"). Inside we were
confronted by what seemed like hundreds of barracks and thousands
of people in striped uniforms staring at us.

The trucks delivered us to the bath house where we were stripped
naked. They took away all our possessions and very thoroughly
searched our bodies for hidden diamonds and gold. Then we were
shaved from head to foot, even those of us who had been allowed in
Ottmuth to keep our hair—the *Judenaelterster*, the *Kapos*, the few
women, and I. A dozen of us at a time were crammed into big tubs
filled with disinfectant to be deloused. Attendants pushed our heads
down into the tubs to be sure we were completely submerged.
Screaming, they ordered us out of the tubs and into cold showers. We
were given rags to dry ourselves with. Then we stood in line to receive
our blue and white striped uniforms, which consisted of a pair of light

cotton long johns, a collarless striped shirt, a jacket, a pair of trousers, a thin overcoat for winter, a cap, and wooden clogs with canvas tops. There were no socks.

Shaved, disinfected, and dressed, we were herded to a barrack where six attendants sat behind a long narrow table. The first one registered us, typing information on cards. He handed each card to the second attendant who wrote a number on it. We were ordered to roll up our left shirt sleeves, and the numbers were tatooed by the other four attendants, half-an-inch high in blue ink along the outsides of our forearms.

I watched the needle puncturing the number into my arm: A-5714. It was over in a moment. It went so fast I can't remember whether or not it was painful. I stared at the number. For the past nineteen months we had been treated like cattle. Now we were branded. Any chance or hope for escape was gone. Identification could never again be hidden. Also gone was Robert Max Widerman. I was just A-5714, a number on my arm.

We were each given strips of cloth with our new identification number, as well as yellow triangles, to be sewn on our uniforms. Yellow triangles were for Jews; red for political foes, underground fighters, and communists; and green for Gypsies and criminals. Pink was for homosexuals, though in Blechhammer I never saw pink or red triangles. Ninety-nine percent of the triangles were yellow.

We were then assembled into groups of twenty on the *Appell Platz*. I became separated from Georges and Shimon, and I didn't see them again for weeks. There were more than three thousand people in Blechhammer, and because we were assigned to different barracks and to work at different jobs, our close friendship was no longer possible. In the nine months I was in Blechhammer, we saw each other once in a great while, and only for a few minutes.

The large barracks slept fifty to sixty men in double bunks in each room. The *Kapos* told us that this was not Ottmuth, this was a much tougher camp, and the work would be harder. They pointed out that we were guarded by the SS and not by the Wehrmacht and that vacation time was over. We would be assigned jobs in a factory outside the camp, and we had better not think of escaping. I felt like laughing.

How could we escape, shaved and branded as we were and weakened physically and mentally by our long ordeal?

We worked in a huge factory, *Obersliese Hydrier Werke*, where synthetic gasoline was processed from coal. Each morning, a small orchestra composed of five inmates would stand just inside the gates and play marching music to send us off.

I worked with a detail constructing bridges on which pipes would be laid to carry the fuel from one end of the factory to the other. On the same work detail were the Fogiel brothers: Louis, Albert, and Bernard. Originally from Poland, they had lived for a while in Belgium but were arrested in France with their father, mother, and sister. The women wound up in Auschwitz. The brothers were strong both physically and mentally. They were nice to everybody, had great senses of humor, and were always optimistic and positive. I felt good when I was in their company. I admired the way they looked out for each other, not fighting the way I did with my brother-in-law Jacques. I had never, in camps, seen people who stuck together like that family. The sons protected their father. I learned much later from them that it was the complete opposite—their father's courage and mental strength held them together and was the main reason for their survival.

My brother-in-law had been put to work in the camp repairing shoes, a relatively easy job compared to the factory work most of us had to do. We never saw each other. Later in Buchenwald somebody told me that Jacques had died there. I have always felt very bad that he and I did not get along, feeling that if we had stayed together, like the Fogiel brothers and their father, maybe he would have survived as I did. But, unlike the Fogiels, we had never been close. Maybe with my father or one of my brothers it would have been different.

At the factory, we Jews were only a part of the work force. Many foreigners were employed there, including requisitioned workers from occupied countries: mostly Poles, Czechs, Ukrainians, and British prisoners of war. The British were guarded by the Wehrmacht. They never seemed to be working, but spent most of the day brewing tea, which they would drink with condensed milk, biscuits, and other foods which came in their Red Cross packages. For the most part, they felt compassion for us, hating to see the way we were treated.

When the SS guards weren't looking, they would offer us tea and milk. It was delicious.

We were fed at noon during our half-hour break, the same watery soup we had been given in Ottmuth. We worked a twelve-hour day, sometimes longer. Then, exhausted, we would trudge the long miles back to Blechhammer where the small orchestra would play us in.

In the camp we stood on endless roll calls, which took even longer than in Ottmuth because there were so many more of us. We were constantly being lined up to hear threatening speeches by the *SS Leutnant Oberstürmbahn Fürher,* in which he reminded us that we were rotten Jews, less than trash, subhuman, lucky to be alive, and privileged to work for the greater Reich.

At other times speeches were made by our new *Judenaelterster,* Demerer. When the SS were around, he sounded tough and strict. He never screamed and he knew how to manipulate the SS so that, despite the cruel treatment we received, there was less torture and fewer hangings than at most other concentration camps.

The *Judenaelterster* at Ottmuth must have told Demerer about me, because on my first Sunday in Blechhammer, I was summoned to a barrack where the Jewish brass lived and asked to entertain them. On Sunday afternoons they all gathered to enjoy an impromptu show put on by some of the inmates. The orchestra that played for us twice a day at the camp gate was there. That day, the other entertainers were Katchka, a Viennese violinist; Manni, a Gypsy guitarist who also played the balalaika; and Harry Post, who was the star of the show. Harry, who was born in Holland, had been in many camps before landing in Blechhammer. He was only five feet tall, even shorter than I, and he had the biggest nose I had ever seen. He would have been ugly were it not for his marvelous soft brown eyes. Out of this tiny man came a strong and beautifully trained voice. Harry, I soon learned, was the star of the camp and was admired by everybody. His closest friends, Yopi, whom he had known in Holland and who was always at his side, looked like a giant next to Harry. Or next to me.

When my turn came, Halbertstock, my *Judenaelterster* from Ottmuth, announced, "I would like to introduce you to a marvelous little Frenchman who entertained us for nineteen months at Ottmuth. We loved him, and I know that you will too. I give you—Didi!" Accom-

My paternal grandparents, Chaya and Ruven Widerman.

My father's children from his first marriage. Top from left: Sarah, Regine, and Adèle.
Bottom from left: Fanny, my father Moishe, and Henri.

Passport photo from Poland to France, 1923. Top from left: Liba (Aimée), my mother Baila. Bottom from left: Ida, Hélène, and Cecile.

Me at four and a half years old, Paris, 1930.

My mother and father, Baila and Moishe Widerman, Paris, 1929.

*Me at my Bar Mitzvah, Paris, 1939.
I was thirteen years old.*

My sister Hélène, Paris, early 1930s.

Plaque in front of childhood apartment house. It reads "In memory of the 112 inhabitants of this house, including forty young children, deported and dead in German camps in 1942."

From left: Jacques Palkenfeld (brother-in-law) with son Bernard and wife, Ida. Jacques Widerman (brother) with wife, Golda. Henri Widerman (half-brother), his daughter Dora, and wife Berthe.

Childhood friends and sisters. From left: Roger Helwasser, Paulette Zelichevsky, Madeleine Widerman, Salomon Schwimmer, me, and Cecile Widerman. Paris, July 1940.

Childhood friends playing kazoos (man on left unknown). From left: Henri Adoner, Roger Helwasser, Georges Goldstein, and me. Paris, 1941.

From the opening number of the musical Seventh Heaven, *New York City, 1956. Photo courtesy of Will Rapport.*

Jiri Zak, my Czech savior in Buchenwald. This photo was taken in 1945 in Czechoslovakia.

Me at the time of my arrival in
the United States, October 1949.
Hair straightened courtesy of Max
Factor Hollywood.

Eddie and Ida Cantor, my future in-laws, in 1950.

The cast of New Faces of 1952. From top, left to right: Joe Lautner, Alice Ghostley, Paul Lynde, Virginia De Luce, June Carroll, Ronny Graham, Eartha Kitt, Rosemary O'Reilly, Carol Nelson, Virginia Bosler, Leonard Sillman, Carol Lawrence, Patricia Hammerlee, Bill Mullikin, Michael Dominico, Robert Clary, Jimmy Russell, and Alan Conroy.

From Thief of Damascus, *1951. Photo courtesy of Columbia Studios.*

Copacabana nightclub, New York City, 1956. From Left: Ricardo Montalban, Gloria de Haven, me, Sammy Davis, Jr, unknown.

From the play Monsieur Lautrec *by Edward Chodorov, Coventry, England, 1959.
Photo courtesy of Richard Sadler.*

Greeting Elizabeth Taylor at a performance of La Plume de Ma Tante *at the Riviera Hotel in Las Vegas, May 27, 1961.*

Me and Natalie at home in Beverly Hills, California, April 1966.

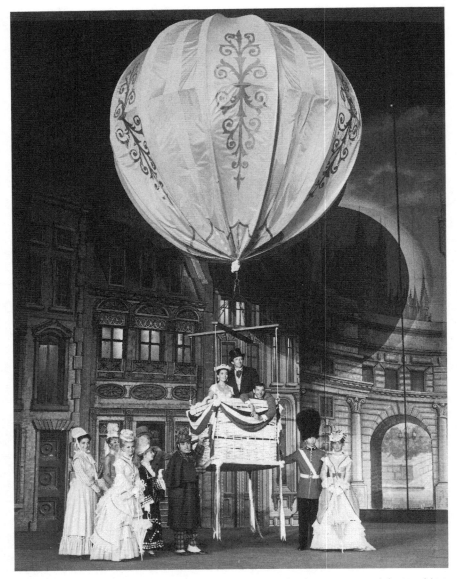

Dom DeLuise, Elaine Malbin, Fritz Weaver, me, and female chorus in Around the World in 80 Days *in Jones Beach, NY, 1963. Photo courtesy of Barry Kramer.*

The cast of Hogan's Heroes, 1965.
From top, left to right: Cynthia Lynn,
Werner Klemperer, John Banner,
Richard Dawson, Bob Crane, Ivan
Dixon, and me.

On the cover of TV Guide
with Bob Crane, 1966.

From TV Guide *article, 1966, "The Strange History of A-5714" recounts my journey from the concentration camps in to a Hollywood version of a POW camp.*

THE STRANGE HISTORY OF A-5714

He is Robert Clary, who has moved from Buchenwald (in Germany) to Stalag 13 (in Hollywood)

BY DICK HOBSON

Robert Clary's role as the French prisoner of war in *Hogan's Heroes* requires that he "intern" himself three days a week on the "Stalag 13" set. Which means that for exterior scenes—the watchtowers, the barbed-wire stockade—he reports to the back lot at Desilu's Culver City studio. For interior shots—barracks and the like—he has to make his way cross-town to Desilu's Hollywood lot 10 miles away. The setting of this make-believe stalag is wartime Germany, sometime in 1942.

During the really true 1942, Robert Clary—a Jew, a French citizen whose name at birth was Robert Max Widerman—was a seven-days-of-the-week prisoner in the German concentration camp "Ottmuth," whose watchtowers, barbed-wire stockade, searchlights, machine guns, SS men, and barracks were located on the same "lot" in Upper Silesia.

Clary survived three years in Ottmuth, Blechhamer, Gross-Rosen and Buchenwald concentration camps. His prison number was **continued**

23

On The Mike Douglas Show *in Philadelphia, June 1968. From left: Mike Douglas, me, and Jimmy Dean.*

With my granddaughters Stephanie and Kimberly in the late 1960s.

With Lou Kaddar in Jerusalem, 1982.

My wife Natalie and me at home in Los Angeles, 1965, a few months after our wedding.

With Bonnie Franklin in Sugar at the North Shore Musical Theater in Beverly, Massachusetts, July 1974.

Escaping the disaster in The Hindenburg, *1975. Photo courtesy of Universal Studios.*

With Fran Ryan in a special musical episode of Days of Our Lives *in January 1979. Photo courtesy of NBC and Corday Productions.*

Lecturing on the Holocaust at Burbank High School in Burbank, California, 1981. Photo courtesy of the Simon Wiesenthal Center.

A gathering of Holocaust survivors in Israel, 1981. From the top, left to right: Tchatkes, Milo Adoner, Henri Wolf, Georges Bendov, Shimon Shiper, Bernard Fogiel, Albert Fogiel, Louis Fogiel, me and Henri Pudeleau.

With Leonard Nimoy and Simon Wiesenthal at a Wiesenthal Center dinner, November 6, 1983. Photo courtesy of Art Waldinger/Tru-Dimension Co.

Showing some of my paintings at home in Los Angeles in the mid-1980s.

On vacation in France, September 2000.

ROBERT CLARY

June 28 through August 23, 1998

The Butler Institute of American Art • Youngstown, Ohio

From The Butler Institute of American Art, Youngstown, Ohio, showing of my artwork, 1998.

At a family reunion in Paris, 1990. From left: brother-in-law Gaston and Aimée Zelonka, Nicky Holland, brother-in-law Jean and Madeleine Wegier, and me.

panied by Manni the Gypsy, I sang, "Bei Mir Bist Du Schoen," "Joseph, Joseph," followed by my imitation of Eleanor Powell, tap dancing in my wooden clogs. Then I did a Mickey and Minnie Mouse routine I had invented, in double talk English, where Mickey courted Minnie, then got fresh with her, and she fought back his advances. I used a high voice for Minnie and a gravelly voice for Mickey, which he didn't have at all. It was probably awful, but they loved it. I was an instant hit.

From then on, along with Harry Post and others, I entertained the brass every Sunday. When we finished there, we would go on to the other barracks to do our show for the inmates. We were well known by practically everybody, Harry by his full name, and I as "Didi."

Because I entertained, sometimes I would receive an extra piece of bread and another bowl of soup. At least once a week they would give me a few more squares of margarine. Food was uppermost on our minds. When you do not get enough to eat, you think about food all the time, remembering meals at home and the bakery where you could get delicious *baguettes;* you vividly remember the candy store with its trays of bonbons and chocolates and the ice cream vendor who stopped in front of the apartment house on hot summer days.

Apart from the rewards, I still had to go to work like everybody else, still had to walk the distance to and from the factory and put in my twelve hours a day.

Around eleven every morning, like clockwork, the sirens would come on, a man-made fog would cover the whole factory, and the Allied bombers would arrive and bomb it. I would think, "What's the logic of the fog on the factory?" The guys in the planes must have said, "Here's the fog—it must be the factory. Bombs away."

The Germans built some very thick cement shelters, but a lot of our people were killed by the Allied bombs because we were not allowed in the shelters. There were signs over the entrances: "Jews not allowed to enter. Verboten." The shelters were so well constructed that bombs could not penetrate them. A direct hit would make a hole, and the shelter would shake as if there had been a tremendous earthquake, but the people inside were safe. Sometimes we would take a chance and seek refuge there, praying to God that nobody would bounce us out. Sometimes we would hide in one of the big cement pipes waiting to be put on the bridges. Once I ran for protection under the trees on the edge of the factory grounds. Fortunately, the earth there was soft and without rocks, because that day a bomb fell close to me, not twenty yards away. I slid down very fast into the hole the bomb made, loose earth coming in with me, covering me. I thought it was the end. I scrambled upward, grabbing at roots until I climbed free. Never again did I go near the trees. Sometimes some of us would go down the stairwells, deep into the heart of one of the main factory buildings, hoping that nobody would make us climb back to the outside. There wasn't a day at the factory that I didn't have diarrhea out of sheer fright of being killed by a bomb.

As in Ottmuth, the barracks had to be kept very clean. We had to scrub the floors on Sundays. The rest of the week the floors had to be swept thoroughly. There were frequent inspections. If the floors were not spotless, the *Stubenaelterster* would beat you and make you do it again until it was right. We were assigned in rotation to get the food from the kitchen and bring it back, where it would be distributed by the *Stubenaelterster*. As with the floors, the tables and benches in the room had to be spotless.

One evening when we returned to the camp, exhausted after the long day's labor, we saw a scaffold on the *Appell Platz*. As we stood at roll call, the *SS Leutnant Oberstürmbahn Fürher* told us that we were going to watch one of our inmates being hanged. It was for some minor infraction of the rules, and by being forced to witness this atrocity, we were being taught a lesson. I stared with horror as the man's hands and feet were bound. He was lifted onto a stool, and the noose was put around his neck. The stool was kicked out from under him. A faint moan came from his throat the moment before his neck snapped. While he stayed hanging all night long, those of us on guard duty had to see that nobody tried to take him down.

That was the first time I saw it happen, and the shock was unbearable. I couldn't sleep that night, and for days afterwards my mind kept replaying the horror of the hanging. At subsequent hangings, the SS reminded us that it was a lesson we had to learn if we didn't want to receive the same treatment. When my turn came to be on guard duty while one of the bodies was hanging from the scaffold, I had a hard time keeping my imagination from running wild. For a kid who had been scared of everything all his life, it was an achievement for me to get through the night.

We had guard duty once every two weeks, and on that night we could get only two hours' sleep. If somebody had to go to the latrine, it was your responsibility to see that he returned to his room when he was finished and did not try to escape. With the electrified barbed-wire fences surrounding the camp, there were few attempts. More than one inmate, in despair and at the end of his capacity to survive, committed suicide by deliberately walking into the fence. When that happened, whoever was on guard duty was held responsible, and would be severely punished. Inmates would sometimes give up their ration of bread to somebody who would stand guard duty for them, but you had to cherish your sleep more than your piece of bread. I always did my guard duty.

It was common knowledge in camp that some people were dealing in the black market, exchanging goods for food. It was always a mystery to me how it was possible for them to acquire anything with which to barter. But somehow there were always those who did it. The *Kapo* in my work detail had the bunk next to mine. He was from Belgium, a huge, burly man named Goldberg. He was one of those screamers and hitters, like the Schmuck in Ottmuth, and was hated by everyone.

Once, without my knowledge, he concealed a small bag of jewelry in my bed. The SS frequently searched the barracks to find things like that, and if you were caught you would be hanged. When I discovered the bag, I yelled at Goldberg because I knew it was his. "How dare you put your stuff under my mattress without asking my permission! I'm not risking my life for your fat ass! On top of it, you didn't offer me even a piece of bread. Why should I hang for you!" Screaming back at me, he hit me hard across the face. I went to see Wolfson, Demerer's secretary, with whom I was friendly, and explained the situation. He went to see Demerer and pleaded my case. The next day, I was moved to another room, grateful not to be involved with fat-ass screaming Goldberg anymore. I didn't object to his dealing in the black market, but I resented his taking advantage of me. Every day in those surroundings we were risking our lives. I had different ways of risking mine, like stealing food from pigsties. But I never involved, innocently or otherwise, another person.

In Ottmuth, we had heard from a few inmates coming from other camps about the inhumanity of some of the SS guards. In Blechhammer we were confronted with a guard whose inhumanity matched the stories we had heard. The inmates had nicknamed him Tom Mix, because he acted like an American cowboy movie star. He wore two pistols in holsters on his hips like a cowboy. He loved to pull them out and, to frighten us, aim close to our feet or our heads and shoot real bullets. Sometimes his bullets would kill. When he didn't feel like sleeping, he would wake up the whole camp soon after lights out, and the three thousand of us would be forced to exercise all night long. He would urge some of the other SS guards to assist him, making us *crawl, stand, sit, stand,* and *run,* faster and faster, hitting us and shooting off pistols in the air. The next morning, without sleep, we would go to the factory to labor for twelve hours.

At the factory, we learned to watch for Tom Mix and not be idle when he approached, because the punishment would be immense. One never knew when he was going to appear. He was a sneak as well as an incredibly sadistic man who felt absolutely no remorse whatsoever about torturing, hanging, and killing.

We all stole things. In the winter we would take old rags to use for socks and empty cement bags to put under our shirts for protection against the bitter wind. There was one incident the camp never forgot. Tom Mix had seen a man at the factory put a piece of wire around his waist. It was scrap the man wanted to use for a belt to hold up his pants. Tom Mix grabbed the man and two others who were standing next to him and proceeded to beat them with a two-by-four he found on the ground, screaming, *"Schweinhunds!* Filthy Jews! You'll pay for that!" The *Kapo* responsible for these men pleaded with Tom Mix, saying it was only a useless piece of wire, explaining that the poor man's pants were falling down. Tom Mix struck the *Kapo* and put him under arrest with the other three. A few days later, in the evening, back at camp we stood on roll call watching those four innocent men with nooses around their necks, while Tom Mix ranted at us that these four dirty Jews had better be a lesson to all of us not to steal German property, or we would wind up like them on the scaffold. Standing there, we endured his abuse for two hours and then saw the stools being kicked out from under the feet of the men. That particular *Kapo*, unlike Goldberg, was loved by everyone. It broke our hearts to see this gentle man hanged. Tom Mix was a typical example of power corruption. After the war he got what he deserved: death by hanging.

Among the SS, there were rare exceptions. In October 1944, we got a new *SS Leutnant Oberstürmbahn Führer,* who, upon his arrival, made a speech telling us not to despair, not to give up hope, that we were human beings, and one of these days we would be free. We couldn't believe our ears. We had heard a German officer saying things nobody in his position would dare to say without being shot instantly for treason. It was a remarkable, brave thing for him to do, and we never understood how he got away with it. Life in camp changed somewhat. Tom Mix no longer woke us up at some godforsaken hour to exercise. And the new lieutenant decided that we should have a theater.

Inmates were assigned to construct a stage in an empty barrack. We needed a long rail from which to hang the curtain. The new lieutenant saw just the right rail at the factory and ordered us to smuggle it out. Leaving the factory that evening, twelve of us carried the rail in the midst of a *Kommando* of a hundred people. We were not searched by the SS. Even Tom Mix, who hanged a man for stealing a useless piece of wire, looked the other way.

The new lieutenant organized a troupe of actors, singers and dancers—all inmates. We had lights, sets, costumes, and wigs for the female parts played by men. I was always chosen, because of my size, to play the girls' roles. I did a lot of dancing in skirts, sang in German Marlene Dietrich's big hit, "Falling in Love Again," and did a French *Apache* dance with Brainine, who was a French dancer by profession and would toss me around the stage as if I were made of rubber.

In addition to playing girls' parts, I did my Ottmuth act. I sang a Yiddish song, "Yir Foor Aheim" ("I'm Traveling Home"). which told the story of a wandering Jew who, being born a Jew, with Jews he must be, and that's why he's going home. I sang it with passion even though the SS guards, who seemed to enjoy whatever we put on, were sitting in the first two rows. What gratified us was that, during the two hours of entertainment, the inmates were able to forget their miseries.

The last two months I spent in Blechhammer, I stopped working at the factory. The new lieutenant told Demerer that the actors involved in the theater should be released from their work outside the camp. I was put into another barrack, as an adjutant to the *Stubenaelterster*, where my job was to supervise the distribution of food. I was able to spend most of my time in the theater rehearsing new routines and sketches with a marvelous Viennese actor, Peter Sturm. Those two months were, for me, like paradise in hell.

CHAPTER ELEVEN

GROSS-ROSEN AND BUCHENWALD: APRIL 11, 1945, THE FLAMES FLICKER OUT

I stayed nine months in Blechhammer. Near the end of 1944, the Russians were all over Poland and very close to invading the eastern part of Germany. Camps in Poland, like Auschwitz, had begun to be evacuated. Suddenly, every day in Blechhammer, hundreds of people arrived from other camps. Quickly, instead of three thousand, we became four thousand. There was an air of excitement and hope, and rumors spread that we would soon be liberated by the approaching Russians.

The SS had a different solution for us. They decided to evacuate the camp. It was announced that this was to be done immediately. A few hours later they changed plans. We would stay and let the Russians free us. The next morning, at roll call, they changed plans again. They were panicking. They told us that we would move out of the camp the next morning and warned us that anybody who stayed behind, trying to hide, would be found and shot.

On January 21, 1945, in the morning, we were assembled on the *Appell Platz*. A heavy snow had fallen, and to our weakened undernourished bodies the cold was unbelievable. We grabbed blankets and, putting them over our shoulders, started out of the camp—four thousand of us in our striped uniforms—on one of those infamous death marches.

Despite the warning by the SS, some inmates took their lives in their hands and stayed behind. The Fogiel brothers, worried that their father could not endure the march, hid under a barrack. The SS, hearing the enemy cannons roaring close by, were in too great a hurry to make good their threats and never searched the camp for those missing from that caravan of striped uniforms. The Fogiel brothers and their father were liberated by the Russians a few days later, and were sent to Paris. I saw them there when I came back.

Four thousand of us walked in the snow for a whole day before the SS changed their minds and made us turn around and start back to Blechhammer. But then they heard the Russians were close to the camp, and they were afraid of being captured. We did another about face, and once again started walking westward into Germany. We marched in deep snow from early in the morning until very late in the evening, holding on and supporting each other physically and mentally. We did this for two weeks. I remember being at the front of that mass of people. We were five in each row. I was with Wolfson, Demerer's secretary, all through this horror. The great terror was knowing that, despite your exhaustion, you had to stay on your feet and keep walking. If you sat down to rest or were too weak to go on, you were shot by one of the guards. On the march we heard constant rifle and pistol shots. Twice during those two weeks, they gave us a piece of bread. Very late in the evening, if there happened to be an empty barn, they would let us get inside for a few hours' rest.

A few times when everybody was asleep, I sneaked out. By then I was so hungry, I didn't care whether I got shot or not. I would knock on the door of the farmhouse and beg for food. The farmers were nice to me. They gave me soup and a piece of bread. As I think of it now, I can't understand why I didn't hide, taking a chance to be freed by the Russians, but I always went back to the barn. I guess I was afraid of the unknown and of being alone even though I had the courage to go and beg for food. At least in the barn I was with people I knew and with whom I shared this particular hell. Wolfson, who was a tall man in his mid-twenties, would comfort me. As Demerer's secretary he was privileged, better nourished than the rest of us, and therefore stronger. We would hold on to each other, helping each other in every way we could to keep from dropping on the road and meeting our deaths that way. We didn't know what our destination was or even if there was a destination. We prayed only that our march would come to an end.

Four thousand of us had left Blechhammer. Two weeks later, on January 26, when we finally arrived at Gross-Rosen, a much larger camp than Blechhammer, there were only two thousand of us. The other two thousand lay dead in the snow on the roads of upper Silesia.

We were jammed into barracks. There were no bunks, no straw on the cement floor, and no window panes—just holes letting in the freezing winds. It was not possible to sit or lie down. We were left there, standing packed together, numb and half-conscious, for several hours; then we were ordered outside for roll call, for more hours of standing, this time in slush up to our knees. Inmates were dropping all around us, their bodies left to die in the dirty snow.

For three days we were shoved in and out of the barracks, *Kapos* at the doors rushing us out, hitting us with clubs and whips, screaming, *"Schnell, schnell, raus, raus!"* To escape the blows, I put myself in the middle of the crowd. During those three days at Gross-Rosen, we were given only one piece of bread and nothing else. Even though I was exhausted, I had the mental strength to do something. I helped pass the bread, just to keep my sanity, and also to make certain that I got my share. There was no way to do it properly. People fought their way to get that morsel of food, and only the strong ones succeeded. The weak were dying fast.

All through this nightmare, I was with Wolfson. I had long since lost trace of Georges, Shimon, and Jacques. One day at roll call, to my horror, I saw Georges' emaciated body sprawled dead in the slush. My dear, sweet friend had not been able to survive the never-ending punishment. I thought I no longer had the capacity to feel any emotion, but looking at Georges, I ached with grief as if part of me had died with him.

On the third day at Gross-Rosen, there were only 1,400 of us left. Early in the morning we were ordered outside and into a long line. I watched people filing into a barrack, the line moving very slowly, and I didn't see them coming out. By then I knew about the so-called "shower rooms." "Oh God," I said to Wolfson, "they are getting rid of us, we are going to be gassed." I had never before felt so intensely afraid of imminent death. I had survived for over two-and-a-half years, and now my time had come.

When we finally entered the barrack, we saw why the line had been moving so slowly. We were being registered again. Even at this time of their crisis and retreat, meticulous records had to be kept by the SS, for history.

After being registered, we were given a piece of bread, a square of margarine, and a slice of sausage, and then we were shoved onto an open cattle train, one hundred wasted, weakened bodies in striped uniforms jammed into each car. We traveled for days, not knowing where we were going. We held each other tightly, trying to keep warm, hopelessly wondering how long we would have to go on like this before dying. The journey seemed endless. The train stopped many times to give priority to German troop trains going to the western front.

We finally arrived on February 9, in Weimar, outside of Buchenwald. When we were ready to get off the train, we saw Allied bombers over us. They were flying very low. The fliers must have been able to see our striped uniforms, our bodies crowded into the open cars, and the German soldiers guarding us. Yet, they started to drop bombs and then came in even lower to machine gun us. In panic, we struggled to climb out of the cars, trying to jump down and hide under them. Fear of death triggered my adrenaline. Hoping that no bombs or bullets would hit me, I jumped as fast as I could and hid under the train. Two hundred of us died at the station that day at Allied hands. Most of us looked like corpses already. The planes left after their slaughter, and slowly the 1,200 of us who were left were forced to walk the six long miles to Buchenwald.

It was late in the evening when we arrived. We were sent into a small bath house. I said to Wolfson, "Here we go. This is it."

The doors to the shower room were open. I said, "Let's wait. Let's not go with the first bunch. If they don't come out after ten minutes, then we're next to get gassed. At least we will have ten minutes to stay alive." We managed to ease our way back, away from the first group being sent to the shower room. My fears, again, were unfounded. Because it was so late and the camp was so overcrowded with prisoners arriving from all parts of Germany, we had been put in the small bath house to sleep overnight.

Some of us slept on benches in the anteroom, others on the floor of the showers. The next morning we were taken to the large bath house, where we were rapidly stripped, shaved, plunged into huge vats to be deloused and disinfected, showered, and then given clean uniforms. We had had the same clothes on our backs for over three weeks, and they were caked with mud and sticking to our skins. Our stench was insufferable. We were crawling with lice everywhere—on our genitals, in our beards. We had scratched ourselves until we bled, leaving open sores. At least it was a relief to feel clean. Now, if we could only appease our hunger.

Buchenwald was divided into two sections, the "Big Camp" and the "Little Camp." The Big Camp was constructed in 1937 by Germans who had been sent there because they had spoken out against the Hitler regime. When we arrived in Buchenwald, most people in the Big Camp were non-Jews—political activists, underground fighters, communists, Ukranians, Gypsies, Jehovah's Witnesses, homosexuals, and Russian soldiers who were in their own compound surrounded by barbed wire.

The Jews who had arrived from eastern Germany were put into barracks in the Little Camp, where there was also a hospital, a whorehouse, a theater, and an experimental barrack where Ilsa Koch made lampshades out of human skins. Because the barracks were overcrowded, the 1,200 of us were put into the theater. They closed the doors and did not allow us to leave the building.

We were kept there for eight days. We didn't know what was going to happen to us. Would they send us on another death march? To the gas chambers? We all had dysentery, and there was only one toilet. Those of us who were able to get up from the hard benches or the floor of the empty stage had to line up for hours to get relieved. Most could not wait until they reached the toilet. Twice in the eight days we were given cold soup, but only the men who were strong enough were able to wait in line outside the theater to receive it. I volunteered to go to the Big Camp and drag back the heavy buckets of soup. I did it because I had to get away from the unbearable atmosphere in that theater, away from all those dying people.

At the end of eight days, when enough people had died to enable those of us who were left to take their place, we were transferred to barracks. I got separated from Wolfson. I didn't know which barrack he was in. I tried to locate him, but without success. There were no windows in the barracks, no beds. We slept on planks stacked five levels high on our sides because the barrack was so crowded. Every morning we awakened to find corpses all around us, and felt lucky not to be one of them. We carried their bodies outside and dropped them on the ground. People rushed at them and took their clothing to add layers of warmth against the winter's bitter cold.

We were dying fast. It was no longer a question of whether or not you were going to die, the question was when.

I'm sure I would have died if it had not been for the delousing supervisor, whose name I think was Karl. A German, he had been in Buchenwald since 1938. The day after our arrival, at the bath house while we were all being deloused, he had taken a liking to me. He asked me many questions, about my childhood, my family, where I was born, how many camps I had been in, and for how long. All this was spoken in passable French. He went to his barrack to bring me back a piece of precious gold: bread.

Karl was a tall husky man in his forties and quite handsome, with gentle eyes. Soft-spoken, he never shouted orders. Looking back and remembering how good he was to me and to a few other young men, I wonder if perhaps he was a homosexual. In my innocence then, and because he never made a pass of any kind, such an idea never occurred to me. He came to the theater three or four times looking for me. He always brought me a few slices of bread, and we would talk. Aware of conditions in the Little Camp, he told me that he was trying to get me transferred to the Big Camp into a barrack with other Frenchmen.

Karl was one of my saviors. Three weeks after my arrival in Buchenwald, he succeeded in getting me transferred to the Big Camp. I was put into a two-story-high barrack occupied mostly by Frenchmen and a few Spanish communists. I had to go through the delousing procedure again. Periodically in that barrack we would be inspected for lice. We would stand in line, dropping our pants in front of a male nurse who would examine our genitals. If we had lice, we would be sent to the delousing bath house immediately to go through the process of getting rid of them. I was given clean clothes, a bunk with a straw mattress, a pillow, and two blankets. I hadn't slept on a mattress since January. I thought I was dreaming. After the last month-and-a-half of incredible inhumanity, I had returned to a semi-civilization.

I had lost contact with everybody connected with Ottmuth and Blechhammer. I was the only Jew in that barrack, which had clean double bunks, tables, benches, and even lockers to keep our personal belongings, though mine had been taken away long ago. There was a bathroom with sinks, toilets, and showers on the upper floor and a large room with tables and benches where, when they were not working, inmates would meet and read.

Karl introduced me to two Frenchmen, Yves Darriet and Claude Francis Boeuf, both in their late twenties. Yves was a short man with deep-set dark brown eyes and black hair worn in a crew cut. It surprised me, in the Big Camp, to see so many people with hair. Yves had a slightly hooked nose and rather thin lips that did not make him look mean. He had been born near Bordeaux and talked with a pronounced Bordelais accent. A pianist-composer by profession, at Buchenwald he had formed a small combo as well as a big orchestra to entertain the inmates.

Claude Francis Boeuf was a scientist and was the complete opposite of Yves. Though they were both extremely bright, intelligent, and sensitive, Yves would at times become intense while Claude was always calm and even-tempered. His face wore a smile, his greyish-green eyes sparkled. He had a brush moustache that was becoming and was never without a pipe in his mouth, though only rarely did he have tobacco to put into it. They had both been underground fighters when they were arrested by the Gestapo.

We became instant friends. More than that, they adopted me. Because I looked like a child, Yves and Claude called me *Bébé*. They nurtured me back to life. It was the first time since my internment, more than two years before, that I tasted sugar, which I spread all over my slice of bread with margarine. I couldn't believe the deliciousness of it. I didn't have to fight for my life anymore. From that day on I was under their protection.

Yves knew a Czech, Jiri Zak, who worked at the *Schreibstube,* the camp's administration office. Zak, as we all called him, became my fourth savior in Buchenwald. He was twenty-eight, a tall, slim, energetic man who wore steel-rimmed glasses. He had been in Buchenwald since shortly after the Germans occupied Czechoslovakia, where he was arrested for being a communist. Working in the administration office, he had access to the files, including the registration papers of everyone entering and leaving the two camps. Yves knew him well, since Zak played bass fiddle in the orchestra. Zak saw to it that I didn't have to go to work, like most of the other inmates in the Big Camp, at the nearby Gustloff armament factory. Like Yves and Claude, I stayed at the camp. All that was required of us was that we stand at roll call twice a day. However, it took hours for us to be counted because there were so many people in the two camps. My number when I arrived three weeks before was 125603, and train loads of people were arriving every day.

After roll call, the few of us in the Big Camp who did not have to go to work at the factory would return to the barracks. Yves had asked me to become a part of his entertainment group, and we would spend what was left of our morning and part of the afternoon rehearsing songs that I would do with the small combo. In the evening we would go around to the different barracks to play and sing for the inmates. The combo was composed of Markowitch, a Frenchman who played the accordion, Zak at the bass, and Tass, who was a marvelous guitarist from Holland. Yves made musical arrangements for the big orchestra, which gave weekly concerts in which I would also participate. Zak had written songs with Czechoslovakian lyrics. He taught me one of them, "Zafouket Na Klarinet." He would laugh like a child every time I sang the song because of my very pronounced French accent.

We kept hearing rumors of how fast the Allies were gaining ground in Germany, forcing the German soldiers to make hurried retreats. We talked a lot about the war situation during those long roll calls, dreaming of the day when all this nightmare would end. We talked about our futures, about what we would do *if* we were liberated—we did not dare to believe it might happen. Claude hoped that his wife who, like him, was a scientist and had been arrested with him and sent to camp, had survived so that they could be reunited, pick up the pieces of their lives, and start over again. Yves seldom talked about his earlier life. I heard him say once that he was married, but he never went into details.

My dream, if I got free, was to go back into show business and have a big singing career in France. We were trying to think of a theatrical name for me. Yves and Claude agreed that Robert Widerman was not a good marquee name. It was too long and sounded too foreign. We racked our brains trying to come up with a good, catchy name. One day, Claude was reminiscing about Sacha Guitry, who came from a long line of actors; his father, Lucien Guitry, had achieved great success throughout Europe. Claude was saying what a marvelous prolific French actor, writer, and director of films Sacha Guitry was and how witty and sophisticated his movies were. Yves and I agreed with Claude that *Le Roman d'Un Tricheur,* and especially *Les Aventures de Désirée Clary,* were remarkable motion pictures. Yves interrupted. "That's the one!" he said. "Clary! Clary! what a perfect name for you, Bébé. That's what you should be called, Robert Clary."

We kept repeating the name. "Robert Clary!" Claude said, "It *is* perfect. It's going to be a lucky name for you; wait and see." That cold day in March, at roll call, on the *Appell Platz* in Buchenwald, I became Robert Clary.

At the end of March, Zak knew that the SS planned to evacuate people from Buchenwald because it had become so overcrowded. First the Jews had to go. Zak hid my file in his office so that I wouldn't have to go with the sixty thousand inmates who were to be sent on death marches to extermination camps like Dachau. For my safety, he moved me into his barrack, which he shared with three other Czechs. Because of his important administration job, Zak had been able to live in a small private barrack, which happened to be in the Little Camp. He issued me a pass that permitted me to go from the Little Camp to the Big Camp.

Although I didn't live with Yves and Claude anymore, I continued to sing with the bands, returning every evening to Zak's small barrack to eat and sleep. I would often take walks in the Little Camp with Zak. From that *Appell Platz* you could see a magnificent view of an immense valley. The sunsets were breathtaking. Zak would keep me up to date on the latest rumors. Some were thrilling, like the news of the Third American Army being close by. Others were horrifying. He told me the SS had given orders that before getting out of Buchenwald they would conduct a massacre of all prisoners left in the two camps. We never stopped living on the brink of death.

On the morning of April 11, 1945, no roll calls were ordered. As we looked at the guard towers, we saw that they were empty. There was an unusual silence hanging over Buchenwald. We knew in our hearts that this was the day. All the SS officers and their troops had fled without fulfilling their plans for the massacre. Suddenly we saw inmates from the Big Camp who had organized underground groups, hundreds of them, carrying arms they had smuggled and hidden for such a day, running toward the barbed-wire fences. They cut huge holes in them, went into the woods to search for fleeing SS. They captured as many as they could find and brought them back as prisoners.

Two small Allied planes appeared in the sky, flying low enough for us to see the American stars on their wings. A huge roar, the cumulative sound of all our voices, rose up as we screamed at the planes. We tore off our shirts and waved them. On the *Appell Platz* in the Little Camp men traced on the ground large letters telling the planes that we were alive. Inmates hugged each other, jumping up and down, dancing, laughing with tears running down their cheeks, and shouting with incredible joy. Those who were too ill and weak could only smile; they understood what was happening. It was almost impossible to fathom that this day had actually arrived, that our miseries had come to an end, that we had survived. Zak kept telling me over and over, "It is *over*, Robert. We have made it. We are free, we are *free!* The American tanks are so close I can smell the gasoline from here. You don't have to hide anymore!" We embraced and cried tears of fantastic relief.

I went to my old barrack in the Big Camp to be with Yves and Claude. From then on I stuck to them like glue. We went to the front gate to watch Patton's Third Army enter the camp. The American soldiers could not believe what they saw. The sight of the *musselmen*—just skin and bones, dead eyes, walking skeletons—and the piles of dead bodies horrified them. They hugged us and cried with us, asking many questions of the people who could speak English.

In the meantime, flags from all European nations had appeared, flying from the tops of the barracks. The whole camp took an entirely different tone. There was constant laughter, mixed with the eerie feeling we had of believing without believing what had just happened to us. The G.I.s distributed food—things that we hadn't seen for years, and in large quantity. The tragedy is that many survivors died from overeating food too rich for them after such a long time of starvation.

The first day I walked out of Buchenwald with Yves and Claude, we felt like wild animals sprung out of cages. We went to the nearby village, just the three of us, repeating, "We are free! We are free!" while looking behind us to see if SS guards were there with their dogs to take us back to the world we knew. The village streets were all deserted; all the windows were tightly shuttered. We were the only three people walking there. The knowledge of being free was incredible and our elation extraordinary. I was bursting with excitement, realizing that I was a human being again and not a set of numbers on my arm and clothes.

The day after the liberation, on April 12, the American soldiers told us that their President, Franklin D. Roosevelt, had died. They flew their flag at half-mast. Even though I didn't know who President Roosevelt was, I understood the grief that death brings.

We started to make plans for our return to France. But first we did something remarkable. On April 19, a week after the liberation, in the same theater in the Little Camp where I had stayed half-alive for eight days not knowing if I would survive, Yves and his big band gave a concert for the G.I.s. The orchestra played ten tunes, mostly American songs like "Dipsy-Doodle," "Solitude," "In the Mood," and "Bugle Call Rag." Yves had made all the orchestral arrangements. The small combo played four songs, "Honeysuckle Rose," "Confession," "Minor Swing," and "Les Yeux Noirs" ("Dark Eyes"). Then I went on and did "Menilmontant," "La Polka du Roi," "Joseph, Joseph," "Zafouket Na Klarinet" (hearing Zak laughing behind me), and "A Tisket, A Tasket" in double talk English. I also did my Mickey and Minnie Mouse skit. The concert closed with a walloping version of "Tiger Rag." We performed on that stage, in our striped uniforms, exhilarated by our new freedom, and gave the greatest show of our lives while hundreds of G.I.s and inmates applauded and shouted. The G.I.s whistled at us, something we were not used to; in Europe, until that time, people only whistled when they didn't like you.

I have a most cherished document, by now old and crumbled, held together by scotch tape—the program of that concert. Along with the letter I wrote on the cattle train to my brother Jacques, it is at the museum of Tolerance of the Simon Wiesenthal Center in Los Angeles. The program lists all the numbers we performed and the names of the musicians who spent years in Buchenwald:

Brass section:	Damek (Czech)
	Hoberg (French)
	Plzak (Czech)
	Stverka (Czech)
Sax section:	Hajtmar (Czech)
	Markowitch (French)
	Broft (Czech)
	Jean (French)
Rhythm section:	Piano—Godschmidt (German)
	Guitars—Tass (Dutch), Muzik (Czech)
	Bass—Zak (Czech)
	Drums—Berdenne (Belgian)
Vocal:	Widerman (French)
Band leader:	Yves Darriet (French)

After the liberation, out of nowhere, we acquired a new mate—a Frenchman my age, Henri Hochberg, who appeared suddenly one day with a violin case under his arm. He had arrived in Buchenwald around the same time as I from other camps in Upper Silesia. Just as Yves and Claude had adopted me, the three of us adopted him, and we became the Four Musketeers.

On April 23, the four of us, with other Frenchmen, were sent to Eisenhar, a city near Buchenwald. We were put into a lovely hotel there for a week. We slept in real beds with clean white sheets! I couldn't sleep the first night, thinking about my family, wondering if I would find any of them alive when I returned to Paris. I felt certain I was an orphan, but more than that, an orphan with no sisters, no brothers, that my whole family had been wiped out. Yves, Claude, and Henri were my family now.

We were last on the list to be repatriated. Survivors who were in worse shape than we went first. Trucks with French drivers picked us up to make the journey back to France. One of the truck drivers turned out to be one of the ladies who had auditioned me for the children's amateur contest and signed me to appear on the Thursday radio show. She recognized my name and was thrilled to see me, as I was to see her.

When we finally left Eisenhar, we traveled by truck through western Germany, crossing the Rhine at Coblentz, then through Luxembourg and into a camp in northeast France at Longuyon. We stayed there for a very long twenty-four hours. We knew we were on the last lap of our homecoming, and the anticipation of seeing Paris was so great that we could think and talk of nothing but that moment. On May 4, early in the morning, we boarded a train that took us to our final destination.

CHAPTER TWELVE

HOME! ALIVE

We arrived in Paris at one o'clock P.M. at the Gâre de l'Est. Crowds of people greeted us at the station, waving flags, and giving us flowers as if we were returning conquerors, which in a way we were. The bus trip to the hotel was entrancing. We didn't have enough eyes to look at the sights of Paris. The chestnut trees in bloom, and the people on the streets rushing, laughing, and sitting at sidewalk cafés brought tears of joy and immense contentment and made us impatient to be back right now to this kind of life.

We finally stopped in front of l'Hôtel Lutetia on the Left Bank. We were told in the buses that we would be staying at the hotel while being rehabilitated—looking for relatives, filling out papers, receiving identification cards, and getting physical examinations.

When Yves, Claude, Henri, and I entered the lobby, we heard someone scream out, "Robert!" Everyone named Robert turned his head to see who was calling. It was my sister Cécile in a dark blue uniform, and she was running toward me! She grabbed me in her arms. We cried tears we didn't know we had, holding on and looking at each other to make sure we were not dreaming. I could not believe that I was in my sister's arms, that she was alive. I kept repeating, "Tell me it's not a dream."

"I had a feeling," she said. When the supervisor had told her to go to lunch, she refused. "I'll wait until the convoy arrives from Longuyon," she had said, "take care of them, and then go to eat."

She was an auxiliary volunteer, helping survivors to get their bearings. She had heard from the Fogiel brothers, who arrived in Paris before me, that they had seen me alive as recently as January. She always questioned French Jewish survivors about the members of our family who had been deported. She would show them photos of us, hoping to hear that we were alive. The lady truck driver who saw me in Eisenhar, and who belonged to the same auxiliary group, on her return from one of her trips asked the girls at headquarters if they knew a Robert Widerman. Nicky (as Cécile was now called) nearly fainted. "Yes! He's my brother!" she said. "What's the matter? Is he alive? Dead? Where is he?"

"He is on his way home," the driver said. "I saw him a few days ago in Germany."

After I introduced Nicky to Yves, Claude, and Henri, she told me the most marvelous news. My half-brother Henri and his family, my half-sister Fanny, her husband, their two daughters, my brother Jacques, his family, my sister Aimée, her daughter, and Madeleine, who was married now, were *all* in Paris, *alive!* They had never been deported. Nicky called Jacques to tell him that I was in Paris. I talked excitedly to him and his wife, Gaby, telling them that I couldn't wait to see them. I stayed at the hotel just for lunch while Nicky took care of the procedure we had to go through. I insisted that Henri, who had no one at all, come with me to my brother Jacques.

Claude and Yves stayed at the hotel to make phone calls, trying to locate their families. Henri and I were told to come back the next day for our physicals and to get the I.D.s and papers we now needed. They gave us military uniforms with Eisenhower jackets. We said goodbye to Yves and Claude until tomorrow.

Claude eventually did find his wife, who also survived the concentration camps. They both joined Professor Picard, a renowned scientist, on his deep-sea explorations.

Yves reunited with his wife for a while but then found out they had nothing in common anymore and divorced her. He got a good job with the French government-owned radio station and later worked in French television as a program director, but he was never happy with his job.

It took a few days to be officially registered and to get identification papers saying that I had come back from Buchenwald. I was allowed to ride the subways and buses free. I passed my physical examination; nothing was drastically wrong. I didn't look like the emaciated survivors. All I needed was a few weeks' rest and nourishing food. Very quickly I locked away the thirty-one months of incomparable nightmare.

You can imagine the feasts that went on for days, with all my relatives coming to my brother Jacques' to visit me. I am the only one out of thirteen of my immediate family who came back from deportation.

Jacques and Gaby couldn't do enough for me. They asked many questions about what I had been through. I was very reluctant to give them answers. I told them briefly that it was horrible but that I didn't want to talk about my experiences in detail—that I wanted to forget what happened to me and to think only of the present and the future.

I had made up my mind to make something out of my life without being supported by the French or German governments. I was determined to do something that would bring me great joy. I was nineteen with lots of big plans for a career in show business. My goal was to become a big singing star. My brother Jacques gently suggested that I should learn a trade, perhaps become a tailor like him. "Are you kidding!" I said. "Six months from now I'll be a star, not only that, but *the* star attraction at the ABC Theater."

Jacques was a tailor specializing in women's clothes. As soon as I returned from Germany, he made me several suits. I insisted and fought with him until he finally agreed to make me zoot suits, with very long jackets and pegged pants and large cuffs. I loved them.

I stayed in Jacques' tiny apartment for the first six months, sharing a mattress on the living room floor with my friend Henri and Gaby's nephew Victor, who had come back from Germany after five years of being a French prisoner of war. Henri, Victor, and I would take long walks in Paris drinking in the freedom and making the most of it. I loved going to the movies and seeing American films that I missed so much. After a while, Henri decided to go his way and see if he could make a career as a violinist. Later, he emigrated to the United States where I saw him in the '50s once or twice in New York City, where he was making a living as a violinist, and never heard from him again.

A few weeks after arriving in Paris, I received my draft notice. I was ordered to report for two years of military service. I had just come back from almost three years of severe regimentation, living constantly with the threat of death. But as far as the government was concerned, I was nineteen years old, a French citizen, and eligible to be drafted. I was shocked and extremely depressed. I had only begun to enjoy my new freedom, making plans for the future. The idea that I had to give up two precious years of my life and endure more regimentation was a tremendous blow to me. But I had no choice. I had either to go into the army or lose my French citizenship.

I reported at the bois de Vincennes military *caserne*, resigned to becoming a French soldier. But when the army officials saw the papers I had brought showing that I spent thirty-one months in German concentration camps, I was exempted. They gave me a stamped paper, and sent me home. I ran out of the *caserne* feeling I had been liberated all over again. I couldn't wait to tell my brother Jacques the good news.

In 1949, when I arrived in California, because I was in the United States on a permanent visa and planned to stay forever, the draft board called me. I had to go, I was the right age, and the Korean war was going on. I was already known in the States because of recordings I had made in Paris which became hits in America in 1948. I passed my physical, and was told I'd be called in due time. Between the time of my physical, and being called to be drafted, I suffered several severe kidney attacks. The day I was called to report for duty I took the medical reports and X-rays describing my condition. The sergeant at the draft board looked at the material and said, "What's the matter—don't you want to serve this country?" I wish I could have told him that I felt I had served my time. I don't know if, because of the number on my arm, the draft board knew what kind of life I had lived from 1942 to 1945 or if they cared, as they did in France. But because of my kidney stones I was classified 4F and dimissed.

Very often, following my liberation from Buchenwald, I had nightmares. They were always the same. I was going to be arrested by the French police and the Gestapo and put into camps again, but this time, being wiser and not wanting to be caught, I would run like mad trying to escape. My legs, running, would kick the covers off the bed. The nightmares were terrible, and I always woke up in a sweat. You can't live that kind of life for practically three years and not have scars. Even though I wanted to erase those memories, they haunted me.

Shortly after my return from Germany, I read the following item in a Paris newspaper: "His work! Only 1.5% of repatriated prisoners of war had TB. But we have counted 25% from people who were sent to concentration camps." It went on, saying, "After examining 200,000 prisoners of war and workers who were sent to Germany, a percentage of 1.5 had pulmonary disease. The proportion rises to 20 or 25% of political deportees." What horrified me was the next paragraph: "Finally, we can evaluate at 92–94% the number of political deportees and 99% of racial deportees who will not come back." In other words, out of one hundred Jews, I was the one who survived. The item reminded me that while the slaughter had gone on, most of the world remained apathetic. The non-Jews were either passive or more than willing to collaborate. In Europe only three countries, in their way, combatted against the extermination of the Jews. The Nazis in Bulgaria arrested the Jews and put them into camps within the country, but the Bulgarian government refused to let its Jewish citizens be deported to the gas chambers in Poland and Germany. Until almost the end of the war, Italy prevented Jews from being handed over to the Nazis. But only Denmark, which had 7,500 Jews, refused to bend to the Nazi's demands. King Christian X said that if the Jews had to wear a yellow Star of David, so would he and his countrymen. He warned the Jews about the Nazi round-ups, and except for 467 older people who were caught, all the others were first hidden, then sent to neutral Sweden.

On my return to Paris I did not encounter anti-Semitism as did Jewish survivors who returned to Poland. Very few of them went back to their native country. They waited in displaced persons camps in Germany for visas to Palestine, the United States, Canada, and other countries. Except in Russia and Poland, the anti-Semites of the world had gone into their closets for a while.

CHAPTER THIRTEEN

L'AL JOLSON FRANÇAIS

I had always loved Al Jolson movies—mostly his numbers in black face. Black entertainers had a special corner in my heart. I admired their great abilities, and the natural, easy way they sang and danced. I thought, I'm going to do that, become a blackface entertainer. I would be the only one in Paris doing such an act. If my act was good, I'd be recognized and get to the top faster.

I bought black makeup and white for my lips, like Jolson and Eddie Cantor wore. My brother Jacques gave me some shirts with detachable white starched collars. I rented a red and yellow plaid suit, put taps on a pair of black shoes, and borrowed a pair of gloves. In France we never made a difference between blacks and whites. Blacks had the same rights as whites had. We didn't have slaves coming from Africa. Blacks who lived in France had the same opportunities to achieve their goals in life. No separate water fountains and separate toilet facilities, no sitting in the balconies in theaters, etc. Having said that, doing a blackface act in those days was a show business tradition so ingrained that we, myself included, never identified we were being racist. For me, on the contrary, it was a tribute to all the great entertainers. But I guess we were dumb enough and unaware enough not to realize a black person might not regard this as a tribute. We need to apologize for this oversight, and I do now apologize.

After I had my costume ready, I proceeded to go to music publishing houses and, by saying that I was a professional entertainer, got free sheet music and orchestrations of songs I wanted to sing.

Line Renaud's husband, Loulou Gasté, was a composer and had a music publishing company. He gave me one of the first French songs I sang, "Daisy Venez Avec Moi" (Daisy Come With Me"). I put the music in my suitcase with my costume and makeup and set off to make the rounds, auditioning for nightclubs in Pigalle. I had five songs in my repertoire as well as my Mickey and Minnie routine. You might say I plunged blindly into show business, but I went with the complete assurance that I would succeed. "Look out world, here I come! Remember my name, Robert Clary, l'Al Jolson Français."

The first club, La Boule Noire, which still exists, was a very cheap place with rowdy customers, but I didn't care. I didn't know better. I auditioned, and the manager said, "You're on, kid, starting tonight." I worked there, doing three shows a night, for a whole week. I hated it. It was a dive. The crowd was lousy—the dregs of Pigalle. Every night after I was through working, I would pack my suitcase, leaving nothing at the club, and walk with it for miles back to my brother's apartment. The subways were not running at that time of night, and I couldn't afford taxis. The walk took over an hour. Very quietly so as not to awaken anybody, I would let myself in, undress in the dark, and get to sleep after four. When the week was over, the manager paid me. I said thank you and, although they were expecting me to sing for at least a few more weeks, never went back. I didn't have a contract or an agent.

The next place, also in Pigalle, was called La Boule Blanche, the White Ball. It was a smaller club catering to a more refined clientele and was run by a tough lesbian. She liked my act, and I stayed there for two weeks, working until two-thirty every morning, schlepping my suitcase home.

My third club—still in the same neighborhood—was called Le Shanghaï and was a comparatively classy night club. José Rémo was the band leader. They had a chorus of dancing girls, most of them not too pretty, and a female impersonator who later became a big name in his field in France. By then I had made some money and could afford to buy a suit rather than rent one. Instead of bothering my brother, I asked my friend Michel Nudel, who was a tailor, to make it for me. We picked out a loud, dark red, yellow, and blue plaid fabric. I wore a very wide, stiff, pink tie, and a little plaid sailor's cap. I was very proud of that costume.

Pigalle was crawling with prostitutes, and a lot of them came to Le Shanghaï. They all thought I was adorable when I sang "The Flat Foot Floogie," which I did in double talk English. I used to jitterbug with the whores when I was not performing. I never went to bed with any of them, but they were my pals. I remember one in particular. She was tall and looked like Joan Crawford. She had the loudest laugh and was a very good jitterbugger. We had a ball on the dance floor.

Nicky told me how, while the G.I.s were in Paris, she went dancing at a ballroom where the Glenn Miller Orchestra, with Johnny Desmond and the Modernaires as vocalists, was playing. I envied her. It killed me that I hadn't been able to be there to dance with her and to hear that orchestra in person. She could get into those places because she was in uniform. The Americans had requisitioned a number of movie houses and theaters exclusively for their soldiers' entertainment.

The Olympia Theater, on the Boulevard des Italiens, was such a theater, where variety acts performed only for G.I.s. Monsieur Margolis, the agent who booked the Olympia, had seen my act at Le Shanghaï and signed me for a two-week engagement. I was very excited and looked forward to singing on a legitimate stage, with a big orchestra playing in the pit. On opening day, we had an afternoon rehearsal. I watched a few acts going through their music, then my turn came to rehearse my four songs. I was a bit nervous, but gutsy, so I didn't panic. It seemed to go quite well.

I was fourth on the bill, following a dog act that always won the audience. The place was jammed that evening with khaki uniforms, and the whole theater smelled of Camel cigarettes. I was ready long before my time to go on, so I watched the other acts from the wings. I listened to the wild whistles, a sure sign of appreciation. My turn finally arrived. The M.C. introduced me as "The Al Jolson of France," and I ran onto the stage and into my first number, "The Flat Foot Floogie." There was polite applause, but not a peep of a whistle when I finished. I thought, all right, they think I'm singing in Polish, and they do not appreciate my double talk. Onward. My next number was "Daisy Venez Avec Moi." I got the same polite reception. I had

two more numbers to do, and I was having flop-sweat. I didn't understand—they loved me in Buchenwald. My two last numbers received
the same negative response. I left the stage extremely depressed. The
stage manager tried to encourage me by saying I would do better
tomorrow.

The next day, at the matinée, I ran on stage and did my act, with
the same result. Flop, flop, flop at the evening performance, too. I
didn't last two days. Monsieur Margolis paid me my two weeks wages,
thanked me, and said, "Let's face it, you are not ready for an American audience. Keep working on your act . . . maybe one day . . ."

I was dejected; my dreams of conquering America were shattered.
Now, in retrospect, I know what went wrong. On top of having little
experience, I should never have been billed as "The Al Jolson of
France," not having done a blackface act for a hip American audience.
However, the experience did not teach me a lesson then, because I
went on doing my blackface act for European audiences for a few
more years, with success.

While I was appearing at Le Shanghaï, a friend told me that they
needed good jitterbug dancers for a scene in a French movie. I put on
my double breasted zoot suit and went to audition at the Billancourt
Studios on the outskirts of Paris. I was chosen and asked to be at the
studio in a week. They told me it would be a two-day job, and I
should be sure to wear the same zoot suit. The week didn't pass fast
enough for me. I didn't know what to expect.

We were at least fifty extras playing patrons at a nightclub where
the stars of the movie were supposed to have a quarrel. The assistant
director coupled me with a very tall girl and told us to walk to the
dance floor normally and once there to do a frantic jitterbug. I
couldn't believe that it would take two days to do that scene. That's
how much I knew about making movies. I came down from my high
cloud very quickly when I realized that I could not mingle with the
stars of the film. In my mind I was always a star. But the assistant
director treated me like the other extras. "Let's have quiet on the stage
while the stars are working. As a matter of fact, just disappear. But
don't go too far, I'm not going to waste my time looking for you.
Understand?"

I saw immediately that I didn't want to do that kind of work for a living. I was much more ambitious. I liked the response of an audience when I did my act in clubs. I guess nobody in France was in a hurry to see me make it in the movies because I never made another one there, and I can't remember a thing about it except for the assistant director always screaming at us and my dancing frantically for two days with a very tall girl.

I worked at Le Shanghaï for six months. In addition to my act, I was given a production number to do with the chorus girls. It is true that you learn your craft by working at it, and Le Shanghaï was a very good school. José Rémo asked me if I wanted to go on tour with the orchestra and the chorus girls. I jumped at the opportunity to travel and also at the opportunity to be with José's sister-in-law, who was one of the dancers and with whom I was having a fling.

We went to Amsterdam and Rotterdam in the spring of 1946 to play in movie houses. We did four shows daily between showings of the feature film. The orchestra performed against a background that had a Mexican motif. The chorus girls did a few numbers, a good looking boy singer sang two songs, and then I went on last and did four songs. I was the featured attraction and a big hit.

We were paid meager salaries. We couldn't afford to stay at hotels, so we shared rooms in private homes, sleeping three guys to a cot in one big room. Breakfast was included in the price. We had fun touring the cities, eating cheese, drinking Dutch beer, and going to nightclubs after our shows were over. We never tired.

In Belgium, we worked in Antwerp in a first-class nightclub. During the month we stayed there, to the displeasure of José's sister-in-law, I had a big romance with the owner's daughter. She must have been eighteen or nineteen. I was almost twenty. We were inseparable. We saw each other every day—going for long walks while she showed me her city, holding hands, stopping in doorways to kiss. We were very romantic. I doubt that her father or mother knew about our goings on. Since I went on last in the show, when everybody was downstairs performing and before I put on my black makeup, she would come to my dressing room and we would kiss until our lips were numb. I really thought I was in love. Well, that love disappeared as soon as I left Antwerp. José Rémo wanted me to go with him and the troupe to North Africa, but I was eager to return to Paris and to get on with my career.

CHAPTER FOURTEEN

LE ZAZOU DU PARNASSE

My sister Madeleine, who worked for the French Air Force as a secretary, had been waiting for her husband Jean's return from Germany, where he had been sent with false papers as an Aryan worker. He finally came back to Paris in September 1945. We all had to find a place to live. I had stayed too long at my brother's. Madeleine and I decided to see the couple who occupied our old apartment and tell them that we were back and rightfully should have our former home. The couple, who had moved into our apartment shortly after we were arrested, understood our position and did not give us a hard time. They agreed to move out as soon as they found a new place for themselves, which they did while I was on tour with the José Rémo band.

Madeleine and Jean took our parents' bedroom, Nicky the other bedroom, and when I came back from my tour I used the dining room. It felt good to be home, but strange. All our furniture and possessions had been stolen. The local town hall gave us a few beds, a table, and four chairs. Madeleine bought a few kitchen utensils. Other things would have to wait until we could afford them. At first we were acutely aware of the absence of our parents and Hélène, who were among the 112 people from the building who did not come back. The building had a new concierge—Madame Froment, the mean old hag, had died—and many new faces were occupying the other apartments. Most of my childhood friends were gone. Only six of us children who were deported had survived the concentration camps. A few others had been sent to farms by their parents and had escaped arrest. A handful of adults who had managed to avoid the round-up retrieved their apartments as we did.

For a long while I didn't dare go to the *Locale.* I couldn't face the memories of all my friends who were gone, all gone.

Nicky, who frequently went dancing at private clubs for G.I.s, met a young Texan. He was soft-spoken, on the shy side, and Nicky instantly felt at ease with him. They started to see each other and before long love blossomed. He asked her to marry him, and she accepted. She married Bruce E. Holland, a Protestant, which I am sure would not have happened had my parents been alive. Because of their deep religious upbringing, they would not have allowed Nicky to marry outside of the Jewish religion. Soon after their marriage, Nicky emigrated to the United States, taking the same ship that returned Bruce to his homeland. She arrived in Texas in 1947 and has been living there ever since. Her marriage to Bruce proved to be a very good one. He has been her guiding light, her friend, her faithful husband, the father of their two daughters, and always kind, sweet, and, still, soft-spoken. For a long time, because of what she went through during the war Nicky didn't tell her daughters that she was Jewish. It was her way of protecting them in the event the world ever allowed another Hitler to come into power.

One day on my way to visit my brother Jacques, I ran into Georges Ostier, a young man who had been in Blechhammer with me. He and his father had both survived the concentration camps. They were in the junk business and starting to do quite well. Georges invited me for dinner one evening at their apartment, and one of the guests was a small, lovely, dark complexioned girl in her early twenties. I instantly took to her. During the whole evening my eyes never left her, and I built in my mind a romance that would never happen. I became very infatuated with her, and although I found out that she was engaged to be married to Georges, I still fantasized being married to her and having children that would look like her. I even wrote her a long love letter, telling her what a better husband than Georges I would make. The next morning, I reread the letter and realized what a foolish romantic I was. I never sent it. I had a tough enough time making money for myself. I still wanted a great career in show business and I was still very selfish; I rarely gave any of my salary to my sister Madeleine to share expenses. How could I take care of a wife and children? I pined for her for days, dreaming of an unreal happiness. But, by the time I was asked to entertain at their engagement party, my infatuation was gone, and I was happy to oblige. This was the closest I came for a long time to contemplating marriage.

After finishing the tour with José Rémo, I auditioned at a nightclub off the Champs Elysées called Le Club and got the job. It was a tiny place and very elegant—the equivalent of the Blue Angel in New York City. Still in blackface, I was the opening act for Bourvil, who was very amusing, the rage of Paris, and later became a famous movie star. Jean Pierre Guerin, who owned Le Club, had just bought the old Lido club, changing the decor of the large place and creating extravaganza revues that became an international success. Guerin liked my act, and I stayed at Le Club for four months.

On my day off from Le Club, I would go to Le Lido and dance until I was ready to faint from exhaustion. One day there, I saw a cute black girl, just my size, jitterbugging on the dance floor. She was superb, and I asked her for the next dance. Immediately it was as if we had been dancing together for years. Carried away by the great band, we danced up a storm. Suddenly, just like a scene in a movie, all the other couples stopped to watch us, clapping their hands in rhythm encouraging us to go on, forming a large circle around us.

There was a man in the audience who owned a night club in Ste. Maxime on the French Riviera. His name was Gaby and his club was called Chez Gaby. He told us that he loved our dancing and offered us a job for the summer. I accepted, but for some reason the girl was not able to go. Gaby, who had seen me at Le Club, hired me anyway to do my act.

I had never been to the south of France. I had heard how beautiful the Riviera was—how chic, exclusive, and very expensive. But nothing I had heard prepared me for my first sight of the Mediterranean. I had never seen a sea so blue, deep blue, or the sun shining so brightly. It was paradise. I wanted to spend the rest of my life there.

Gaby picked me up at the Ste. Maxime railroad station and took me to a *pension* a few blocks away from his club. I was still dazed by what I had just seen from the train. I couldn't get enough of the clear blue skies and the bright colors of the flowers and the houses.

"Is the Riviera always so colorful?" I asked Gaby.

"It's everything you've always dreamed of and more. As soon as we check you in, I'll take you around. I'll show you the club, we'll have lunch and take a drive through the town and go to St. Tropez, which is the town next to here."

At the *pension* I was given a small room with a wash basin. The bathroom had to be shared with the people living on the same floor. I knew right away that I was going to enjoy my summer. The woman who ran the *pension* was very charming and made me feel at home. She told me that breakfast, lunch, and dinner were served at specified hours; otherwise, there were no formalities. I had brought with me summer clothes, sandals, swim trunks, and, of course, my loud plaid suit for my act. I intended to bask in the sun and get a marvelous tan.

The club had a quartet composed of piano, bass, guitar, and drums. The guitarist was Joseph Reinhart, the brother of the famous Django Reinhart who, with Stephane Grappelli, had formed Le Hot Club De France. Joseph, like his brother, was a gypsy and as good a guitar player as Django, and they looked like twins, with the same dark eyes and heavy moustaches. We worked every day from eight-thirty in the evening until at least two in the morning, which suited me fine. I would have worked twenty-four hours a day if Gaby asked me to. After watching the rehearsal of my blackface act, Gaby had a brilliant idea. "How would you like to be the band singer, and sing with the quartet?" I had never done that, and the idea appealed to me greatly. It was not the Ray Ventura orchestra, but it would do. Gaby also asked me to dance with the female clientele who would love to have a good jitterbug dancer as a partner. I gladly said yes to all his requests. I was young and full of energy that I had to let out of my system. Gaby was as energetic as I, and ran his club with an enthusiasm that was catching. He would have the audiences wear funny hats and participate in silly games, and they loved it. They were eating out of the palm of his hand. Word of mouth was so great that the club was jammed with people every night. Gaby, for quite a few seasons and even in Paris, was the talk of the town and Chez Gaby the place to be seen.

I very quickly made friends in Ste. Maxime, especially with three girls and a boy my age who were staying at my *pension*. We would spend our days on the beach, sunning until we were golden brown. We laughed at everything and nothing; everything amused us. We rented bicycles and went to St. Raphael and St. Tropez and had marvelous lunches. We enjoyed ourselves without a care in the world. I spent every day with my friends until it was time for me to get ready to go to work in the evening. Life couldn't have been better for me; it was a wonderful combination of vacation and work I loved doing. We swore to keep in touch with each other once the vacation was over, but because the boy was from Lyon, and the three girls from Avignon, we never saw each other again after that marvelous summer.

My act went well. I loved singing with the combo, and with my smattering of English I was able to get through the lyrics without really understanding what I was singing about and at least well enough to satisfy the French audiences. I was never idle. When I wasn't performing I would dance with the customers to the point of exhaustion.

One night during my last month there, a small round-faced man came into Gaby's with a beautiful young woman, and at the end of the evening approached me, saying that he was staying in Ste. Maxime for a month and that he had a project he wanted to discuss with me. He was a North African Jew; I don't remember his last name. Everybody called him Marcel. He was a very astute businessman who could be tough when the situation demanded, but he had a heart of gold. After watching me work for a week, he told me that in the fall he was opening a new nightclub in Paris in Montparnasse that he was calling Le Parnasse. It was to be a very chic club with a big orchestra, and he wanted me to work for him not only as a singer and dancer but, like Gaby, as *Le bout entrain*, M.C. and greeter. I accepted his offer, delighted to work for him in all those capacities.

Reluctantly, I saw the summer coming to an end. I thanked Gaby for three glorious months and a wonderful experience. The Riviera was the most beautiful place I had ever seen, and I made up my mind that I would return as often as I could. Marcel offered to drive me back to Paris with him and his girlfriend Suzanne. The trip was very comfortable in his big American car.

Le Parnasse was scheduled to open in October. The workers were putting on the finishing touches for the grand opening. The club's colors were dark purple and pink, the decor in very good taste. I told Marcel that I had gone to art school, and he asked me if I would do a design for cards advertising the club. The cards, to be put on tables and sent to future customers, billed me as "Robert Clary, *Le Zazou du Parnasse*." *Zazou* was a colloquialism of the period for a person who was energetic, hip, and always on—a kind of dynamic jester.

I persuaded Marcel to hire an orchestra with Jo Boyer as band leader. I had known Jo when he played trumpet with José Rémo's orchestra at Le Shanghaï. Not only was he a remarkable musician, he was an excellent jazz arranger. Jo formed a very hip band with good musicians. But a week before opening, when Marcel heard the band rehearsing, he knew that it would not be able to play the kind of dance music he needed for the club. He had to have a more versatile orchestra. Fernand Clare had just arrived from Nice, where he had made a name for himself as a band leader with a terrific sounding orchestra able to play all kinds of music and tempos. Marcel hired him with the condition that Fernand fire his singer and that I replace him.

I worked at Le Parnasse for two years. The club was very successful. During the winter season, Marcel ran a nightclub in Megève, a ski resort in the French Alps. He would send me there for a month, and I would sing with the band and do my blackface act. Marcel did the same thing with Henri Rossotti, the band leader, that he had done with Fernand Clare. "Get rid of your singer. Robert is now taking his place; he's going to M.C., do his act, and sing all those popular songs better than the singer you have. That's it, that's my final word." Henri, like Fernand, accepted his wishes. Nobody argued with Marcel.

Marcel thought I was extremely talented. What I had on my side, with some talent, was energy. I had as much vitality as Sammy Davis at his peak. I never stopped. We worked from nine P.M. to three A.M. I never had a low moment, I was always on. I made them laugh, and they always asked for more. I was very ambitious. I thought I was the best—that nobody could do what I was doing.

It was a little more than two years since I had been liberated from

Buchenwald, and except for an occasional nightmare, all that seemed distant and unreal. It was as if I had taken a wet sponge and erased what had been written on the blackboard behind me. During my thirty-one months in Germany I had acquired a hard shell. Things like death did not worry me anymore. Sometimes I cried thinking about the loss of my parents and the others in my family and the way they died. But not often. A toughness had taken hold inside me. I did not get emotional and for a long time could not be compassionate.

One evening while I was at Le Parnasse, Yves came to see me. He told me that he had received a letter from Zak, saying that he would be in Paris for a week and wanted to see Claude, Yves, and me. The thought of seeing Zak again pleased me enormously. I was always happy to see Yves, who was proud of me and what I was doing with my life. Yves promised, "As soon as I hear from Zak, I'll let you know and we'll come with Claude and his wife to see you at the club, and we'll have a nice reunion."

The four of them came to *Le Parnasse* on Zak's first night in Paris, and even though I was very busy, I spent as much time as I could at their table. Yves was in a good mood and glad to see his old pal Zak, who looked marvelous. Zak was happy to see us all. He told us what a good life he had in Prague, working in an important post for the Czech government. But somehow he seemed to me like a stranger now. We had little in common; he was a communist, and I was not; he lived in Prague, and I lived in Paris. Nonetheless, it was a happy reunion. I watched Claude, smiling and relaxed and, as always, with his pipe in his mouth, removing it only when he sipped champagne or danced with his wife. None of us talked that evening about the past, but only of the present and the plans we all had for the future. Claude and his wife were going on another deep-sea exploration with Professor Picard. Yves was very optimistic about wanting to write music again. I looked at these three men, my three saviors, with love in my heart and deep gratitude. They told me how happy they were to see their little *Bébé* playing in a fashionable club, admired by the audience. It was a memorable evening.

I saw Zak once more before he went back to Prague. We had lunch at his hotel. It was a brief and somewhat sad meeting, because some-how we both sensed that it would be the last time we would see each other. God knows I didn't intend to visit him in Czechoslovakia, and he never returned to Paris. I don't know what happened to him or if he is still alive, but the memory of this great man will stay with me forever.

Tragically, Claude and his wife died a few years later in a small plane crash, returning from an expedition in North Africa. Yves and I saw each other rarely while I was in France. Once I moved to the United States we exchanged letters occasionally. I would try to see him each time I went to Paris on a visit, and I learned to my great sorrow that he died in 1980.

I did not become a big star, as I had so cockily told my brother Jacques, and I never played the ABC Theater. It is just as well, because I don't think that I would have been ready for the big time and might have flopped as I had when I entertained the G.I.s at the Olympia Theater.

I gave up doing my blackface act and went on working as a band singer, appearing with two good orchestras. Fernand Clare's orchestra was especially good. He had two vocalists. One was Yolande Cora, a beautiful, buxom woman with red hair and sensual lips and looked a bit like Dinah Shore, who sang mostly ballads. I was Fernand's male vocalist, singing up-tempo numbers. I stayed with his orchestra from 1947 to 1949, until I went to the United States. We worked in a huge dance hall called Le Dancing de l'Olympia, on the Boulevard des Italiens, between La Place de l'Opéra and La Place de la Madeleine. It was a tremendous room, situated directly under the Olympia Theater. We gave matinee and evening performances six days a week. On Christmas, New Year's Eve, and other holidays we would work all night long. The matinees went from four-thirty to seven P.M. We called them *thé dançant,* teatime dancing. The place was full of single people seeking partners to go to bed with and also lots of not-so-single people looking for a quickie. There were two orchestras. Quintin Verdu's small combo played tangos and latin rhythms, and Fernand's big band would do "up" tunes, jazz, and ballads. We had *Le quart d'heure de charme,* where, with the lighting turned low for fifteen minutes without a break, we would do slow ballads, and sing French and American love songs. The customers loved the fifteen minutes of charm, dancing very close, taking advantage of the darkness to know each other better.

In the back of the dance hall there was a lounge where we could go and rest between sets, and there we would mostly play *Fussball.* At seven P.M. we would break for dinner, returning to work from nine to midnight. Usually I went home. My mode of transportation, like that of most of the other musicians, was a bicycle. We worked long hours, but I enjoyed singing with that orchestra and being in that place. It was also a steady job. We even made some recordings, and every Sunday afternoon, for a year, we would perform on a very popular radio program starring two comedians, Pierre Court and Francis Blanche.

I became friendly with Charles Aznavour, who had a partner in his act named Pierre Roche. They, like me, had been working steadily and writing songs that many singers wanted to do. I particularly loved singing their "Le Départ Express," "Le Feutre Taupé," and "J'Aime Paris au Mois de Mai." We would see each other very often at Pierre Roche's apartment on the Right Bank, where Charles, with great enthusiasm, would sing their latest songs. We would talk about the business, our ambitions, and our plans to become big stars.

CHAPTER FIFTEEN

HARRY BLUESTONE

I n 1947, the American musicians went on strike, refusing to make records. There was a company called Standard Radio Transcriptions, which made recordings for radio-station use only. Because of the strike, the company sent their Artists and Repertoire man, Harry Bluestone, to London and Paris to record material. While he was in Paris, Harry was told to go to the Olympia dance hall to hear a vocalist named Yolande Cora. Yolande, who came from Nice as did most of the musicians in the band, had a marvelous voice and singing style.

Harry Bluestone did not speak a word of French, and he hired a translator, Morris Porter, a native of Switzerland, who spoke fluent French and English. After listening to the band for a half-hour, Harry sent Morris backstage to the musician's lounge.

I was in the lounge, between sets, playing *Fussball,* when this energetic man, in his twenties, walked up to me and said, "Excuse me, Robert, may I see you for a minute?"

I had no idea who he was. Reluctantly, I gave my place at the *Fussball* table to the bass player. "Yes, what do you want? I'm winning the game. Make it fast."

"There's a man in the audience from America who would like to have a word with you."

"What about? I don't speak English."

"Don't worry about that, I'm his translator. He really wants to meet with you and talk business."

Intrigued, I followed Morris to their table. He introduced me to

Harry Bluestone, a big imposing man who exuded great charm. With a wide smile, Harry invited me to sit down and have a drink. Wasting no time, he said, "Robert, I'm in Paris looking for talent to make records for the United States. I just heard you sing. You are very good. I would like to record you." United States! Where the streets were paved with gold! The land of my favorite movies, the land of Fred Astaire, Eleanor Powell, Ella Fitzgerald! Me! Recording for America! A dream coming true! I said, "Sure, Monsieur Bluestone, I'll be happy to. When do you intend to do the records?"

"In a week . . . to give you time to learn four songs."

"Four songs! I have only a smattering of English; I don't think I can learn four songs in a week."

"Don't worry," he said. "Morris will teach you the words phonetically, and you'll be all right." Smiling broad smiles, we shook hands. Morris said that he would stop by the following day with the four songs, and that we would work on them.

He was a good teacher, and I learned the songs quite rapidly. The day before the recording session, I met with the arranger. I knew his work, and was impressed, because he was the one who made the charts for the show at Le Lido. Harry had gotten the best arranger in Paris.

With my heart in my mouth I went to the recording studio. A big orchestra was waiting for me. That fateful day I recorded "Johnny Get Your Girl," "Put Your Shoes on, Lucy," "Hollywood Bowl" and "I'll Slip Around and Do It in My Dreams Tonight." "Put Your Shoes on, Lucy," was a mouthful of lyric, even for a native American, and I had a tough time recording it, missing words, my accent sometimes changing the meaning. I did take after take, getting more and more annoyed with myself because I was unable to master the lyric all the way through. Finally, after ten takes, and to everyone's great relief, I got it right. I have always thought it ironic that this song turned out to be the one that brought me to America. I was paid very little for the session. Harry seemed pleased with what I had recorded, thanked me, said goodbye, and that was it. I was back that same day at L'Olympia, telling all the guys about the fun I had recording with the big band. And then I put the whole thing out of my mind, regarding it as another job done.

Almost a year later, Morris Porter appeared one evening at the dance hall. "Robert," he said, "your records are making noise in America. Harry Bluestone wants me to tell you that he will be coming back to Paris specifically to make some new recordings with you. And, brace yourself, he also wants to give you a contract and bring you to the United States." My recording of "Put Your Shoes on, Lucy" had sold a half million records there in 1948! I had made the *Variety* and *Billboard* magazine charts. It was difficult for me to realize that Morris was talking about *me*. During this time, while I had been singing at L'Olympia in Paris, totally unaware of what was happening, I had become a recording hit in the United States.

Harry returned to Paris in early 1949 to woo his little star, who was very naive about the situation, and to offer him a seven-year contract. I didn't read the small print, couldn't read it anyway, and never thought of having a lawyer look at it. I would have signed my life away for the opportunity to go to America. As Morris translated as best he could what was written in those many pages, I thought, "Yes, yes, I'll sign. Where, where?" I was twenty-two, not married, and had no parents to support and no responsibilities. What did I have to lose? It was thrilling. The contract guaranteed me a hundred and fifty dollars a week, work or no work, more money than I had ever made. But, when I earned money, Standard Radio Transcriptions would get 20% of my salary. If I made forty thousand dollars a year, a lot of money in 1949, they would take 40%. If I made over forty thousand dollars, the percentage would go up to 60%. What did I care? It was nothing but numbers to me. All I could see was my going to America, becoming a big star, working and living among the heroes of my childhood.

Harry told me what Morris had told me before, that my records were doing well. Aside from the minimum payment I had received when I made the recordings, I never saw a penny from their sales.

At the end of 1947, when I did my first records, I had a very heavy French accent. Since then, I had worked on my English, and I was more American than Harry wanted me to be. At my second recording session—this time for Capitol Records—when I sang "Give Me a Little Kiss Will You, Huh?" Harry insisted that I use a thicker accent. "Don't say 'kiss,' Robert. Say, 'kees.'"

"Like dees, Harry? Geeve me a leetle kees?"

With a big grin, he gave me his nod of approval.

Harry took my signed contract to the American Embassy in Paris, to apply for a permanent visa allowing me to work in the States. He told me that he didn't know how long it would take to get the visa, that it could be a matter of several months. He made a call to his office in Los Angeles and then told me what Standard Radio was going to do for me. "We want you to stop working completely," he said. Harry knew that I had a hernia and was wearing a truss, which was uncomfortable, and that I didn't have the money for an operation. "Let's get your hernia taken care of. Don't worry about the money. Then, while you're waiting for your visa to come through, we'll send you to the Riviera with Morris, where you can recuperate, and at the same time he can help you with your English."

I gave my notice to Fernand Clare. He was genuinely happy about my wonderful break. The musicians all envied me, knowing that I would have the opportunity to see in person all the great orchestras we loved, like Duke Ellington, Stan Kenton, Woody Herman. My last night at L'Olympia was mixed with sadness and jubilation. Everybody at the dance hall, including all the waiters, wished me the best of luck and great success. I had had a marvelous two years with them, and it was tough that night to say goodbye . . . I'll see you . . . I'll write . . .

I went to the best hospital, the American Hospital in Neuilly on the outskirts of Paris. A few weeks after I was discharged, I went to Ste. Maxime with Morris and his wife. He was supposed to talk to me in English so that I would know at least some of the language when I got to America. But we very quickly got tired of it and spoke French again. We had the most beautiful time on the Riviera, two months of fun, enjoying the sun and the beaches.

Robert Dhery, with his wife Colette Brosset, were in Ste. Maxime, taking a break from their tremendous hit stage show called *Les Branquignolles,* a revue very similar to *Hellzapoppin.* When they saw me, they asked me to join their company in the fall. I had to refuse, explaining that I was on my way to America. I eventually saw them again in 1958, when they brought to New York City their famous and successful revue, *La Plume De Ma Tante.*

Milton Blink, who was the vice president of Standard Radio Transcriptions, was vacationing in France with his wife and his daughter. We met on the Riviera and had an immediate marvelous rapport. He told me that he was anticipating my arrival in the States and had big things cooking for me. He said we were all going to be rich and famous.

In Paris, Milton and his family were staying at the Georges V. One evening, when I met them there and we were in the lobby on our way to dinner, we ran into Eddie Cantor and his wife Ida. Milton introduced me. I had seen Cantor in many movies in my youth. I was facing a shrine. Eddie told me that he had heard about me, and the recordings I had made, from his daughter Natalie. He wished me good luck and said he hoped to see me again when I was in the States. I couldn't get over the fact that Eddie Cantor had shaken my hand.

My visa finally came through at the end of September, and I was summoned to the American Embassy to pick it up. After swearing that I was not now nor had ever been a communist, or had venereal or other diseases, I was given the piece of paper that would allow me to go abroad. I was in heaven.

On October fourth, I packed my two brand new suitcases with everything that I possessed, and I said goodbye to my family. I felt very lonely on the plane. It was my first flight, and a long journey. In 1949, the trip took forever. I couldn't sleep. I was excited about my new adventure, and nervous about not really knowing what was going to happen to me.

The plane landed at La Guardia Airport, where Milton Blink was waiting for me. He had come especially from Chicago where he lived, to welcome me. After going through immigration, we were driven by limousine to the Pierre Hotel in Manhattan. I left my suitcases in my bedroom, which was part of a suite I was sharing with Milton. "What do you want to see first?" he asked me.

"Can we go to Times Square?"

We stood across the street from the Bond sign over the clothing store, watching the waterfall coming down like Niagara Falls. I couldn't believe what I was seeing, all the neon lights making the evening look like daytime, the huge animated electric signs, the smoke coming out of the mouth of the man on the Camel Cigarette billboard. Even though I was exhausted from the long trip, I was com-

pletely fascinated by all the sights, the noise, the traffic. I had never
seen so many people in one place. For a born Parisian, I felt like a
farmer on his first visit to the big city.

We went from Times Square to the famous Copacabana for dinner
and to see the floor show. Milton kept introducing me to people and
most of the time I had no idea what they were saying. I kept answering yes, to everything. I found out quickly that my smattering of
English was just that. Everybody was talking much too fast. I tried so
hard to concentrate and to understand what they were saying that it
gave me a headache. Joe E. Lewis was the star attraction, and the place
was mobbed with his fans. We were sitting at a ringside table. On the
same bill was the singer Kay Starr, and I was very surprised to hear
the people talking loudly through her act. The production numbers
were very impressive, at least to a greenhorn, all those beautiful
chorus girls dancing on a handkerchief-size stage, while the stiff-as-
cardboard boy singer tried to be heard over the noise. Then Joe E.
Lewis came on. The audience adored him, laughing at everything he
said. I watched this phenomenon with a straight face. Holding a glass
of Scotch in his hand, Lewis mumbled drunkenly into the microphone. I couldn't understand a word he said. I remember his introducing Martin and Lewis who were in the audience. People cheered
when they took a bow. They had just started to make a name for
themselves and were appearing at the Paramount Theater.

When we left the Copacabana, Milton said, "Are you tired?"

"No, I'm fine. Why?"

"I know what you like and I'm going to take you someplace
you're really going to enjoy." He took me to an upstairs club on the
corner of Forty-Ninth Street and Broadway to hear Duke Ellington
and his orchestra. This time, I didn't have to try to understand the
language. Even though my eyes were starting to close, I stayed wide
awake during the whole set. What a beautiful way to end my first
night in my new country. We went back to the Pierre, where I took a
bath in the most luxurious bathroom I had ever seen. I was exhausted,
but so stimulated I couldn't sleep.

We stayed in New York City for two days, sightseeing. I saw my
first Broadway show, *Lend an Ear,* the hit revue that had originated
in Los Angeles and featured a new comedienne with a big voice and

big eyes, Carol Channing. The show, and especially Carol, impressed me greatly.

Then we took the Twentieth Century to Chicago, traveling first class. In France, I had been used to going second class, sleeping on benches. Now I was in a private room with berths, sleeping in a bed— Wow! I was living like a king.

Milton Blink couldn't have been nicer to me. In Chicago, I checked into a hotel very close to where he was living. Again, he showed me the town. We went to see Danny Thomas at the Chez Paree. I understood him a little bit better than Joe E. Lewis, but not much. Two days later Milton put me on a plane for Los Angeles and the main headquarters of Standard Radio Transcriptions.

I was greeted at the airport by a smiling Harry Bluestone. He drove me in his new Rambler to his home in Canoga Park, in the San Fernando Valley. The palm trees, the sunshine, the casual way people were dressed, made me feel that I was back on the French Riviera. Harry's wife Le welcomed me to their home. She was a stunner, blond, slim and tanned. I wondered if all American girls were as beautiful.

At dinner I was served corn on the cob. I thought, this is what the French feed their animals, but I fell in love with it immediately; it was delicious. Merv Griffin tells the story on his show about how I ate corn at his parents' home in San Mateo, in 1950, and when I was through, I gave the corn cob back to his mother and said, "May I have some more, please?" It makes for a funny story when he says that I thought his mother would put some more corn back on the cob I had just handed her.

Harry Bluestone found me a place to live in the heart of Holly-wood, behind Grauman's Chinese Theater, on Orchid Avenue, a small single room with a Murphy bed, a bathroom and a tiny refriger-ator. It was the best and most spacious place I had ever had in my life. I loved living in that neighborhood. I would take walks on Holly-wood Boulevard—which, in 1949, was more reputable than it is today—watching for movie stars. The only one I saw was Ricardo Montalban. That gave me something to write home to my sister Mad-eleine. One of the first things I did, after arriving in Los Angeles, was to call my sister Nicky in Texas. I told her how excited I was to be in

America, that everything was super, and that I hoped we would visit each other one day soon. She was really happy to have me in the same country.

Later on that day, I went with Harry to the office of Standard Radio where I met the president, Jerry King. He and all the employees made me feel so welcome and at home that I realized all over again how lucky I was. Jerry told me that I would have GAC (General Artists Corporation) as my agents, as well as Jimmy Saphier, who represented Bob Hope, as my manager.

They were all going to make me a big star, even if it killed me, which it nearly did. I was sent to a very good vocal coach, Sy Miller, five times a week. His office was at Harms Music Publishing Company on Hollywood Boulevard, a few blocks from where I lived. Sy had coached Doris Day, who was then the vocalist with Les Brown's band. I was flattered to be in such fine company. Sy loved Gershwin songs, and so did I. With his help, we put an act together.

I was in complete awe of everybody: manager, agents, coach, Jerry King, Milton Blink, and mostly Harry Bluestone who had been my mentor. At twenty-three, I was being represented by some of the most important people in show business. It was a tremendous change for a kid who had never even had an agent. I obeyed like a trained dog, doing everything they asked. If they said turn left, I immediately turned left—with a smile. Put your tongue out and make a silly face, the tongue would be out with the silliest face. I felt all these people had much more experience than I and knew what they were doing. How could they be wrong? I trusted Harry Bluestone implicitly. His batting average was very high. They wanted me to be a great success, to our mutual benefit.

They even hired a choreographer who worked magic with some Warner Brothers musical films. He was charming, and went to work on two numbers for my act. One of them was "Give Me a Little Kiss, Will Ya, Huh?" The gimmick he devised was that during the song I would sit on a chair, with a pink balloon attached to the back of it and a woman's red coat with a white collar draped around the balloon. I would sing to that make-believe woman in my most pronounced French accent . . . "Geeve me a leetler kees." The other number was as terrific as the first. I was supposed to sing "I'm in Love with a

Wonderful Gal" (changed from "guy," from the score of *South Pacific*), working with two microphones set apart. Each time I started to open my mouth to sing, that particular mike would supposedly go on the blink and I would then have to run to the other, which would also not work. And so I would go back and forth between the two mikes for the whole song until, completely frustrated, I would stand in the middle of the floor and belt out the song. You had to be there to see how bad it was. If they had asked me to do my act naked, I would have complied.

Between all my tutorings, to help me learn the language, I read American novels and magazines, with the aid of a dictionary, and went to the movies. At first I didn't understand three-quarters of what was said on the screen, but I didn't care. It was entertainment, and gradually I got used to the rhythm of the English language and began to comprehend more and more of it.

It was also a tremendous help that I didn't know any French people, because I was forced to speak English, no matter how badly, or not speak at all. Later, in 1950, when I met Natalie, I said to her one evening, "It's time for me to go back to my apartment to sleep, because I have to stand up tomorrow at eight o'clock." More often than not, I put the accent on the wrong syllable. After seeing that marvelous movie with Humphrey Bogart and Katherine Hepburn, I told Natalie, "I just saw a perfect movie with Bogart and Hepburn, *The Afreecan Queen*."

"The what?" she said, her green eyes widening.

"*The Afreecan Queen*! You didn't see it?"

She burst out laughing. In those days, Natalie was always laughing at my fractured English. Once, when she asked me about the concentration camps, I said, "The least you ask, the better you'll be off." Most of the time Natalie corrected my errors. She did it for years.

Jules Green, who was Jimmy Saphier's associate, was assigned to educate me about American customs. When we went to restaurants, he would teach me what to look for on the menu. He took me to Sy Devore, the "in" tailor in Hollywood to buy the proper clothes. He even chose the right kind of shoes for me to wear. Jules was a man with impeccable taste; I liked the way he dressed, and what he selected for me. He told me that I should go to Hollywood High School to

learn English grammar. I said no to that, feeling ashamed at my age
to go back to school with teenagers. Instead, I learned the language
the hard way. Jules never forced me to do things I didn't want to do.
He was a very easy person to be with, a gentle man with an even temper. He was optimistic about my future, as were Standard Radio,
Jimmy Saphier and GAC. They wanted me to get my act in shape as
quickly as possible in order to take advantage of my being in the
States while my recordings were still being played and my name was
still hot. I had made more recordings for Capitol under the baton and
orchestrations of Lou Busch, and they would be coming out soon.

My act was finally ready and GAC had me signed to break it in at
The Tops, a club in San Diego. In my custom-tailored Sy Devore tux-
edo, I was determined to go on with everything I had been taught,
and show them what a good student I was. I did what I had learned
to perfection. I gave it everything I had. And I flopped. Those two
special material numbers no sooner got off the ground than they went
down in flames. My managers, agents, publicity agents, and everybody from Standard Radio were there watching their discovery take
a huge dive. I mean *huge*. The audience sat on their hands, with their
mouths sealed shut, and stared at me, obviously puzzled by what this
overcranked little foreigner thought he was doing with a balloon, a
woman's coat, and two mikes. Nothing worked. Here I thought I was
going to conquer the world, and I couldn't even move an audience in
San Diego. They had fabricated somebody who wasn't me. The act
was not what Harry had signed me for. They had manufactured a
French robot.

After the first show, all my sponsors came to my dressing room
with the good news. Harry was the spokesman. "Listen, Robert," he
said, "it is not working. I know you can do better than this. I think
we've led you down the wrong path. We've decided that you should
sing what you feel like singing. First of all, let's cut out those two

GAC booked me for an appearance on a daily television talk
show, hosted by Al Jarvis, on KTLA. Betty White was his girl Friday.
Al liked me and I was signed to be on the show at least twice a week.
It was a marvelous exposure. I had never done television, but I
jumped into the new medium with ease. I had fun being fresh, saying
all kinds of nonsense in broken English, and singing a lot.

special numbers right now. When you finish this engagement, and you're back in Los Angeles, you and I will revise your act."

GAC had already booked my act into Detroit, New York, and Montreal. As soon as I returned to Los Angeles, Harry and I agreed on the kind of act I should do. We held auditions for a pianist to go on the tour with me. I wanted a jazz pianist, somebody who could swing, as well as read music and conduct. We finally selected Claude Williamson, who had been with Charlie Barnet's orchestra, and who I felt was the right pianist for me. Claude and I worked very hard on choosing songs, tempos, and arrangements. He was young and willing, and we were very compatible. The act was a mixture of French and American songs, a distinct improvement over what I had done in San Diego, and I felt good about it.

Before going to Detroit, I was booked for my first network TV appearance on the Ed Wynn Show, on CBS. It was done live in Los Angeles, then kinescoped for the Middle West and the East Coast. Ann Sheridan was the guest star. Ralph Levy directed the show. I sang my hit song, "Johnny Get Your Girl," and did some talk with Ed Wynn. He meant nothing to me because he wasn't known in France, but being with Ann Sheridan was exciting. What a thrill it was, even though she never talked to me, not even to say, "Bug off, kid."

I went to Detroit in February 1950 to The London Chop House, a first-class restaurant and night club. The customers enjoyed my act, and my confidence was restored. The reviews gave me hope. One reviewer said, "Robert Clary, a recent importation from France, is one of the most promising young singles to hit the Midwest recently. Although his size and bounce are reminiscent of Mickey Rooney, the protruding lower lip of Maurice Chevalier, the husky accent of Charles Boyer, and the crooning style of several top male singers, Clary still has his own distinct personality. He had much to offer . . . plenty of animation, poise, and an obvious enthusiasm for his work."

After Detroit, Claude and I opened in New York City at Fanchon and Arnold's Park Avenue Restaurant on East Fifty-Second Street. Billy Daniels worked there just before me, had packed the club for six months, and had been the talk of the town. Maxine Sullivan, who was billed as the "Loch Lomond Lady" because of the record she had made famous, was my opening act. A few days after I opened I read a review in *Downbeat*, written by Will, which began, "Robert Clary is a small Frenchman with an equally small voice who is currently being subjected to a build up in this country . . ." Then after comparing me with Mel Tormé, though saying I was not nearly as talented, he concluded his review by saying, "If and when he stops pushing so hard, Clary might develop into a good turn for intimate clubs, but in his present status he seems to be missing the boat all around." With my limited understanding of English, I thought he was telling me to take the next boat to France.

When performers are new on the scene, they are always compared to celebrities they may look or sound like, or in no way resemble. In 1950, I was usually described as a combination of Frankie Laine, Mel Tormé, and Maurice Chevalier. I should have taken it as a compliment, but I didn't because they allowed me no personality of my own, no originality, and of course did not find me as talented as the stars they compared me to.

I truly looked forward to going to work every evening. Fanchon and Arnold's was doing okay business and the customers liked me. I loved being in New York. It reminded me more of Paris than Los Angeles did. I was able to catch Broadway matinees and see the current movies at the Roxy, Capitol or the Paramount, with their live big-star, big-band stage shows. My first visit to Radio City Music Hall was a revelation. The Rockettes knocked me out. I went back again and again to see the same show and still did not get enough of them.

After finishing my month at Fanchon and Arnold's, I went to my last booking, in Montreal. My act did not overwhelm the people there. But I was happy, because I got to spend time with Pierre Roche and Charles Aznavour, who were trying to make a career in Canada. It was fun to be with them, and a relief to speak French again.

When the tour was over, I returned to Los Angeles. There were no future bookings waiting for me. My Capitol records weren't selling at all. One of them, "C'est Si Bon," for which they had high expectations, had come out at the same time as the big selling versions by Louis Armstrong and Johnny Desmond. Harry Bluestone said to me, "You know, your career is not working as we thought it would.

Maybe you should go back to France, where I'm sure you will do quite well."

I thought that it was nice of him to say that. Nonetheless I told him, "No, Harry, I'm here now, on a permanent visa, and I would like to stay." I didn't want to go back to France with my tail between my legs. Harry did not insist that I return to Paris or that we tear up my contract.

My life was at a standstill. I would get up in the morning, trying to find a way to occupy myself for the day. After having breakfast at the Betsy Ross coffee shop across the street from Grauman's Chinese Theater, I would take my walk on Hollywood Boulevard, stop at the Las Palmas news stand to buy French magazines, and browse through the book and record stores. Then I would eat lunch at Betsy Ross again, where I would have my daily conversation with Harry Ruba- loff, the owner, who was very sympathetic about my being alone and not having friends. In the afternoon, I would usually go to a movie. Three times a week, I took a bus to the office of Standard Radio to meet with Harry Bluestone and talk about my career. Our conversa- tion always went like this:

"Harry, did you talk to the agents at GAC today?"

"Yes, Robert, they still have nothing right now. They are trying to set an audition for you at the Mocambo."

"The Mocambo?"

"Yes, but don't hold your breath."

"Okay, I won't. Did you talk to the people at Capitol Records?"

"Robert, your records are not selling, and they are not renewing your contract. They are dropping you."

"So what other cheerful news do you have for me, Harry?"

"Look, Robert, don't let it discourage you. That's the business. Something will turn up. Keep your chin up. If you go home to Paris, you'll probably get work right away. But since you want to stay here, it's just gonna take longer."

"Thanks, Harry, you've made my day."

Every Thursday his secretary Ginger would give me my weekly check. Occasionally, Harry would invite me to his house for dinner. American food was one of the hardest things for me to get adjusted to. It was so different from French food, in taste and quantity. Everything was put on the same plate and in such abundance that it killed my appetite. Most of the time I had dinner alone at the Pig'n Whistle Restaurant next to the Egyptian Theater or, when I felt like splurging, at Musso & Frank, both on Hollywood Boulevard. It was not the kind of life I had planned. I wanted to work and to make money. I didn't want to spend my days walking on Hollywood Boulevard. I knew almost no one. I had met people living in my building, but nobody I cared to make friends with. It was a lonely time.

CHAPTER SIXTEEN

NEW FACES OF 1952

One night, Red Doff, the publicity man at Capitol Records, took me to the Palladium to see Freddy Martin and his Orchestra. Merv Griffin was Freddy's vocalist. Red Doff must have told Merv that I was in the audience, because he rushed over to our table and said, "How very nice to meet you. I know all about you. I love your recording of 'Johnny Get Your Girl,' " and proceeded to imitate me singing a few bars of the song.

"I want to introduce you to some people who are big fans of yours," he said. "Are you free tomorrow afternoon? I want you to meet these people." Merv had, and still has, great warmth and enthusiasm, and it's catching. Suddenly I was his friend.

The next day he picked me up at my place and took me to meet Jeanie Plant, Natalie Cantor, and her sister Margie, at Natalie's home. Jeanie was Freddy Martin's private secretary, and it was through her that they had all become acquainted with the first record I had made while in Paris. Mike Gould, a song plugger for Bourne Music, had given Jeanie my recording of "Johnny Get Your Girl" and "Put Your Shoes on, Lucy," together with a brochure telling about me. He also gave her the sheet music, hoping that Freddy Martin would put the songs in his repertoire. Jeanie had flipped over my record and the way I sang. She played the record for Natalie, who was her best friend, with the idea of getting Natalie's father, Eddie Cantor, to listen to me. She knew Cantor was interested in discovering new talent and thought I would be perfect to appear on his radio program.

Natalie and Margie had loved my American beat and thought my accent was adorable. Natalie played the record for her father who reacted with the same enthusiasm. A short time later, Mike Gould had asked Freddy Martin what he thought of the songs. Freddy said, "What songs?" It turned out that Jeanie had been so excited about me and her plans for my future that she had forgotten to give the record and material to Freddy. Eddie Cantor had been interested in sponsoring me to come to America, but by that time I had already signed with Standard Radio Transcriptions.

Natalie, Jeanie, Merv and I became fast friends. It happened like lightning, like love at first sight. And it was the end of my loneliness. We were together constantly.

Merv was single. So was Jeanie. She was tall and pretty, had an engaging smile, and was an excellent jitterbug dancer. She talked a lot, as we all did, often all at once. Merv was a great story teller, very witty. They all had a great sense of humor, and a tendency to be loud. Natalie, who talked less than the rest of us, in her quiet way usually came up with the best lines. She was a striking woman, with large green eyes and dark hair with an attractive premature white streak she refused to dye. She was divorced and had a young son, Michael. She introduced me to her parents, Ida and Eddie, who remembered having met me at the Georges V, and to her sister Edna. Marilyn and Janet, her other two sisters, lived in New York. Very often, Natalie and I would travel to San Diego, San Francisco, Oakland, and other cities in California to be with Merv and Jeanie and the Freddy Martin Orchestra. We never stopped laughing. Everything amused us. Natalie, Jeanie, and Merv often teased me about my English. By that time I understood at least 80 percent of what people were saying. Merv, for example, would say, "You're behaving like a brat today, Robert."

"What does it mean, a brat?"

In unison they would answer, "It's a compliment, Robert, say thank you."

Harry Bluestone still got no work for me. GAC dropped me, and so did Jimmy Saphier. Eddie Cantor thought that with my talent I should be doing things. And he took over. He had a marvelous quality of wanting to help people when he felt they had talent. There's a long list of his protégés, including Dinah Shore, Joel Grey, Bobby Breen, Eddie Fisher, Deanna Durbin.

He arranged an audition for me with the William Morris Agency. He had been with them for years and knew everybody there.

"Robert," he said, "all the agents will be there to hear you sing."

At William Morris, I waited in the conference room with my pianist, and when all the agents had arrived, I sang five songs from my night club act. I received a warm round of applause and many compliments and was signed by the agency.

Eddie didn't stop there. He knew the people who owned the Bar of Music, a night club on Beverly Boulevard in Hollywood, and talked the owners into hiring me. My act was a success and I stayed there for six months. The great female impersonator Arthur Blake was the star attraction. It was a big room, with the stage behind a huge bar, so you had bartenders and people sitting on stools directly in front of you. You had to project beyond the bar for the people who were sitting at tables. Working in one place for six months had its advantages, I found out which numbers worked and which to drop out of my repertoire. I learned what fitted me, and what to say between songs.

When I finished my engagement at the Bar of Music, I was hired to work the very next day by Jimmy Dolan who owned a tiny, chic club on the Sunset Strip called Café Gala. It had two pianos and no microphones. I worked for Dolan a whole year. I was paid a hundred and fifty dollars a week, and never got a raise. Sometimes the checks would bounce, even when business was good, and I would complain to Dolan who always said, "Put it back; it's good now." The list of people who entertained there was impressive. Bobby Short had been a fixture for years, and was still doing his marvelous tasteful show tunes. Like Bobby Short, Portia Nelson sang romantic and witty songs from Broadway shows. Felicia Sanders sang like an angel. The breathtakingly beautiful Dorothy Dandridge had her night club debut there, with an act fantastically put together by Phil Moore. She stayed at the Gala for three months, and while she was there you could not get into the place unless you made a reservation weeks in advance. We would do three shows a night. It was great for us who were working with her, because we were seen by all the important

people in Hollywood. Bobby Troup, with Al Viola at the guitar and
Lloyd Pratt at the bass, would entertain as well as accompany the acts.
One night, I said to Al, "Let's do 'But Not for Me' with just the guitar, no bass, no piano, just the two of us." In this intimate club, it
worked like a charm, and we did it that way from then on.

Burt Lancaster, who was producing movies with Harold Hecht,
was ready to film *Ten Tall Men,* a story about the French Foreign
Legion. They came one evening to the Café Gala and, after seeing my
act, told me that they were interested in casting me as one of the lead
Legionnaires. I was very excited, not only about the possibility of
being in my first American movie, but about playing with Burt Lancaster, and having one of the lead roles. The film was to be produced
in tandem with Columbia Pictures, and at the last minute, a big shot
at the studio made them hire Nick Dennis to do my part. I was terribly disappointed. Hecht said that they would use me for another part.
But it was much smaller. I played the role of Lancaster's orderly, a
little Arab called Mussel, with just a few scenes.

In my second movie, *Thief of Damascus,* I was cast again as a little
Arab. In the 50s, Sam Katzman was the king of the B-minus movies.
They were made in two weeks, maximum. I had just finished filming
Ten Tall Men. Sam called me into his office at Columbia Studios. He
said, "Kid, I'm giving you the break of your life. I have a big part
for you in *Thief of Damascus.* I know you can sing, but can you do
comedy?"

"No," I said. "Can you?"

He laughed and hired me for the part. It was the seventh lead. Sam
made his low budget movies by hiring stars who were no longer box
office. The cast of *Thief of Damascus* starred Paul Henreid, and featured Lon Chaney Jr., John Sutton, Helen Gilbert, and Jeff Donnell.
Elena Verdugo and I were the only newcomers. With a two-week
shooting schedule, Will Jason, the director, didn't have time to explain
every little move, let alone motivation. It was only my second movie.
I didn't know a thing about camera angles, close-ups, or key lights.
Most of my scenes were with Lon Chaney Jr. I was Aladdin and he
was Sinbad the Sailor. Chaney was an old pro and knew every trick
in the book. After a few days of watching him chew the scenery, I

learned how to defend myself so that my face, and not just the back of my head, would be on camera.

I was afraid after these two movies that I would be cast as a Sabu character, playing little Arabs for the rest of my life. But I didn't have to worry, because I didn't make a movie until two years later, when I filmed the stage version of *New Faces*.

The Cantor girls had been raised on Broadway musicals, and Natalie and Margie made me more aware than I had ever been of that world. I would listen in fascination as they described in detail all the shows they had seen, from *Ziegfeld Follies* to *Oklahoma.* I fell madly in love with the songs from *Guys and Dolls.* And at the Café Gala I sang practically the whole score. I was dying to do *Sue Me,* a duet between Adelaide and Nathan Detroit. But it wasn't published. I met Frank Loesser, the composer, at the club, and asked him if I could do the song. He said, "Yes, why not? But don't mention that I gave you permission." I had a ball doing that number. It was unusual for a performer to do both parts. The audience loved it and I kept that song in my repertoire for a long time.

I saw Natalie every day. I would have dinner with her and her son. Mike and I liked each other and got along fine. I remember him playing "Marines" a lot, putting ketchup on his face, faking being wounded. He was very theatrical. After dinner, Natalie would chauffeur me to the Gala. I didn't know how to drive in those days. She was always there when I needed her, her generosity never faltering.

Eddie Cantor opened doors for me. He featured me prominently on one of his TV Colgate Comedy Hours, and he arranged a New York night club engagement for me. "There's a new room called La Vie En Rose," he said. "I'm going to see that you sing there. I'll pay for your trip, and you'll stay at the Sheraton Hotel on Seventh Avenue." He was able to book me at La Vie En Rose because he was friendly with the co-owner, Milton Blackstone, Eddie Fisher's manager. The other owner was Monte Proser, who instantly took a great dislike to me because Milton hired me without consulting him. Let's face it, the place was called Monte Proser's La Vie En Rose. Opening night Eddie Cantor reserved a big table and invited a lot of people to see my act. He even recorded an introduction praising me. My opening was very successful.

Subsequently, the audiences liked me, and all the trades and newspapers gave me good reviews, but Monte was determined to make my life miserable. He would put me on only when he felt like it, mostly for the third show when there were fewer people in the room. Sometimes he would do me a favor and let me do the second show. If he was in a very good mood, I would get to do all three shows. Nevertheless, I stayed at the club for almost four months. Dorothy Dandridge was the main attraction, and we enjoyed working together again. She was represented on the East Coast by Eric Bernay, who later on became my manager. Seeing how Proser was treating me, Eric reasoned with him and succeeded in getting him off my back. After that, I did all the shows, and my engagement became more enjoyable.

Merv Griffin was singing with Freddy Martin's orchestra at the Roosevelt Hotel. Since neither of us could afford to spend too much money on hotel rooms, we became roommates. We found a huge room at the Royalton Hotel, across the street from the Algonquin. Merv, at that time, was going out with Judy Balaban, who was a close friend of Peggy Ann Garner. Peggy was separated from her husband. The four of us would go out and have great fun. I liked Peggy a lot. I thought I was in love. She was a very lovely, sweet girl, I enjoyed her company, and I was very impressed that she was who she was, the child star from *A Tree Grows in Brooklyn.* In those days I was taken with celebrities.

One evening at the club I received a call from Morty Halpern, the stage manager for *New Faces of 1952,* a new revue currently in rehearsal. He asked me to come and audition for the show the next morning at the Broadway Theater. I didn't think I stood a chance, so I went to the audition with a very cool attitude. I sang three songs, "Fleur Bleue," "Shrimp Boats," and Johnny Ray's "Cry" in French, exactly as I had been doing them at the club. When I finished, Ronny Graham ran onto the stage with the director John Murray Anderson, raving about my audition. They were joined by Leonard Sillman, the producer, who insisted that I stay there while he called Charlie Baker, my agent at William Morris, to come over right away to talk contract. And, just like that, I was signed to join the company at rehearsal the next day. I learned later that Leonard had caught my performance the night before at La Vie En Rose, and hadn't particularly liked me. He said something happened on the Broadway stage that wasn't there at the club.

I was making seven hundred and fifty dollars a week at La Vie En Rose. I was still under contract to Standard Radio, who, after my disastrous first tour, gave up on me. It bothered me that they were taking 40 percent of my salary. If it hadn't been for Eddie Cantor, where would I be? I decided with Eric Bernay to drop them. Standard Radio wanted to sue me for breach of contract, maintaining that they had invested thousands of dollars in me and, now that my career was going fine, I wanted out. They considered me ungrateful. Finally, we settled out of court by my paying them money for a year until we reached the agreed upon amount.

During my first week of rehearsal of *New Faces*, nothing was written for me. They had no plans for how they were going to use me in sketches and songs. In the meantime, they thought it would be funny to do a quick walk on between set changes in which a pimp is beaten up by his prostitute. Eartha Kitt who, like me, had been given nothing to do, played the prostitute. The skit wasn't funny at all. Eartha was so frustrated that she would hit me as if she meant it. She was a strong girl. When we did the first run-through, John Beal, the sketch director, saw how bad it was and decided, to our great relief, to throw it out.

Arthur Siegel, who composed half the songs in the show and who doubled as the rehearsal pianist, came up with a bright idea. He said to me, "There's a song written by Ronny Graham that would be perfect for you to do. You should learn it, and sing it for Leonard, Ronny, and Murray." He played me "I'm in Love with Miss Logan."

I said, "My God, it's beautiful." I couldn't wait to learn it. I've always been a child at heart, and I felt a strong identification with the song. Originally, Logan had been given to Bill Mullikin, but it didn't work for him and had been set aside.

When Arthur told Murray, Leonard, and Ronny that he thought I should do the song, they said, "But he's French."

"Listen to him sing it," Arthur said. "I think you'll be surprised."

It was not the first time Arthur helped me. He was the one who had told Leonard to see me at La Vie En Rose.

I sang "I'm in Love with Miss Logan" for them, and it was instantly agreed that the song was mine. I was thrilled. Ronny was delighted with my interpretation. "I'm going to write another song for you," he said.

I will never forget when Ronny came in the next day and sang "Lucky Pierre" for me. My face must have shown how I hated it. I said, "What is this crap? I don't want to sing this cliché ridden song. Forget it, Ronny. I'm not going to do it." I wanted so badly to be American. I never wanted to be a professional "zeez" and "zoze" Frenchmen, "ron, ron, ron," and all that.

"Don't fight me," Ronny said. "It'll work, believe me. I know what's good for you. Once you get over the shock of feeling like Maurice Chevalier, it will fit you like a glove." I still resented it. Not only that, I was fighting Richard Barstow's choreography for the number. I thought I knew everything. I said, "Richard, I don't want to do this step. It doesn't feel good."

Richard said, "It'll feel good when you learn it. I don't have the time to argue. Do it." He choreographed "Lucky Pierre" with Virginia De Luce, Pat Hammerlee, and Rosemary O'Reilly as three ladies falling all over the little Frenchman who had just arrived from France. It was a fast paced number, and Ronny was right. All the clichés worked without being corny. Because of Ronny's two songs I became a hit in *New Faces*. For years afterwards "Lucky Pierre" was my opening number in night clubs.

June Carroll and Arthur Siegel, who wrote "Love Is a Simple Thing," asked me to write a French lyric. Rosemary O'Reilly, Eartha, and I sang different versions of the song, followed each time by a couple dancing in that particular tempo. Carol Lawrence tap danced Eartha's version. The song became a standard and was recorded by many popular singing stars.

We went to Philadelphia for the tryouts, and received mild reviews. During our two weeks there, a few cuts and changes were made. The night before the Broadway opening, when we did the preview, we all felt low. The audience reception was cool. We thought we had a flop on our hands. On Friday, May 16, 1952, opening night, in the first act, Alice Ghostley stopped the show cold with her rendition of "Boston Beguine," written by Sheldon Harnick who later on, with Jerry Bock, wrote the score of *Fiddler on the Roof.* Then in the second act, I stopped the show with "Logan." I couldn't believe that I had to go on stage to take an extra bow. And then the same thing happened with Eartha when she sang "Monotonous" written by June Carroll and Arthur Siegel. Paul Lynde's monologue (a man returning from an Africa safari, bandaged and on crutches) had the audience in stitches. So did the take off of *Death of a Salesman* with Ronny, Alice, and Paul, written by Mel Brooks.

That evening, Walter Chrysler, who was a big backer of the show, gave a marvelous party for the cast. He had the ballroom of the Metropolitan Opera House opened just for us and a hundred guests. When the reviews came out and were read aloud, we all cheered. We couldn't believe our good fortune.

The next morning, the lines at the box office were long. We were a hit, such a tremendous hit that people would talk about it for decades. We were the toast of Broadway. We had the cover of *Theater Arts.* *Life* did a feature story, and *Time* did one on me alone. The show was a major breakthrough for all of us.

During the Broadway run of the show, I was booked at the Village Vanguard night club. As soon as the curtain came down at the Royale Theater, I would take a cab downtown to the Vanguard to do the 11:45 and the 1:30 shows. Then several of us would go to Lindy's to eat and be seen. I would finally quiet down and get to sleep around four.

My life changed. Eric Bernay hired Eartha's press agent, who was very good, and got my name in the papers. I was constantly in demand and appeared on major television variety shows, like *The Patti Page Show* and *This Is Show Business,* with Abe Burrows and George S. Kaufman on its celebrity panel.

At the Village Vanguard, I was on the bill with the comedian Phil Leeds, and with Sylvia Syms, who indirectly taught me how to sing a ballad. I learned a great deal by watching her every night. She had a way of singing that touched me and made me understand the sadness or the joy she was feeling. Often after our last show, Sylvia and I would go to Barbara Carroll's place. Barbara played great jazz piano, and Sylvia would sing, and I absorbed it all. Harry Belafonte, whom I knew well, came down to the Vanguard one evening with Marlon Brando. It was an off night, unusual for us, and the place was half-full. They sat at a ringside table and talked and laughed noisily during my act. I was furious. Afterward, I grabbed Harry, who is a tall man, and took him to the kitchen and bawled him out. I said, "Wait until *you* work someplace. I will sit right in front of you, and make such a racket, you'll never forget it!" He may not remember that incident, but I do. I will never forget once at La Vie En Rose, when Marlene Dietrich came with Harold Arlen, and all she did during my act was stare. Never applauded, or smiled, just stared.

Pops Whitaker, who did night club capsules for *The New Yorker,* reviewed me at the Vanguard: "The minute and Parisian Robert Clary is a magnificent example of concentrated animal magnetism. His songs, as often edged with pathos as with laughter, are all topnotch." Pops had a trenchant wit, but was always very kind to me. He rarely repeated himself, but week after week, for the thirty-five weeks I was at the Vanguard, he was always complimentary: "Robert Clary has become a clown in the round, all the way from quiet pathos to out-landish merriment. You'll rarely see as expert a job of gamut-run-ning."

John Murray Anderson, who staged *New Faces,* was a brilliant direc-tor and a gentle person. He was also mischievous. "Don't go out with Peggy Ann Garner," he would say to me. "She's not the right girl for you." He didn't even know her. When I asked him why he felt that way, he would shrug his shoulders. "Trust me," he would say. He felt fatherly toward me and wanted to see me happy, but not with Peggy. He didn't have to worry. Peggy and I had a very short romance. I dreaded getting serious and attached to anyone.

Murray, in his late 70s, looked much younger than his age. Tall, slim, erect. With a beaked nose and a devilish twinkle in his eyes, he had enormous energy. He also had a dry sense of humor. He gave everyone nicknames. Mine was "Guignol," which means "puppet." He called Ronny Graham "Scraps," Alice Ghostley "The Phantom," and Paul Lynde, who was addicted to sun lamps, "Suntan." Like everybody who came in contact with him, I was very fond of Murray.

After the success of *New Faces,* Murray was involved with Bette Davis' revue *Two's Company.* When he was putting the finishing touches on a show, he worked at a large board in the middle of the orchestra seats, with a microphone in his hand. He didn't want anyone around him, ever. But he asked me to come to the Alvin Theater, where *Two's Company* was in its final days of rehearsal. I would go there every afternoon, except when we were having matinées. He wanted me there, next to him and his board and his microphone, because he knew I would not say a word while he worked. In his wicked way, he told Bette Davis to pat me on the head for good luck, and every day Bette Davis, believing or not that I was a good luck charm, would pat me on the head. I felt like a dog who had just done a great trick. I don't know if things worked well for her on Wednesdays and Saturdays when I was doing the matinées. I was amused by the whole thing, and pleased that Bette Davis was touching my head.

One day, in panic, her voice hoarse with laryngitis, she phoned Murray. "I can hardly speak," she whispered. "What should I do with my throat?"

"Cut it," he replied, and hung up.

Merv Griffin went on the road with the Freddy Martin band and I moved to the Gorham Hotel, on West Fifty-Fifth Street. I had a big room with a double bed, a small refrigerator, and my collection of records. I had discovered classical music, starting slowly with romantic and melodic composers like Tchaikovsky and Rachmaninoff. I was beginning to understand why my father loved that kind of music.

Life for me in New York City in the fifties couldn't have been better. What an exhilarating city it was! Broadway was overflowing with hits. One wasn't afraid to walk on the streets late at night. Between the show and doubling at the Village Vanguard, I was making five hundred dollars a week, substantially less than I had earned at La Vie En Rose, but I was happy and felt successful.

In May 1953, after a year's run, *New Faces* was scheduled for its national tour. Leonard Sillman wanted to keep the original cast. Eric Bernay told Leonard that I would not go on the road. He felt I should go forward with my career in New York and embark on new projects. But Leonard, who could have gotten another small man to do my part, very badly wanted me. "Okay, Leonard," Eric said, finally. "We will go on the road if you pay Robert a thousand dollars." To our surprise, Leonard agreed. It was a coup to get him to pay that kind of money.

We opened the tour successfully in Boston, then went to Chicago. The show was such a hit there that we settled in for a six-month run.

My sister Aimée, without her husband, traveled for the first time to America to visit me and my sister Nicky. At that time I was commuting twice a week from Chicago to New York to do the Garry Moore television show. Aimée came by boat, and I had arranged for Eric to meet her at the pier in New York. She was panicky because she didn't know what Eric looked like. When he finally located her, she was in tears. Eric took her to my room at the Gorham Hotel. The next day I flew in from Chicago for my appearance on the Garry Moore show. After the show, we flew back to the windy city, where the same night she saw me in *New Faces.*

I showed Aimée the town, and took her to the best restaurants. Once, in a steak house, she asked for roast beef; when her plate, filled with huge portions of beef, baked potato, and vegetables, was put in front of her, she exclaimed, "That's for my whole family!" In Paris, she was used to many courses, but in small quantities. She was amazed by the amount of food American restaurants served to one person. Aimée was very happy to be with me, and to see my success in the theater. Her warmth, friendly attitude, and the charm of her broken English won the hearts of the whole company. She had always been very emotional, and two weeks later, when I put her on the train to visit my sister Nicky in Texas, she was in tears, certain we would never see each other again.

I continued to commute twice a week to New York to do the Garry Moore show for three months, taking a red-eye flight after the performance. I would nap on the plane, then go to the Gorham and catch an hour or two of sleep before going to CBS. I would rehearse the show, do it live, and then take a cab to La Guardia to make the three P.M. flight back to Chicago. In my room at the Ambassador West, I would have time for dinner before getting ready to go to the Great Northern Theater for the evening performance. You had to be young. I loved doing the Garry Moore show. I was on the air twice a week, nationally. But it was exhausting. I would say to Eartha, "I don't know how long I can keep up this pace."

"I don't want to hear any complaints out of you!" she would say. "Look at the exposure you're getting. If you're a good boy, I'll give you a present when you finish."

At the end of my three-month guest appearance on the Moore show, Eartha gave me a medal that said, "Bobby—Good boy." She was the only one in the cast of *New Faces* who called me Bobby. I'm not a Bobby or even a Bob. Most people call me Robert.

Eartha and I were close pals. Our relationship depended on what mood she was in, how she woke up in the morning. She could be cold and difficult, ignoring you, or she could be very thoughtful, charming, sweet, warm, generous, and fun to be with. If you didn't want to be hurt by her temperament, you accepted her as she was. Love her when she's lovely, and ignore her when she ignored you.

I was always made up and dressed early and would go to visit Ronny in his dressing room while he was getting ready. It was a ritual. I liked Ronny, and admired his involvement with life. If he read a book about mountain climbing, he would want to go and climb a mountain; he'd buy all the necessary equipment and go and do it. In Chicago, he decided to play golf, and got me involved. We bought all the gear and started to take lessons. I was very bored with the game. I hated the pains in my shoulders, the calluses I got on my hands from gripping the clubs too tightly. I said, "Who cares about running after a little ball? I love to walk, but I don't have to go looking for a ball that I can't see in the first place." Ronny was intense about everything. In a way, I envied that quality in him, but sometimes I wondered why he had to get so intensely involved with everything in life.

Alice Ghostley was marvelous, extremely kind and very funny in the show, as well as in life. She was accused years later of imitating Paul Lynde's mannerisms. Actually the opposite was true. During the run of *New Faces,* they were extremely close friends, and their comedic styles developed simultaneously. But the basic nervous, anguished quality was Alice's.

Paul Lynde had a sharp wit, and he was a funny man. Once during a matinee in San Francisco, a very drunk lady in the balcony would loudly say after each number, "I don't get it! I don't get it!" disrupting the whole mood and pace of the first act. At intermission, the police were called to take her away. As they escorted her through the theater alley, Paul leaned out of our dressing room window and screamed, "*Now-w-w* you're gonna get it!" Despite his wit, there was a meanness about him, an unhappiness, even with the success he later achieved. When he drank, he could be very cruel. I was aware that, most likely because of his upbringing, he was anti-Semitic. He always had hostile words to say about Jews. He used all the clichés: some of his best friends were Jews; Jews ran the government, the banks, show business, etc. It bothered me. Often I wanted to tell him to shut up and grow up. But there would be no reaching him. Whenever I did say something, he accused me of having no sense of humor. When people make jokes, they often reveal their true feelings.

Arthur Siegel had been a close friend of the Cantor family since the days when he had known Marilyn at the American Academy of Dramatic Arts. He was practically adopted by the Cantor girls as their brother. A gifted composer and musician, he played double piano, and accompanied Eddie Cantor at his Carnegie Hall concert. Six-foot tall, bespectacled, Arthur had the hugest laugh I have ever heard. He was liked by everybody, and would go out of his way not to hurt anyone's feelings. He knew everything about the theater, and had an enormous collection of playbills and LPs, which were stacked all over his apartment, even in his kitchen cupboards. He possessed files of sheet music of obscure songs written by great popular song writers. A bachelor, Arthur enjoyed his freedom. He was never lonely, and relished his time by himself, so that he could read his newspapers, magazines, and books. He loved the theater and saw absolutely everything that opened and closed on Broadway, as well as every movie he could fit into his schedule. Arthur and I had a lot in common, not only our love of the theater, movies, music, and books, but our close friendship with Natalie and Jeanie. During the run in Chicago, when Jeanie was there with the Freddy Martin Orchestra, Arthur and I saw her constantly.

Natalie joined us there for a week. We always loved to surprise each other. During my Garry Moore Show period, I was living at the Ambassador West, where my routine was to arrive in Chicago from New York, go to my room, and call room service for dinner. One evening, after I had showered and was trying to relax and get myself together for the night's performance, there was a knock on the door. Assuming it was room service, I opened the door and, instead of the waiter, there was Natalie, pushing the table with my food. She had just arrived from Los Angeles without telling any of us. It was a joyful surprise.

Natalie and I discovered that we had an affinity for each other. There were strange coincidences. Once, talking to her on the phone, I mentioned that the big toe on my right foot was hurting. She said she had the exact same pain in the same toe. Often we'd be reading the same book at the same time, and we would discover that we were practically on the same page. Our phone numbers, 3,000 miles apart, were almost the same, with a few digits reversed. It was eerie.

I have never been late in my life for anything. One day in Chicago, Leonard told the cast that we were going to make the movie version of *New Faces* for Twentieth-Century Fox. We were all elated. That evening during intermission I was telling Ronny and Paul about making movies. I got carried away, showing off to both of them my experience and knowledge. Two movies had made me an expert. We were in our dressing room in the basement when suddenly I heard my music cue! I was supposed to be on stage in "Coocoo's" (Virginia De Luce's) arms, while she carried me across the stage to introduce the next number. Because I was so reliable none of the stage managers or Coocoo had looked for me. Coocoo had gone on stage with her arms out singing as though I were there, "I take him off my income tax, etc." I panicked. I felt unworthy of being in the theater—*me*, missing an entrance! It was an actor's nightmare, except it was for real. I apologized ten thousand times to everybody—cast, crew, stage managers, ushers, box office people, bathroom attendants, until everybody said, "All right, shut up about it. We know you are highly professional and reliable. Nobody's holding it against you!"

After Chicago, *New Faces* played for a month at the Biltmore Theater in Los Angeles. Then, before going to San Francisco, we took a week off to make the movie. It was done on a shoestring. We were paid our usual salaries. The studio used our sets and costumes. A thin plot was incorporated, because they didn't believe that the movie would sustain with only skits and songs. Harry Horner, the famous set decorator, was making his debut as a director. Lucien Ballard was our cinematographer. The entire filming took six days. It was the first musical put out in Cinemascope and did tremendous business wherever it played. It stayed in one movie house in London for over a year. We all had a small percentage of the net profit, but naturally never saw a cent of it.

After making the movie, we resumed our tour. We were playing at the Curran in San Francisco when we heard the news that Murray had died. Leonard Sillman did something very touching that night at the curtain call. He came on stage and told the audience that John Murray Anderson, the man responsible for our success, had just died. Then, as one by one we stepped forward in silent tribute, Leonard called each of us by the nickname Murray had given us—Scraps, The Phantom, Suntan, Coocoo the Bird Lady, Mrs. Harrison Williams (June Carroll), Guignol, etc.

After touring for a year, and being together for two, we all felt sad when we gave our last performance in Detroit. When you have to cry on stage, you can't do it every night. When I did *Logan,* once in a while I would cry real tears. On our last night, knowing it was the last time I would do the number in the show, I did not have to pretend.

CHAPTER SEVENTEEN

LA PLUME DE MA TANTE

After *New Faces,* I resumed my nightclub career, opening as the headliner at The Blue Angel in New York City. I worked there and at the Village Vanguard repeatedly over the next few years.

One of the performers with whom I shared billing at The Blue Angel was Lenny Bruce. He was crucified by the reviewers. They all said, "The evening is saved by Robert Clary." Lenny was brilliant. I would watch every show he did. The club was jammed, and most audiences adored him. Some would walk out, shocked by his use of foul language. How mild it was compared to the comedy of today. Lenny was incredibly inventive. He wasn't as spaced out then as he became in later years, near the end of his life. One night, Herbert Jacoby, the owner of The Blue Angel, told Lenny that the police would be there, and to clean up his act or they would close the place. Lenny went on that night without using one dirty word. It was still a great act, and it proved that he didn't have to use foul language to make his point. But profanity was part of what made Lenny Bruce Lenny Bruce.

I played a lot of night clubs in the fifties and early sixties. The William Morris Agency booked me frequently in Miami Beach. I worked all the hotels there, from the Fontainebleau to the Diplomat. I enjoyed working in the big hotels. I never had a bad audience. It was a good change for me, because for a long time I had been known as a sophisticated entertainer who worked only in intimate chic night clubs. My act had been considered to be above the interest of average people, but I thought it was commercial enough to be enjoyed by everybody. George Kane at the Morris office agreed with me, and persuaded the owner of the Town Casino in Buffalo to book me there. I was frightened by the size of the place. Suddenly I was a mile away from the nearest table. The Town Casino had an enormous stage, and I felt I wouldn't be able to reach the audience. It took me at least a couple of days to get adjusted to the place. I made no changes in my act, except to use larger orchestrations, and work broader. The Goofers were the main attraction. They were six guys doing all kinds of things—playing instruments, singing, swinging on a trapeze—a very visual act, to say the least; I was glad I didn't have to follow them.

My first big supper club engagement in New York City was in the Cotillion Room at the Pierre Hotel. It was the height of success for people who worked the clubs.

In 1956, I was cast in my second Broadway show, the musical version of the Janet Gaynor and Charles Farrell movie *Seventh Heaven.* It was Peter Gennaro's first job as a choreographer for a Broadway musical. He had talent, enthusiasm, great kindness, and a big smile for everybody. Along with Victor Young, who wrote the music, and Vertes, who did magnificent sets and costumes, Peter was the most professional and inventive person involved in the project. But because the show was in deep trouble with the book and lyrics, the producers gave him a hard time, blaming him for everything.

Ricardo Montalban and Gloria De Haven were the stars of the show. Featured were Paul Hartman, Fifi D'Orsay, and me. Chita Rivera, Pat Hammerlee (who had been in *New Faces*), and Gerrianne Raphael were playing three adorable whores. We went to New Haven, Philadelphia, and Boston for tryouts. After a few days in New Haven, Fifi and Paul were replaced by Kurt Kasznar and Bea Arthur. Paul was too American for the part of a Parisian cab driver, and I think Fifi wasn't fast enough learning her lines and songs.

Our first director, John C. Wilson, who had a long list of theatrical hits to his credit, was a very nice person, but he had a drinking problem. Most of the time, he didn't seem to know what to do with the show. Gloria was supposed to sing the opening number with the dancers and singers. When it didn't work, Wilson decided that everybody should whisper the number. He thought it would be an original way to start a show. That bombed, too. Then, thinking it would be livelier, he shoved me into the number instead of Gloria. It didn't work with me either.

Wilson, however, was a witty man, never at a loss for a *bon mot.* After the third week of rehearsals, working on the opening number, I said to Wilson, "John, it's not working—*I'm scared!*"

He replied, "You're scared—like Ethel Merman."

Wilson was replaced out of town by Morton Da Costa, who had just directed the Broadway hit *Plain and Fancy.* He was called "Teek." He had a tough job on his hands. In the second act, Pat Hammerlee and I had a number in one (in front of the curtain, while the set was being changed) called "Love Sneaks Up on You," and we used to stop the show at every performance. Teek didn't want us to do the number in front of the curtain, and made us do it on a huge street set, with the chorus looking at us. We never stopped the show again. I begged Teek to put the number back in one. He said, "I don't care if it doesn't stop the show; it's not important to me. The story has to have continuity." We opened at the ANTA Theater in New York to poor reviews, and closed after a seven-week run.

It was back to the clubs again. In January 1956, I was on the bill with Sophie Tucker at the El Rancho in Las Vegas. She liked me and asked me to appear with her again when she worked in Philadelphia and Brooklyn. I would always tease her. She had very little sense of humor, at least not my kind. I would have early dinner with her every evening at the El Rancho coffee shop. She never ordered anything there. Her Las Vegas friends would send her home-cooked meals. A pot of chicken and matzoh balls, a beef ragout, enough for a regiment. I would always pretend that her food looked marvelous. "Sophie, what you have looks and smells delicious!" I would say. She would never offer me a taste. Never. She was a kind person, but she was stingy.

Sophie had a Japanese maid named Missa, who was always in the wings with a box of Kleenex, because Sophie would wipe her nose before going on stage to do her act. While she wiped her nose, she would watch my last number, and always had a comment for me when I came off stage. "You did very well tonight, Robert," she would say toughly. "Take another bow." One night I changed my

closing number, doing a song, "La Vie Française," that had been written for me by Michael Brown for an industrial show in New York.
One of the lines in the song had something to do with Davy Crockett,
which was appropriate when Michael wrote the song in 1952. I knew
it was a bit outdated in 1956, since the TV show with Fess Parker had
been off the air for a while. But it didn't hurt the song. It was a good
song, with a funny point of view of a Frenchman in America. After
the show, Sophie called me to her dressing room. She said, "Robert,
I like your new song, but let me tell you a few things about America.
Davy Crockett is dead!"

With a shocked look on my face I replied, "No kidding, Sophie,
when did he die?"

"Don't be funny," she continued. "I know what I'm talking
about. The line has got to go! You have to be up to date when you do
special material!" I kept the song and never changed the line. Poor
Sophie, I guess she meant well. After her shows, she would be out in
the lobby, selling her records and books. She hated to fly—she'd
rather be on a train for days than be on a plane for a few hours. I
would tease her about that. "When it's your time to go, you go, train
or plane—it doesn't matter."

She would say, "Stop talking like this, Robert. Don't tell me what
to do with my life. Just let me tell you what to do with yours."

My agent at William Morris booked me in Detroit for nine days at a
place called The Gay Haven, which was not a homosexual club. They
were having a bowlers' convention. The money was good and I had
top billing. I arrived in the afternoon for the rehearsal, early as usual,
and waited for the big band to show up. The place was large, ugly and
looked dirty. After a while three musicians appeared on the big stage.

"Where are the other guys?" I asked.

"What other guys?" the pianist said. He had a patch over one eye.

"The rest of the orchestra!"

"This is it; this is what you are getting, Mr. Clary. Just a trio." It
consisted of the pianist, a trumpet player, and a drummer. I was frustrated, and annoyed with my agents who had not bothered to check
out the details. To them it was work, and the money was good, and
they were getting their ten percent. I was as much to blame. I should

have asked about the job . . . the kind of club, accommodations, the number of musicians. Now there was nothing to do but try to make the best of the situation.

I started to rehearse with the trio. They were a peculiar combination. I had never encountered a trumpet player in a trio. The piano was out of tune. I asked the pianist if it was going to be tuned before the show.

"Not that I know of," he said. "And don't panic if you don't hear my left hand. There are some strings missing on the bass." He was not very good at reading music and my orchestrations were too complicated for him. The sounds that came out of the trumpet were a disaster. The drummer read music as poorly as the pianist. We rehearsed four songs, for a long time. We were getting nowhere, and I was disgusted. Finally, I told them that it was enough. We would wing it tonight somehow. I didn't know how, but we would. Then I went to my dressing room. It was a real pig-sty, filthy, full of empty beer bottles, cigarette butts, used tissues all over the floor. All that was missing were pigs. I paid one of the bus boys to clean up my room and, to calm myself down, walked the few miles to my hotel.

I had been told to be at the club at eight, which was when the show would start. I arrived promptly. The place was packed and noisy with visiting bowlers wearing their team shirts, drinking beer.

There turned out to be an hour and a half show before I went on, consisting of B girls doubling as bad dancers, an emcee doing corny jokes for ten minutes, followed by a local girl singer, who was not going to go places. Then the B girls again, with grease-stained costumes, doing another dance. Then an encore from the MC, doing ten more minutes of the worst material. I had made up my mind not to use the pianist and the trumpet player, but to do my whole act with only the drums. I was getting nervous, sweating, worrying how people were going to sit patiently for so long to hear me sing with just drums. I knew I was going to bomb.

Finally, the MC introduced me. Giving the drummer the tempo I wanted, I started to sing "Lucky Pierre." I did my whole act with only drums. Miracle of miracles, the bowlers enjoyed it. They even made requests. I was a hit. I did the same thing for nine days and got away with it.

At Eddy's, in Kansas City, I could not believe the audience. I did maybe two satisfying shows out of twenty-four. It was February and the weather was freezing, and so was the audience. For the first few days, I put up with people talking loudly while I was singing. They didn't look at me when I came out for my first number, didn't even give me a chance to prove myself. And it was always the ones sitting at ringside who were the noisiest. Finally, one night after my opening number, I said, "I don't mind your talking and being rude once you have looked at me and found me too short, too tall, too fat, too skinny—but you don't even have the decency to let me try to entertain you. I wonder why you bothered to come here. There are lots of bars where you can talk your heads off. It will cost you much less money. You know there's a floor show at Eddy's; you know I'm here, so why not give me a chance?" After my speech they quieted down. They listened, or left, which was fine with me. The only thing I can say in defense of performers who get annoyed by rude customers is that they do want to give a good performance. They get involved with their songs or routines, and suddenly they are confronted with a bunch of drunks who are ruining the mood, the continuity of what they're trying to do, not just for them, but for everybody who has come to see them.

For years, whenever my tolerance was pushed too far, I would single out and attack the person who was making the noise. Eventually I realized it was wrong to do that because, for one loud mouth, you upset and antagonize the rest of the audience. Now, when it happens, I rise above it and ignore the rude ones and try to continue to entertain the others who came to hear me. I let the ones in the audience who are bothered by the noise do the shushing. It works much better that way.

I did a movie with Paul Newman and Joanne Woodward, in 1958, called *A New Kind of Love*. Mel Shavelson was the writer and director. I played the part of a French pimp, selling girls, postcards, anything to make money. I said to Mel Shavelson, "Do you want me to put on a French accent?"

He said, "No, no, speak naturally, it's fine." I didn't think I had a strong accent. I never thought I talked like French people, because they talked like "zees." I don't hear myself speaking with an accent.

The next day I went to see the rushes, and I said to Mel, "You're right. I don't have to put on an accent. It's there. It's thick."

After all these years people in the industry still think of me as a professional Frenchman. Not only am I French, but I'm small, which limits me further. In show business, you get stamped and categorized. I have a huge stamp on my name. It says in big letters "TINY FRENCHMAN." I have been living in the United States since 1949. I became a citizen in 1954. I vote, pay taxes, and do everything American-born citizens do. I am as American as apple *tartelette*.

When I played at the Café Gala in 1951, I was approached by Pierre La Mure, author of the then current best-seller *Moulin Rouge* about the life of Toulouse Lautrec. He had written a dramatization of his book and wanted me to play the artist. I began to read everything available about Lautrec. I understood and identified with him, and was convinced that I was born to play the part. It was all I could talk about. But John Huston bought the film rights to the book and hired Jose Ferrer to walk through the part on his knees. I was bitter, jealous, and disappointed. A year and a half later, while I was in *New Faces*, Edward Chodorov, the talented playwright and screenwriter, and author of the Broadway hit *Oh Men! Oh Women!* wrote a play, *Monsieur Lautrec*, and asked me to do the title role. I was eager to have the chance to do the part, but I had just resigned for another year with *New Faces*.

In 1959, seven years later, Chodorov called me. "Old boy, I still want you to play Lautrec in my play. We're going to do it in England and then take it to Broadway after the run in London." I gratefully accepted his offer this time.

I was the only American actor in the cast; the others were very British. I tried hard to say "cahn't" instead of "can't." My accent was a combination of heavy French, fair American, and awful English. We rehearsed one week in London and two weeks in Coventry, the town the Germans had bombed practically to ruins during World War II. We were supposed to be in Coventry to work out the kinks of the play, and then take it to London. Before leaving New York, I grew a beard so that I would look like the image of Toulouse Lautrec. When I arrived in London, the first words out of Chodorov's mouth were, "Old boy, shave that off. We want Lautrec in the first act to be young and innocent, arriving in Paris without a beard." So off it came. It was a three act play, and for every performance I glued on the beginning of a beard in the second act, and a full one in the third. It was very irritating to my skin—I hated it.

The reason for taking a play out of town is to see what's not working, and do rewrites before the play is reviewed by the major critics. On opening night in Coventry, all the British critics were there. Most of the reviews were kind to me and liked my performance, but they crucified the play. The show was a tremendous flop. Chodorov, who also directed the play, got so depressed by the reviews, he said, "I don't know what else to do to improve it." He left shortly after the opening. We stayed in Coventry for the two-week run, and closed there forever. I was extremely disappointed. I went back to New York with my tail between my legs. But at least I had played the role and had gotten Lautrec out of my system.

La Plume de ma Tante was a very funny French revue which, after playing two years in London, opened at the Royale Theater in New York in 1958. Robert Dhery, the writer and director of the show, also starred in it, with a company of mad Frenchmen. It was a tremendous hit. I had met Dhery and his actress wife Colette Brosset in the summer of 1949, when I had gone to Ste. Maxime on the French Riviera before coming to the United States.

When *La Plume de ma Tante* opened in New York, I went backstage and reintroduced myself to Dhery. He remembered me well, reminded me how he had wanted to have me in his show, *Les Branquignolles,* and we became friends. The summer of 1960, when Dhery and Colette were scheduled to take a three-month vacation and go back to France, he told David Merrick, the producer of *La Plume,* he would like to have me as his replacement. Dhery and I had nothing in common physically. He was a tall, slim man, with greying hair. He also had a slight, but charming, speech impediment that worked to his advantage. Merrick agreed to have me. Liliane Montevecchi was hired as Colette Brosset's replacement, to costar. The salary was small, five hundred a week. David Merrick was well known for not paying actors big salaries. But it was an opportunity to be back on Broadway.

I watched the show every night for several weeks before starting rehearsals. There is a very famous sequence in *La Plume,* the bell ringing number, in which four monks stand sleepily holding ropes. It starts very quietly and ends up in total madness, as the monks amuse themselves with the ropes, jumping and running in a circle, as though on a carousel. When one of the monks pulls on the rope, another is lifted up off his feet. Pierre Tornade, who pulled the other end of my rope, weighed at least a hundred and seventy-five pounds to my hundred and eighteen. Because I was so light, Pierre would make me fly over the orchestra pit, close to the first rows of the audience. I used to scream, really out of fright, because my hands would slip to the big knot at the end of the rope, my arms stretched to the maximum, until I thought I was not going to be able to hold on anymore, and that I would fall into the orchestra pit. The audience loved the sight of me flying over their heads. By intermission I would be in such pain that my dresser would have to massage my arms and legs.

After doing the routine for as long as I could endure it, I told the stage manager that I wanted out of the number. Robert Dhery had never done it. He thought it would be fun for a tiny person to play one of the monks. It's a shame that it made a wreck out of me, because except for the physical discomfort, it was very enjoyable to do.

As the show neared its two-year run on Broadway, Merrick decided to take it on the road and open at the Riviera Hotel in Las Vegas. It was the first Broadway show to play a room in Vegas. Robert Dhery wanted to leave to write and do a movie called *La Belle Americaine,* which eventually became a tremendous international success. He told Merrick, "I'll do *La Plume* for the first month in Vegas, and then replace me and Colette. Take Robert Clary and Liliane Montevecchi, who did such a good job last summer."

Merrick called me and asked me to come in to his office to discuss my replacing Dhery. He insisted that I see him alone without my agent. I listened to him telling me how great it was going to be for my career, to be seen nationally in this magnificent revue, that it was going to be a long engagement, six months minimum in Vegas, etc. He said I had done a good job on Broadway in the show. I could tell he hated to say that, afraid I would ask for the moon. Then he said, "This is what I can pay you . . . five hundred a week." I looked at him, shocked. "Mr. Merrick," I said, "I would love to do the show because I enjoy it a lot, but your offer is ridiculous. I make much more working in night clubs. You are asking me to lose a lot of money, and I can't afford that." At five hundred he was getting me a lot cheaper than Robert Dhery.

Merrick said, "I'm sorry you feel this way, because I can get Claude Dauphin, Jean Pierre Aumont, Louis Jourdan . . ." He gave me all the well-known French actors who worked in America. I was surprised he didn't include Charles Boyer and Maurice Chevalier.

I said, "Why don't you get them then! Be my guest, and hire any one of them for that price."

Finally, reluctantly, he gave me more money. I went to Las Vegas with Liliane Montevecchi. We played two shows nightly, seven nights a week, for five months. It was an abbreviated version of the original show. We were very fortunate to have a great company. Liliane was fun to be with. We got along well, never had a fight. She was a kookie, charming, crazy, sweet, beautiful, stunning, full of life, loud woman. I adored her. In Vegas, most of us in the company would spend our days together, going to Lake Mead, to the desert—and the mountains. We picnicked and celebrated birthdays. We were a happy family.

We toured after Vegas for a year and a half. Our first stop was Los Angeles at the then Moulin Rouge. The whole tour was extremely successful. From February 1961 to August 1962, we played major cities across the country and in Canada, from San Francisco to Boston, ending up in Chicago. We had been extremely well received everywhere. We thought we'd be held over in Chicago for at least six months.

We had been booked into the McVickers Theater, originally a movie house and not planned for a legitimate show, a long narrow theater with a balcony five miles away from the stage. The Chicago critics panned us. It was a shock, because we were used to rave reviews. We stayed only a month in Chicago, and closed the show there. It was sad to say good-bye. We all felt so close to each other; it was tough suddenly to go our separate ways. Most of the cast returned to France. I missed all of them for quite a while.

* * *

In November 1962, I was signed for a two-week engagement at the Statler Hotel in Boston. During the first week, the audiences were noisy, usually at the second show, but I kept my cool, not saying anything, trying to rise above the noise. It was tough. On Saturday night, second show, the room was jammed, and I might as well have been working at Grand Central Station during the rush hour. Nobody cared, and I mean *nobody.* After doing the first five songs and suffering sheer agony, I just thanked the people and walked out. I went to my room. The manager of the hotel called me immediately and said, "You'd better come down and do your act."

I said, "I've done my act."

He said, "You'd better come down, on the double, and finish your act."

I said, "I finished my act."

He said, "You're fired."

I said, "Thank you very much." And hung up. I called my agent and told him what had just happened, went downstairs, picked up my orchestrations, packed my bags, and took the next train to New York, greatly relieved not to fight unruly patrons anymore. The hotel tried to sue me. Breach of contract, they said. But because of my excellent record all those years, never walking off a job, or being fired, there was no suit. I had not refused to do the show. I had just shortened my act.

I was in Dallas on the day John Kennedy was assassinated. I had opened at the Statler Hotel the day before. In the audience that night was a large group of Pepsi Cola representatives, including Richard Nixon, who was their lawyer, and Joan Crawford with her husband Alfred Steele, the head of the company. My sister Nicky, who at that time lived in Irving, a suburb of Dallas, came to the opening with her husband and her two daughters. During my act, I introduced the celebrities, something I never relished doing. Unless I admired them a lot and could be totally sincere in my praise, I felt uncomfortable. Most of the time, you had to lie through your teeth, and pretend they're great, fabulous, extremely talented, and wonderful human beings. I was never a big Joan Crawford fan. I would laugh at her

exaggerated acting, especially in her later movies. Still, when I introduced her, respecting the big superstar she was, I was very kind. Then
I introduced Nixon, and I couldn't help myself. I began by saying,
"This next person—you either like him or you don't." I went on, in
a subtle way letting the audience know that I didn't. When he stood
up to take his bow, he received the biggest hand from the audience,
bigger than Joan Crawford got. It was an ovation.

The next morning I went down to the hotel coffee shop to have
breakfast. It was late morning, and suddenly, right before my eyes,
while I was eating, the history of the world changed. People rushed
in and out of the place shouting, "The President has been shot!"
Chaos took over that city. The hotel was invaded by journalists and
television and radio crews—it was a madhouse. Nobody could really
believe what had just happened. At first I thought it was a prank,
because Kennedy and the Democrats were not liked in Dallas. Adlai
Stevenson, a few days before, had been booed and harassed there.

I had been booked for a three-week engagement at the Statler, but
the room was closed until further notice. The town was deserted,
except for the media. The whole world was glued to the television. It
was fortunate for me that my sister Nicky lived nearby; I went to her
home and did what everybody was doing—watched TV. It was a
shocking, sad, sad experience. Dallas was a big dark cloud.

A week after President Kennedy's death, the supper club at the
Statler reopened, but they might as well have kept it closed. I did my
act for no more than ten people a night. Who wanted to be entertained, especially in Dallas where it happened?

CHAPTER EIGHTEEN

HOGAN'S HEROES

In 1963 and 1964, my career was at a very low ebb. I was not hot anymore and my agents could not get work for me. The only bright spot in those two years was that I was hired for the summers to play Passepartout in the musical version of *Around the World in Eighty Days.* It was produced at the huge outdoor theater at Jones Beach in Long Island by Guy Lombardo and Michael Todd Jr. The season went from July to Labor Day. The first year I costarred with Fritz Weaver as Phileas Fogg, Elaine Malbin as the Indian Princess, and Dom De Luise as Fix, the detective who follows Fogg and Passepartout. The second year, my costars were David Atkinson, Jan McArt, and Dom DeLuise again. The show was beautifully staged, with an enormous cast, including an elephant and a camel. There were barges, boats, and a large balloon carrying Fogg and Passepartout high over the stage very effectively. I received great reviews. I loved playing Passepartout and looked forward to going to the theater every night, where we would do the show for an audience of more than four thousand. It was a thrilling experience.

For the rest of the year, my manager, Lenny Ditson, would occasionally book me in Brooklyn at the Elégante Club or at one of the hotels in the Catskills.

In 1964, around Christmas time, Arthur Siegel said to me, "I'm going to Los Angeles for a couple of weeks and staying at Natalie's. Maybe you should come with me, just for the fun of it." I didn't have money for the fare, so I borrowed it, and went, without telling Natalie

I was coming. She was at the airport expecting only six-foot tall Arthur. I hid my five-foot-two frame behind him so that Natalie couldn't see me at all, until the last second. She was happily surprised, and immediately invited me to stay at her house. "We'll manage, we'll make room." It was a small house, with two bedrooms. Her son Michael was already married, Arthur had his room, and I slept on a cot in the den. As usual, we had lots of laughs, and Natalie's fabulous meals. It did me a world of good to be there, and it brought me a change of luck. It was on this trip that I was signed to do the pilot for *Hogan's Heroes.*

One of my agents, Bill Donohue of The Agency for the Performing Arts, had met with Edward H. Feldman, the producer of the pilot of *Hogan's Heroes,* regarding Godfrey Cambridge, who was supposed to do the Ivan Dixon role of "Kinchloe." For some reason, he didn't want to do it. Bill Donohue asked Ed Feldman, "Who else do you need in the cast?" Ed said, "I need a Frenchman." Because I was in Los Angeles and had met Bill the day before, he said, "Robert Clary is in town. Would you like him to come in and talk to you?" Ed said, "Robert Clary is here?" he remembered me from the Café Gala in the early fifties. He said, "I want to see him tomorrow. I'll give him the part right away. He's exactly who I want."

The next day I went with Bill, and Ed said, "The part is yours, if you want it. It's yours. I have no idea what will happen. The role can be big, medium. I don't know for the moment, but it's yours." I didn't even have to read for it.

Reviews for *Hogan's Heroes* in 1965 were from excellent, "Genuinely creative farce comedy, well conceived and played," to very negative ones: "How could you make a comedy series set in a concentration camp?" The *New York Times'* Jack Gould said, "Nazis are silly old buffoons, hopeless oafs who have more in common with Desilu than Hitler." In spite of the bad reviews the show became an instant hit with the viewers and it is liked to this day. It was a satire not to be taken seriously. Every week we made fools of our captors. Klink and Schultz were not "lovable Nazis;" they were members of the Luftwaffe and not automatically Nazis. Richard M. Powell, who wrote the pilot of "Hogan's Heroes" and twenty-eight episodes for the show, said, "I always tried to show the Nazis and the Gestapos in an unfavorable light and achieved it quite well, while still writing funny scripts."

When the show went on the air, people asked me if I had any qualms about doing a comedy series dealing with Nazis and concentration camps. I had to explain that it was about prisoners of war in a stalag, not a concentration camp, and although I did not want to diminish what soldiers went through during their internments, it was like night and day from what people endured in concentration camps. Prisoners of war were protected by the Geneva convention, received Red Cross food packages, and could write and receive letters, even though they were censored. Soldiers were not forced to work in German factories, they were not guarded by the SS, but by the Wehrmacht, and they were not sent to the gas chambers. I was an actor who was asked to play the part of a French corporal prisoner of war and not a little Jew in concentration camp, and I never felt uncomfortable playing Louis Lebeau.

When we all met for the first day to read the script for the pilot, I didn't know a soul in the cast. I had never heard of Bob Crane (Hogan), who at that time had a local CBS radio show interviewing celebrities, playing records, and sometimes his drums, which he was mad about. Everybody who had heard his radio show thought him very clever and greatly entertaining. He had also been featured in the TV series "The Donna Reed Show." Werner Klemperer (Klink), the son of the world renowned classical conductor Otto Klemperer, had done many movies and plays on Broadway, but wasn't as yet a household name. John Banner (Schultz), who was a big, huggable bear, had struggled for many years until he got his well-deserved break with "Hogan's Heroes." He had arrived in the United States from his native Austria just before the beginning of World War II, having lost all his family under the Nazi regime. Richard Dawson (Newkirk), whom we all called Dickie, had had some recognition on local television in Los Angeles. Ivan Dixon (Kinchloe), had understudied Sydney Poitier on Broadway in *A Raisin in the Sun,* and had made a marvelous small black and white film called *Nothing but a Man.* Larry Hovis (Carter) had a part in the pilot, but had not yet been signed as a regular. Very often on the set, Larry and I would sing old standard songs, harmonizing, to the delight of the cast and crew.

Also in the cast was Leonid Kinskey, the veteran character actor, playing a Russian soldier. We all sat at a huge table reading the script for the first time and were greatly amused by Leonid changing his lines, ad-libbing all over the place, trying very hard to make the show center around a Russian prisoner of war. He appeared only in the pilot. His part was cut out of the show.

There was an immediate camaraderie among us that went on for the next six years. I had a small part as did all the Heroes except for Crane, Klemperer, and Banner, who were the stars of the series. As the days went on, Ed Feldman kept adding to my role. I started as the cook and the man who tended to the German shepherds. Then I became the tailor and finally the barber.

While we were filming the pilot, my agent, Lenny Ditson, called me from New York to tell me that he had gotten me a job in London, to appear on a variety show on TV with Shirley Bassey, produced and directed by Buddy Bregman. The *Hogan's Heroes* pilot was supposed to be filmed in ten days, but the director, Bob Butler, was taking his time to make sure the finished product would be perfect. I got panicky, because I had to leave for London a day or two after the completion of the pilot. Every day, Ed Feldman kept telling me, "One more day, Robert, and we will be finished, then you can go to England." Time was running short. Friday evening, Ed told me that he would be needing me through Tuesday. "Ed," I said, "I have to be in London by Wednesday, I have to finish Monday, not later than that. It's a long trip." We did our last scene on Tuesday evening. I grabbed my bags and took the very next plane to England, making the rehearsals just in time.

When I finished with the TV job, as long as I was in London, I made a quick trip to Paris to visit my family. My sisters all wanted to know about Natalie. They had met her the previous year, and had been very taken with her. At that time I had been staying at my sister Madeleine's apartment when I got a surprise phone call from Natalie in London. I shouted with joy. She had not told me that she had decided to go to Europe on a vacation. She had made the trip with our friends Kaye Ballard, Arthur Siegel, and Sandy Dody, a very witty writer, with an amusing affected British accent. Natalie was calling to tell me that they were flying to Paris for the weekend.

I showed them my Paris, and Natalie decided not to go back to London with the rest of the group, but stayed for a week, and we flew back to the United States together. Kaye insists that's when love bloomed. We got married a little more than a year later, after I realized that, through all those years, there was something more than friendship between Natalie and me.

I asked Natalie to marry me before moving permanently to Los Angeles to begin shooting *Hogan's Heroes*. The pilot had been sold almost immediately. I had made up my mind to move to the West Coast even if *Hogan's* wasn't a hit. I told Arthur that there wasn't any woman in the entire world that I would like to spend the rest of my life with except Natalie, and I was going to ask her to marry me, which I did, over the phone. When I proposed to her, she was shocked. Out of the blue, her best friend was telling her he loved her and wanted to marry her. I remember saying, "Natalie, I do love you tremendously, and want to marry you." There was a big silence. She must have thought I was kidding, or drunk. Jeanie Plant, who was at Natalie's that night, couldn't believe it either; her reaction was a mixture of he's crazy and how marvelous if it happens.

I called Natalie every day during the next weeks, repeating that I loved her, that she was the only woman for me. I told her that I was buying a car in New York and driving to Los Angeles and, once I got there, we'd get married. She kept saying, "We'll discuss it when you get here. We can't make a decision like this over the phone." I think I broke all records driving across the country. I phoned her every evening to ask if she had decided yet. "We'll talk about it when you get here," she said.

I stopped en route to visit my sister Nicky and her family in Texas, phoned Natalie to suggest that she fly up to meet me in Las Vegas and we'd drive back to Los Angeles together.

As soon as we saw each other again, Natalie finally realized that I was serious, and deep down her feelings were the same as mine. As friends, we had so much in common, but had never thought of love. I married my best friend, and vice versa.

Natalie suggested that instead of getting married in Los Angeles, it would be simpler to do it in Las Vegas, and I agreed. We got our license, rings, and made the appointment at the Little Cupid Chapel for the night. Nobody knew we were getting married. The only ones who knew I had been asking Natalie to marry me were Arthur, Jeanie, Natalie's sister Edna, Nicky, and Lenny Ditson.

We had a hilarious wedding. Liliane Montevecchi was starring at the Tropicana Hotel in the *Folies Bergere.* She was thrilled that we asked her to be our maid of honor. Her boyfriend was our second witness. He could not remember Natalie's name and kept calling her Esther. Because we had to wait until Liliane was through working, we were married around two in the morning. We were in front of the chapel, in complete darkness, and I was screaming, "Where is that peace of justice?" Finally the door opened, and an old man told us that the justice of the peace had overslept and would be coming out soon. Liliane was very elegantly dressed in white, with a huge white hat, her arms filled with flowers for Natalie. The old man thought Liliane was the bride-to-be.

We giggled like kids all through the ceremony. When it was over, they presented us with the customary gifts from the chapel—a box of laundry detergent for the bride, and a tape recording of the ceremony. What an evening. After the wedding we went to Liliane's home where we had champagne and caviar to celebrate.

The next day, elated, we drove to Los Angeles as man and wife. We telephoned everybody and told them the news. Natalie laughed about what I said when I called some friends of mine who lived out of town and didn't know her. They asked, "Whom did you marry?" And I answered, "Oh, a friend of mine." I didn't know it was funny. I think everybody was very happy for us. Natalie wrote her son Michael, who was on vacation in Europe with his first wife Carolyn, a long letter telling him about the marriage. He sent us a beautiful reply saying how happy he was for both of us. Natalie's sisters in New York were surprised by the news, but very pleased, because they thought we were a good combination. My family was ecstatic. I was thirty-nine years old, and they had about given up on my ever getting married, and now, I had a wife and work on TV.

Edward H. Feldman was the main reason for the show's success. In a television series, if you don't have a good producer, the show's not going to work. He is the one who hires the cast, the writers, the directors, and the editors. He oversees everything, and Ed was very,

very good at it. I have never heard anyone involved with *Hogan's* say anything bad about him. He was kind to everybody. He held the reins. It was his baby, and he made the show what it was: a fun show. Richard Dawson, Larry Hovis, Ivan Dixon, and I were signed to do seven out of thirteen shows. Ed saw to it that we worked on all the episodes and changed that clause in our contracts. He knew that we were as valuable as the three big stars. We were very fortunate to have worked for him and to have known him. Not only was he my producer, but he and his wife, Mary, became good friends to Natalie and me. I was immensely saddened by his death in 1988. The memory of his kindness will last forever with all of us who worked on *Hogan's Heroes.*

The routine on *Hogan's* was organized like a well-oiled machine. On Friday morning at 10:00 A.M., the regular cast—Bob Crane, Werner Klemperer, John Banner, Ivan Dixon, Larry Hovis, Richard Dawson, and I—and the guest stars who had big roles that coming week would meet in an office with Ed and the director assigned to shoot that particular episode. We would read the script to see if it worked or if it needed changes. The four Heroes were always thrilled if the scripts were written by Laurence Marks, Arthur Julian, or Phil Sharp, because we knew we would have more to do. Friday was a short working day. We had the weekend off. On Monday morning we would go to the Desilu Studios to rehearse and block the scenes on the sets, under the supervision of Ed and the director, making dialogue changes if necessary. Monday was also a short working day. Tuesday to Thursday we worked from 7:00 A.M. to 7:00 P.M.

On Tuesday, weather permitting, we would go to do all the exterior scenes at a place called Forty Acres. That's what it was: forty acres of land in Culver City. The first year I had a brand new Mustang, and we had assigned parking places. One day, at the end of the day's filming, I got into my car and put it into reverse to back out. I didn't see a box on the ground that contained live wiring. My gas tank hit the box, and suddenly my whole car was in flames. I got out just in time without being hurt. What a lucky break *that* was! Believe me, I watched those boxes from then on, and so did everybody else.

On Wednesday and Thursday we would be back at the studio to try to finish that episode. It would be made certain that all the scenes involving guest stars and semi-regular actors would be in the can. If the director did not finish filming the script, and when there were enough scenes accumulated from different shows to make up a day's work, the regular cast would work on Friday (instead of the reading day) and do the episodes that needed to be finished. As I said, it was a very well oiled machine.

During the first year on the show I was very frustrated and unhappy. Most of the time all I had were lines like "Shultz's coming" or "Krautz's coming" or "How are we going to do that, Colonel?" "But how, Colonel?" One day, when Howard Morris was the director, I was actually placed with my back to the camera, because I had no dialogue. I felt I should not be in the scene at all, and I told Howard to take me out of it. From what followed I learned an important lesson. By not forcing me to be part of the scene, I realized how kind and understanding Howard was. Any other director would have insisted that I do the scene regardless of whether or not I had dialogue or whether my face was seen by the camera. I was grateful to him, but then I realized that I had done something very unprofessional. Later in the day I reasoned with myself: Should I go see Ed Feldman, tell him how unhappy I was because of the smallness of my part and that I wanted out of the show, or should I get with it and do the best I could with what was offered to me, ignoring the jealousy I felt toward the other cast members who had bigger parts that week? My conclusion was just to enjoy my work. Besides, I was getting a weekly salary and staying in one place instead of looking for jobs that would take me away from Natalie, my family, and friends.

Thanks again to Ed Feldman, we were lucky to have a great group of directors, starting with Robert Butler, who really established the marvelous atmosphere we had on the set, with his inventive camera moves and ability to deal with the huge cast. Of all the directors, Gene Reynolds directed the most shows. Gene had been a child actor at MGM, being a classmate there of Jackie Cooper, Mickey Rooney, Judy Garland, and many others. After serving in the Navy in World War II, he became a casting director, because he wanted a steady job, he said. He then became very much in demand as a director. Before joining *Hogan's*, he worked on *My Three Sons*, starring Fred MacMurray. After three seasons with us, he left to work for the Fox Studios, where he produced and directed shows like *The Ghost and Mrs. Muir, Room 222, Anna and the King* with Yul Brunner, and *Lou Grant* with Ed Asner. The most successful show he did (with Larry Gelbart) was *M*A*S*H*. Gene was a meticulous director, who took great pride in doing the best work he knew how. I learned more about movie making by watching him than if I had taken a course in film. I would not stay in my dressing room, but would very often stand next to him, sponging it up. What a wonderful teacher he was, and so were the other directors, like Howard Morris, Bob Sweeney, Marc Daniels, Bruce Bilson, Richard Kinon, and Jerry London. Jerry was first our editor, then assistant producer, after which Ed gave him a chance to direct the show. By then we were all very much established in our parts. All he had to do was concentrate on his setups and not give us motivations for our roles. Jerry, later on, became very much in demand for TV mini-series. Michael Kahn was Jerry's assistant editor, then chief editor for our show. Michael went on to greener pastures, working for Steven Spielberg as his editor, and won an Oscar for the job he did on *Schindler's List*.

The mood on the set was always jovial, cordial, and extremely pleasant. We, the regulars, made the guest stars feel part of the family. We had our dressing rooms on the stage. Bob Crane had two of them. In one he kept his drums, his stereo machine, and great jazz records, where, while the next scene was being lit and made ready to shoot, he would play his head off. It was his way to relax, and the assistant director knew where he was and didn't have to look for him when needed. It was very clever of the company to let him play his drums (very loudly). They saved time and, I'm sure, money.

Most of the cast members were Democrats, except Bob Crane, who was a conservative Republican, as it was his right to be. His way of thinking about life in general was not the same as mine. When we talked about politics, however, if he didn't agree with us (which was most of the time), his voice would reach four octaves higher than it should. I would say, "That's not the way you are going to win your point, Bob, so lower your voice and join the group." Except for politics, he was very easy to get along with.

After divorcing his first wife, Pat, Bob married Sigrid Valdis who played Klink's secretary. The wedding took place on the set of

Hogan's Heroes, which I thought was kind of weird. The cast and crew were all invited. I felt that we should have worn our uniforms. I wouldn't be surprised if Bing Crosby Productions paid for the whole shebang. There were hundreds of guests, and CBS filmed the event. Years later, I felt saddened by Bob's death, especially the way he died. No one deserves to be murdered (except Hitler and the likes of him). He was too young to die, and it was so strange. It puzzles me that they never found out who did this heinous crime.

I remember, during the pilot, Gordon Avil, who was our cinematographer, saying to me, during a scene involving the entire cast, "Robert, you see this light? (pointing to a light way up on the set) It's your key light. All you have to do is look at it and switch your position slightly, and you'll be in the clear." Those are the tricks of the business that you learn, but you need the kindness of the people who know the tricks. Gordon was also one of the most patient and endearing people I've ever met.

Richard Dawson told very amusing stories and entertained us with imitations of everybody in the movie *The Maltese Falcon* from Humphrey Bogart to Sidney Greenstreet. He was "on" a lot. I kept thinking, if the pilot is sold, I will go mad with Richard's constant monologues. But, I must confess, my fears were unfounded. During the six years of filming *Hogan's Heroes* he was amusing, witty, ahead of you on all kinds of subjects and, most of all, never boring.

Ivan Dixon was the most serious person in our cast. He always wondered what he was doing with these crazy "hyper" people. He was a marvelous actor who, once in a while, was given a part that he could sink his teeth into. He did not renew his contract after the fifth season, even though it was a steady job. He felt he had stayed as long as he could. I think he did the right thing, because he became a very good director and was involved in many shows for television, both comedy and drama. He lives in Hawaii and owns a radio station. He seems very happy, which pleases me a lot.

Larry Hovis is a multitalented person, not only a good actor, but also a comedian. He sings quite well and is also a writer. After *Hogan's* he and Richard Dawson became regulars on *Rowan & Martin's Laugh-In,* where he also contributed material. On *Hogan's* he and Richard were inseparable, always playing cards, drinking thousands of cups of coffee, and smoking miles of cigarettes. They were always plotting jokes to amuse us. Today Larry is a widower, living in his native Texas, where he teaches acting and directs plays and musicals at a university in San Marcos.

I adored John Banner. I had lots of scenes with him, and it was a wonderful challenge. In show business there's a saying, "Never work with children or animals, because they will always steal the scene from you." Well, the same applied to John. He knew how to make his part even better than it was written. Even though I'm quite a scene stealer myself, I learned a lot from him. What a joy it was working with him. He was married to Christine, a fantastic lady who was born in Belgium. She was a most accomplished cook. It was a privilege to be invited to their dinner parties, and she and John were fun company. John died in 1973 in his native city, Vienna, on the eve of his sixty-third birthday.

Ed Feldman cast actors who had backgrounds authentic to their roles. Richard Dawson was born in England; Banner and Leon Askin were both from Austria; I was born in France. Werner Klemperer was born in 1920 in Cologne, Germany, and spent his childhood in Berlin. His father married an opera singer, who gave up her singing career to be his wife. Werner has a younger sister. Music was always a great part of his life. He often said, "Music is around me from morning until night." Because his father was Jewish, their lives changed dramatically when Hitler rose to power. His father saw the handwriting on the wall long before the concentration camps and genocide started. In 1933, while his father was out of Germany to fulfill a conducting engagement, he called his wife and told her to leave Germany in the next twenty-four to forty-eight hours with the children. Werner was thirteen. They took the train from Berlin to Switzerland and then to Austria. When they left, the Jews were not allowed to take out money or belongings—just a suitcase. The border lines were already being watched very carefully. Werner told me, "We were on the train, going out of the country. My mother, just before the border line appeared, decided we were going to have some afternoon coffee and cake. She had brought a cake—one of those cakes, like Jewish coffee cake with a large hole in the middle. We sat down. She had coffee, and we had whatever kids drink, and we had this cake. In come the border guards, and they say, "All right, passports, open the suitcases" . . . while we are having our afternoon cake . . . end of story. Later on I found out my mother had arranged for the cook to put in the cake 100,000 marks (which was an enormous amount of money in 1933) wrapped in a special paper like wax paper and was able to smuggle the money out under the nose of the border guards." His mother had done that daring thing very cleverly and bravely.

Ed Feldman's close friend, Richard Crenna, told Ed that Werner would be perfect to play Klink. Ed thought that Werner was a dramatic actor and could not do comedy. After making a film test with Crane, he got the part and consequently won two Emmys for it. Werner married quite a few times. With his second wife he had two children, Marc and Erica. When he divorced Louise Troy, his third or fourth wife, I told him not to get married anymore, but live with whomever he loved at the moment. Well, I was wrong. He was happily married for quite a while to Kim Hamilton, one of the sweetest ladies I know. He lived in New York City, where he did what he loved the most, theater and concerts. We were very close friends, and I saw him whenever he was on the West Coast. In his last few years, Werner was in poor health and he died on December 6, 2000.

Bernie Fox was very funny as Colonel Crittendon. Richard M. Powell wrote great scripts for his character, a pompous, foolish Colonel in the Royal Air Force, who always fumbled things and made our missions so much harder to accomplish. As funny as he was, so was Nita Talbot as the mad Russian, Marya. She always called "Lebeau" "My little one," and he was madly in love with her and never thought she could do anything wrong. Richard M. Powell created very odd characters that worked well in the show.

Once in a while we would do musical numbers, which was fun for Larry and me. In one of the episodes Richard, Larry, and I sang the Irving Berlin song, "This is the Army Mister Jones." The number worked well with the story line. I enjoyed doing what little choreography there was. In another episode we put on a show in the barracks for the prisoners and the German soldiers and officers. I sang "Alouette" with Ivan Dixon playing the bass fiddle. Dawson did his imitations, while Crane and Hovis were sabotaging some factory nearby. I also staged a number for Marlyn Mason, who that week played a chanteuse named Lily Frankel. She was singing the song that Marlene Dietrich made famous years and years ago, "Falling in Love Again." Marlyn told the director that I absolutely saved her, because she didn't know how and where to move in that singing sequence. We took one hour, during lunch time, to figure it out, and she was thrilled. I loved being able to help her.

Dell comics published a series of magazines making fun of *Hogan's Heroes*. There were also lunch boxes illustrated with our faces. Bob Crane put out an L.P. playing his drums. Richard, Larry, Ivan, and I recorded for the Sunset label, *Hogan's Heroes Sing the Best of WWII*. It is by now a collector's item. It was never a financial success. The album was a terrific one, with great orchestrations by Jerry Fielding, who wrote the theme for *Hogan's Heroes*. I think no one took advantage of the popularity of the show. The record was distributed only in super markets, with no advertising whatsoever. On other hit TV shows, like *The Beverly Hillbillies, Gunsmoke,* and many others, the actors would go on weekends to the opening of markets and to fairs. God knows there was enough talent on our show to get an audience and woo them. We proved it when we were asked to entertain at the affiliate banquets in Washington and Chicago. Larry had a superb stand up comic routine; I did my night club singing act; Crane played his drums; Dawson did his brilliant imitations; and Klemperer and Banner did skits involving their characters.

In 1971 the FCC ruled that prime time would start at 8:00 P.M. and go through to 11:00 P.M., instead of starting at 7:30 P.M. Therefore, after our sixth season, even though we were still doing well in the ratings, we were canceled, along with other shows at CBS that included *The Beverly Hillbillies, Hee Haw, Mayberry R.F.D.,* and *Green Acres.* Too bad. We could have gone on for at least a few more seasons. *Hogan's* is still playing all over the world. I have seen it dubbed in Spanish, Japanese, Italian, and French. I never thought that it would be seen in Germany, since all the German characters were really buffoons. Somehow it became a huge hit there, being shown twice a day. It is titled, *A Cage Full of Heroes.* The dubbing makes the Germans even more bumbling fools than the American version. Kids over there love it, according to the fan mail I still receive. I do not regret having been a part of *Hogan's Heroes*. It was a delightful six years, and I forged lasting relationships with Werner Klemperer and Gene Reynolds. It is always nice to hear from Larry Hovis and Ivan Dixon. As for Richard Dawson, who is a neighbor of mine, I never see or hear from him, and that is a pity, because I enjoyed his company.

A year after Natalie and I were married I decided to play the tape of our marriage ceremony that the Little Cupid Chapel had given us. I wanted to recapture that wonderful moment. As we listened to it, I almost fell off the chair. They had given us the wrong tape. Two strange people were exchanging vows. Somewhere in this world another married couple has our tape, and I hope they laughed as much as we did when we listened to theirs.

Our marriage keeps getting better as the years pass by. We trust each other. Natalie sees through people very quickly. She's understanding, compassionate, very honest, and outspoken. She will not tell you something she doesn't mean—ever. To me, that's a most beautiful quality. You know where you stand with her. She is never rude, and has great kindness. We help each other, but neither of us is helpless. We're not on each other's backs constantly. We are not fighters or screamers. If something bothers us, we talk about it. At the beginning of our marriage, when I became angry my first reaction was either to explode or pout. Only afterward would I try to reason the situation and find out why I got angry. My normal voice is not particularly soft, and it goes up an octave when I get excited. Sometimes Natalie will confuse my loud voice with screaming, when, to me, it's just a little excited. I say, "No, I'm not screaming, Natalie—THIS IS SCREAMING!"

I think that one of our greatest assets in our marriage is that we both have a sense of humor. Sooner or later, we laugh about almost everything. I always felt that I would not get married as long as I wasn't able to be responsible. I would not have taken the step, no matter how much I cared for Natalie, if I had not outgrown my selfishness.

After *Hogan's* was canceled in 1971, I didn't work for a whole year. The phone never rang. I felt I was through in the business. When I called my agent, he would say, "You've been over-exposed." When you're new in the business, they say, "Nobody knows who you are," and it's tough to get that first job. After you're established, they give you the line about over-exposure.

During that year of unemployment, I started to paint. It had been years since I had done anything, and it was fun to draw again, and good to realize that I hadn't lost my touch. I was getting residuals every month, very big ones the first year, so I wasn't worried. I loved painting, and the weeks flew by.

Hal Gefsky, my agent at APA, called me one day and said, "How would you like to do *Days of Our Lives*?" I didn't know what *Days of Our Lives* was. I had never watched soap operas. At that time they weren't fashionable, and you only took a job on a daytime show when you couldn't get arrested in the business. Hal said, "The show is a lot of work, and it pays very little money. If you want to do it, they would like to have you." Since I had been out of work for a whole year, I decided to try it. I had nothing to lose.

I worked on *Days* for three months without a contract. At the beginning, I was frightened. It is the most difficult job in all the media. It was especially so in 1972 when you really couldn't afford to make mistakes while the camera was rolling. Because tape was so expensive, they could not allow the actors to stop and go. You had to be on your toes.

After the three months with *Days*, I was hired to be on a new soap on CBS called *The Young and the Restless*. On *Hogan's Heroes* I had played a feisty little man—that's the way Ed Feldman saw me and asked the writers to write my character—who was always ready to fight with anybody, and constantly dreamed about girls. That was Louis Lebeau. On the soaps, I was the complete opposite. On both of them I played identical people, lovable, sweet, very *nebbish*. The writers of both shows wrote how they imagined a French person talked—"Ees true. You are in love not weez me, non?" It was extremely difficult for me to learn the dialogue. They never thought of Pierre or Robaire having sex. Both characters married women who had been rejected by their lovers and were pregnant. In order to give the children legitimate names, Pierre/Robaire came to the rescue, unselfishly.

John Conboy, who was the producer of *Restless*, could be very nice and charming, but would rarely give you a compliment. One day, after we were through with the day's work, he came into my dressing room. That day I had done some very nice scenes and I thought he was going to tell me how good I was. Instead, he said, "We're going to kill Pierre."

I said, "Oh, you are?"

He said, "We don't know what else to do with him, so we're going to kill him in a month. Please don't say anything to the cast."

I replied, "Well, that's life, John. Onward—I always say, and thank you for having me for the year." I thought it was decent of him to warn me a month in advance. Usually in soap operas, they don't give you much notice. You don't know you're dead until you read it in the script. At least I had a month to try to get another job.

Soap operas, for a long time, were a one-way street. Everything was worked out to the advantage of the producers and the networks, and very little to the actors. Even if you signed a long-term contract, they could fire you whenever they felt like it, by not renewing you after a thirteen-week period. Overtime didn't count if you had a contract and they paid you more than the minimum. It has changed a great deal since then, thanks to the efforts of our union.

What always amazes me is that they give you a big cake when they get ride of you. On *Days,* I used to kid Jack Herzberg, one of our producers, who was in charge of "death cakes." I would say to him, "When I leave the show, don't give me any cakes. I will not stay to celebrate my departure. 'Good-bye' will suffice."

It's a funny thing about soap opera fans. If you play a villain, they will hit you when they see you in person. They think that's the real you on the screen. The day after the episode of my death on *The Young and the Restless* played on the air, I went to the supermarket and a woman came up to me and said, "What are you doing here?—I thought you were dead!" They believe you are the character they see on television. On *Restless,* Bill Bell, who invented and produced the show wanted to call me Frenchy. I said, "That's a no-no. Please do not call me Frenchy. I don't want people calling me that for the rest of my life, as you know they would. Give me any first name you want, but not Frenchy." So it was Pierre. Now when fans recognize me on the street, I can tell which show they watched by the name they call me—Lebau, Pierre, or Robaire.

After I left *The Young and the Restless* most of the soaps went to an hour instead of a half-hour. Because they needed more characters, Betty Corday, the executive producer of *Days of Our Lives,* asked me if I wanted to come back. I said, "Yes, I will come back, but only if I have a contract. And please tell the writers to write my part as they would a normal American character. My own accent will carry the foreign part of it." I worked for the next five years on *Days,* and later returned for another two years. The cast was very easy to work with, no tantrums, no temperament. There was no time for any of that nonsense. We started every morning at six A.M., blocking scenes, without arguing with the director. If he told you, "On this line, you go from the chair to the couch and then turn around," you did what he said and made it work. A soap director had very little time to open doors for actors who do not understand their motivations. He's too busy putting an hour show on its feet every day. Therefore, you rely on your fellow actors a lot to rehearse the lines and solve what doesn't work. You get a camera blocking at 8:30 A.M., and a camera rehearsal. Then lunch for an hour. Then makeup, costumes, dress rehearsals, notes, and finally you tape the show. It's practically a twelve-hour day's work. Between dress and tape, the director and producers give you notes, add dialogue if the show is too short, and cut lines when it is too long. You have to be alert all the time. To survive on a soap opera, you have to be a damn good actor.

But working on *Days* was great fun once you got over the fright of having to learn so many pages of dialogue in such a short time. The atmosphere on the set was always without pressure, and what made it more rewarding was that I worked with a bunch of actors who made the job a breeze, particularly Bill Hayes (Doug). Most of my scenes were with him and Susan Seaforth Hayes (Julie). Bill and I sang, either solo songs or, very often, duets. Bill is one of the sweetest men living on this planet, and it's not just my opinion. Ask anybody who knows him. He and Susan were the king and queen of the soap opera in the 70s, and they deserved their crowns. The most memorable time I recall on *Days* is when the whole cast did something for which they were not well known—singing and dancing. It was three-day's work.

The plot was that a telethon was being held to raise money to buy a CAT scanner for the University Hospital. We all did musical numbers. I even played Shirley Temple, tap dancing. Frances Reid played Groucho Marx; Bill, Chico, and Susan, Harpo. Big Jed Allan played Margaret Dumont. We had skits and numbers choreographed by Jack Bunch. Mark Tapscott played the trumpet. Suzanne Rogers danced beautifully. What a cast it was—from MacDonald Carey and Frances Reid, who were in the show since 1965, to John Clarke, Ed Mallory, and Susan Flannery, who joined the cast very soon after. I worked on *Days* from 1972 to 1973, 1975 to 1980, and in 1986.

In the summer of 1973, Dania Krupska was directing musicals at the Northshore Theater in Beverly, Massachusetts. Scheduled were *Kiss Me Kate* with Chita Rivera and Hal Linden, *Sugar* with Bonnie Franklin and Arte Johnson, and *No No Nanette* with Nanette Fabray. For some reason Arte Johnson couldn't do *Sugar*. Dania, with whom I had worked in the 50s in an industrial show, called me and asked if I'd like to do the part. *Sugar* was the musical adaptation of the Jack Lemmon, Tony Curtis, Marilyn Monroe movie, *Some Like It Hot*. I hadn't done theater for a long time and missed being on a stage. I told her, "Yes, I would like that very much."

I immediately listened to the recording of the original show and began to study the script, because I knew when you did summer theater you had only two weeks of rehearsals. By the time I arrived in Massachusetts, I was prepared. All I had to worry about during the rehearsals was which aisles to use to make my entrances and exits and to understand the role better.

I hit it off immediately with Bonnie Franklin, who played Sugar, and we had fun working together. Dania was remarkably inventive. She had a very good concept for staging shows for theater in the round. In staging my musical numbers, she did what Peter Gennaro and June Taylor had done with me. They let me move in order to see what steps I could or couldn't do, then created movements within my limitations.

While I was rehearsing, every evening I studied Chita Rivera's performance in *Kiss Me Kate*. I looked at her ways of posing, and what she did with her hands, hips, body, and I copied her, because she breathed femininity. I looked very ugly as a girl, but nonetheless I was a girl, not winking at the audience and not silently saying, "You know me; it's all in fun. I'm not really a girl; I'm a boy."

When we opened, everything seemed to fall into place. The critics, who did not rave about the book or the score, raved about our performances. The Boston critic Elliot Norton wrote: "Robert Clary is riotously funny. Tiny and nimble, he creates an uproar as the bass player named Joe who converts himself into a lady called Daphne. In a blonde wig, wearing a white gown and a notable smirk, Mr. Clary affects a piping high voice. He doesn't swish, he swoops. With his chin tilted up, a silly smile on his cherubic face, his hands pertly placed on his hips, he is artfully and idiotically funny for two solid hours and when he takes off his wig and drops his voice from soprano to bass, the effect is happily nonsensical." The audience loved the show very much, we got big laughs, and I was delighted to be on the stage again.

For his film *The Hindenburg,* director Robert Wise wanted an all-star cast. He had signed George C. Scott, and was trying to get Sophia Loren, and also Joel Grey who had just won an oscar for his brilliant work in *Cabaret* and was very much in demand. Somebody told me that Joel didn't want to do the part of the circus acrobat, Ben Dover, so I called my agent John Gaines at APA and asked him to get me an appointment with Robert Wise. He said, "Robert Wise will not see you in person before he sees films of yours. That's his method of casting actors." I didn't want him to see clips of *Hogan's Heroes,* where my character was played on one level. I felt that if I could go and talk to him I could woo him. Well, that was the end. Gaines said, "Robert, if you don't want me to send him film, there's no use in my calling him. I know he won't see you."

I asked my friend Stewart Stern, the writer of such hit films as *Rebel without a Cause,* and *The Ugly American,* among many others, if he knew anybody connected with Robert Wise. He knew Stan Musgrove, who was very close to Wise and, through him, arranged an appointment for me. I went to see Wise at his office at Universal, and talked to him for about ten minutes. His graciousness made me feel completely at ease. He called in his associates and we talked for another ten minutes. I never read for the part. A month later, while I was doing *Sugar,* Hal Gefsky called me to say the role of the acrobat was mine if I wanted it.

I had a good relationship with Robert Wise. He was a meticulous director, highly organized, and always prepared, qualities which appealed to me.

It was a privilege to work with George C. Scott, whose career I had admired for years. He was a gentleman and a true professional, everything an actor should be. Anne Bancroft, who costarred with him, had a great sense of humor. One day when we were waiting for our cues to make an entrance, I asked her, "How is Mel?" referring to her husband, Mel Brooks.

"Short!" she replied.

In the movie, I had a musical number with Peter Donat singing and playing the piano. We rehearsed the number for a few weeks with Michael Kidd. Michael is very acrobatically minded in his choreography, as is apparent in *Seven Brides for Seven Brothers.* If you're a great dancer and an acrobat, he's perfect. Ben Dover, the character I played, was a circus acrobat, and though I'm a fair dancer, I'm certainly not an acrobat. I kept telling Kidd, "I can't do those steps or jump over balustrades." He said, "What do you mean, you can't do them? I'll show you how easy they are." He tripped while showing me what he wanted, nearly breaking his neck. I said, "You see—that's why I can't do them." Eventually he simplified the routine, giving me jumps and steps I could do.

During the filming I received a lot of compliments. The still photographer took many pictures of my scenes and my character, and people said I stole the movie. I should have known better, but in my mind I began to accept the Oscar for best supporting actor. I had my acceptance speech all prepared. This was a great departure from my usually realistic way of thinking. I thought *The Hinderberg* would open doors for me for other films. It didn't. The film was neither a critical nor a commercial success.

CHAPTER NINETEEN

REVISITING THE HOLOCAUST

When I go to high schools and talk to students about the Holocaust and my experiences, at the end of my speech I look at the many minority faces in the audience. "If Hitler had his way," I tell them, "if he had conquered the world as he wanted to and had his thousand-year Reich, none of you would be here today." Then I quote Pastor Martin Niemoller, who was German and was sent to the concentration camps and survived: "First the Nazis went after the Jews, but I wasn't a Jew, so I didn't react. Then they went after the Catholics, but I wasn't a Catholic, so I didn't object. Then they went after the worker, but I wasn't a worker, so I didn't stand up. Then they went after the Protestant clergy, and by then it was too late for anybody to stand up." I tell the students that the worst thing they can do, if they want to live in a free society, is to remain apathetic.

I remember being tremendously shocked, when I first arrived in the United States in 1949, to see how the blacks were treated. I could not believe or understand how, in certain parts of this great land of democracy, freedom, and liberty, blacks were second rate citizens, who could not go into the same restrooms as whites, drink from the same water fountains, who had to travel in the backs of buses, sit in the balconies of movie houses, and were refused entrance to hotels, restaurants, and clubs. How dare we think ourselves superior to other human beings? Why can't we see people for what they are, and not judge them by the color of their skin or their religion?

It is deplorable how we are taught at a very early age to hate. In

1981, I attended a conference of Christians and Jews in Los Angeles, organized by the Anti-Defamation League, to discuss the Holocaust. A German woman described to us how as a young girl she belonged to the Hitler youth movement. She told how the first words her parents taught her to say were "Heil Hitler," how those words were uttered before she could say "Mama" or "Dada," and how proud her parents were that she could say "Heil Hitler" first. She enjoyed being in the Hitler youth movement and believed she was doing good because they were taught that Jews were evil people and had to be extinguished form the world or they would take over and kill you.

Increasingly, over the years, I would read in the newspapers about the rise of Neo-Nazis, watch reports on the television news about Jewish cemeteries being desecrated and synagogues bombed in European cities. Swastikas were painted on Jewish buildings and temples, and there were rumors of professors writing books and articles in magazines denying the Holocaust. Nonetheless, though I was disturbed to see signs of the 30s all over again, I stayed in apathy, caring mostly about my family and my career.

In 1980, Natalie and I were watching an English-made documentary on public television called *Kitty: Return to Auschwitz*. It was done simply, but it moved me profoundly. The documentary showed Kitty Felix-Hart, who spent two years in Auschwitz and had survived along with her mother. After the war, she went to live in England, got married, and had two sons. *Return to Auschwitz* details Kitty's journey back to this infamous extermination camp with one of her sons, who today is a doctor in Canada, to show him where and how she survived two years in hell. It is one of the things she said that woke me up. I'm paraphrasing: "The reason I'm doing this documentary is because thirty or forty years from now most survivors will be dead, and anybody can write whatever they want about the Holocaust, denying it left and right, and we won't be here to tell them and the world that they are liars. We went through it, we barely escaped it. How dare they!"

That's when I turned to Natalie and said, "She's right. I'd better stand up and be counted. Thirty-six years of silence is enough."

I made up my mind to ask my good friend Merv Griffin if I might go on his show and for the first time talk about my experiences during the Nazi regime.

I needed facts and documentation to disprove the so-called revisionists, most of them professors and Ph.D.s, who were writing articles denying the Holocaust, calling it a myth, a fragment of Jewish imagination, a Zionist plot to gain the world's sympathy for Israel. Some of them were even saying that the gas chambers were there to kill lice, the ovens to bake bread, that extermination camps never existed. All this was done and is still being done, with great authority, and to me that is dangerous and extremely alarming. They have the gall to call most of my family, including my mother and father, lice and bread. I cannot let them get away with it.

These professors and Ph.D.s write lengthy articles in a magazine published four times yearly called *The Journal of Historical Review.* A man named Arthur Butz, who is a professor at Northwestern University in Illinois, has written a book that is the Bible for these so-called revisionists. His *The Hoax of the Twentieth Century* makes a mockery of the six million Jews, including a million and a half children, who died in shooting pits, gas chambers, and ovens.

It was suggested to me that I would most likely be able to find the facts and documentation I needed at the Simon Wiesenthal Center in Los Angeles. The Center was founded in 1978 by Rabbi Marvin Hier, Dean of Yeshiva University there. The Center has embarked on many major projects to keep the memory of the Holocaust from fading into oblivion. It was named for Simon Wiesenthal who, after his liberation from Mauthausen concentration camp in 1945, had dedicated his life to hunting Nazi war criminals all over the world, in order to bring them to trial and record their crimes for history. I called the Center and was connected with then director Alex Grobman, who gave me what I wanted and more. I proceeded to do my homework before appearing on the Merv Griffin show.

On the show, being very impassioned, I talked for over twenty minutes. I received lots of phone calls and letters from people telling me how courageous I was. It had never entered my mind that I was courageous. I was doing something that finally I had to do.

I learned that The Simon Wiesenthal Center had an Outreach Program, under the supervision of Rabbi Abraham Cooper, in which survivors were sent to high schools to talk to students in order to give them a clearer insight into what happened during the Holocaust and the events leading up to it. By 1980, 60 percent of the population had been born after the event and knew nothing about it. In the history books, the Holocaust is mentioned in one sentence. Only a few states have made it mandatory to teach about the Holocaust, but in most it is ignored. Too many innocent people, Jews and millions of non-Jews, died at the hands of the Nazis. Current and future generations must be made aware of the dreadful facts. History professors in public schools must not let themselves be influenced by the magazines and books denying the event and teach those lies to young children.

More than willingly, I joined the Outreach Program. I feel it is my duty to open eyes and minds, no matter how painful it is for me to relive the experience. When I go to high schools and talk to thousands of students, if a hundred of them get my message, I feel that I have accomplished something worthwhile, and maybe next time I'll reach a higher proportion.

The Wiesenthal Center has a project called *Testimony to the Truth,* a collection of video tape interviews with concentration camp survivors and liberators. The object is to provide a visual encyclopedia of the Holocaust, with tapes that will be available to colleges, universities, churches, synagogues, and for broadcasting on TV news programs.

I have been giving talks for a number of years now, traveling all over the country, strictly voluntarily, going to high schools, colleges, universities, and to civic organizations and religious congregations of all denominations. I would have thought that by now it would be easier for me to talk about the Holocaust. On the contrary, it is still very painful. But, to quote Simon Wiesenthal, "I owe it to the people who died in the ovens."

At the end of my talk, I have a question and answer period. I was once asked by some history professors from Nevada, who were in Los Angeles to study the Holocaust, "Do you feel guilty for having survived?"

I answered, "No, I don't feel guilty for having survived. I didn't do anything during my thirty-one months in camps to feel guilty about. I didn't kill people, I didn't take their food from them, I didn't torture them, inform on them to the SS. Why should I feel guilty? It is true that some survivors do feel guilty, asking why God chose them and not their families. Very frankly, I never felt that. I am extremely, painfully sad that six million of my people died, including twelve members of my immediate family. But I'm not guilt ridden for being alive today."

After I found out that none of my family who was deported came back, my prayers ended, and so did my belief in God. What did my parents, who were extremely religious, my sisters, and the rest of my family do to deserve such an end to their lives? Where is the justice? These gentle people who tried to make decent lives for themselves—why would God take them away so cruelly? To teach a lesson? Nothing has been learned from their deaths. Man's inhumanity to man still exists.

I may contradict myself when I say I'm a very realistic person, because, in a way, I'm a dreamer. I want the world to be something it isn't. Why can't a world be without armament and wars; why can't we get along together; why can't we realize that we're becoming over-populated, that we will eventually die from starvation? Why can't we all get together and do something intelligent and peaceful instead of destroying one another constantly? It's a shame that we all want to be superior to others. We seek power, and, once we have it, most of us misuse it. We're *very* selfish, jealous, small-minded, and narrow in our thinking. We're wonderful builders—isn't it too bad we have to destroy. Look at it—so many people are starving, education is inadequate, and people don't try to understand each other, to love each other. We are *all* guilty.

With anticipation, in June 1981, I went to Israel for the first time. I knew I would find people I hadn't seen for many years, people who had been in the camps with me, like the Fogiel brothers who had emmigrated to Israel in 1946. I also wanted to see Lou Kaddar, who was one of our social workers in the *Locale* when we were children in Paris, and who had been Golda Meir's private secretary and companion. First I wrote, then talked to her at great length on the phone. She was as anxious to see me as I was to see her.

My friend Louis Fogiel, who works for TWA, was at the plane

when I arrived. He greeted me and the others from the Wiesenthal Center. After going very rapidly through customs, the others went to a hotel in Tel Aviv, and I went with Louis to his apartment, where I met his wife Martine. She and I hit it off from the first moment we met. Martine urged me to go to sleep after that endless trip, but I didn't feel tired, and Louis insisted that we go out and eat in Jaffa, in the Arab section. After a very pleasant meal, we went back to the apartment. His brothers Albert and Bernard came and visited for a while. By then I was exhausted, but happy to be with them.

I left the next morning, by taxi, for Jerusalem. It was only an hour's ride from Tel Aviv. The breathtaking city of Jerusalem is elevated, very hot during the day, but cool in the evening. They had warned me in the United States to take sweaters and jackets, so I wouldn't freeze. I arrived in Jerusalem on Friday, shortly after noon, and went to the Plaza Hotel. The lobby was full of people from all over Europe who had come to attend the World Gathering of the Jewish Survivors of the Holocaust. We were supposed to be registered, in order to have our names put on badges showing what countries we came from. The Sabbath is very sacred in Israel. At one P.M. on Friday, the Jews close everything until sundown on Saturday. There is no transportation, no stores are open, and we were told that we would have to wait until Sunday morning to be registered.

The central meeting place, Binyanei Ha Ooma, a huge building, had been converted into the Survivors' Village, where every day we would meet, hoping to find people we knew. Computers had been set up to help us track people down. Six thousand survivors with their wives or husbands, children and grandchildren were expected at the Gathering. At the opening ceremony there were eight thousand of us. At the closing we were ten thousand.

The entire reunion was extremely well organized, but at times, for me, chaotic—masses of people constantly looking for each other, hoping to find somebody who had been in the same camp, or had come from the same small town in Poland or France or Holland. It was so sad to see people searching, looking into each other's faces to see if they recognized somebody who shared those terrible times. Like the others, I still hoped to find someone alive whom I had given up for dead. There were three thousand of us from America, and my ego was inflated quite a bit, because so many of them recognized me. They had seen me on the *Merv Griffin Show* and Sandy Freeman's cable network show, when I talked about the Holocaust, and told me how proud they were of me.

I was pleased to see that there were lots of media people, journalists and TV reporters from all over the world. I felt it was very important that the whole world witness this mass reunion. I had been sent by the Wiesenthal Center for the purpose of being interviewed by Dr. William Rader, the psychiatrist and ABC TV commentator, for a documentary he was making on the gathering. I did my interview that first Sunday afternoon, along with other survivors, including Simon Wiesenthal, as well as children of survivors.

My interview was going smoothly—I was answering Dr. Rader's direct questions—when suddenly, while I was talking about being saved in Buchenwald by Yves and Claude Francis Boeuf, he said, "I denote a sadness in your voice."

I answered in a meek, "Yes." And I started to weep and couldn't stop.

The camera kept rolling. Dr. Rader urgently asked me, "Why are you crying? Why the tears suddenly?"

I couldn't answer. I was choking. I had no voice, just tears. Finally, in a weak whisper, I told him, "I don't know."

"No, no, no—tell me, it's important—why are you crying now?"

It felt as if a whole minute passed by before I recovered. Then I said something to him which I find very strange. I said, "Maybe I should have died."

He said, "Why are you saying that?"

I never think about dying. I love life, and find it worth living. I know now exactly why I said it and why I cried. It was the environment, it was being in Israel amongst all those survivors, thinking about my father and mother, the rest of my family and the six million Jews who did not come back. The whole thing overwhelmed me, and everything that had stayed bottled up inside me for all those years finally exploded. Also, I missed terribly those two saintly Frenchmen who had saved my life in Buchenwald at the last moment. I guess it dawned on me while I was doing the interview that I had never pursued our friendship the way I should have. After the interview, I became very sad and emotional. I found it difficult to talk to people. The least little thing made me cry.

The same night, we went by buses to Tel Aviv, where a big celebration was held in Eliahu Sports Stadium for the preopening night. The weather was hot and humid, and there was a huge crowd. All the speakers talked beautifully, saying how thrilling it was to see us all there, so that we could tell the world not to forget, and that we were the ones who had to tell the truth. But the speeches, the fanfare depressed me. I was with Walter Kirschenbaum, the press representative for the Gathering, and his wife. In the middle of the festivities, I said to Walter, "I cannot stand it anymore. I'm leaving." My depression was a culmination of everything—being bused to Tel Aviv, being in this big place, and feeling that I was back in that camp taking orders (go to door G, not H; stay in line; wait your turn; stand up; sit down; salute; sing; stop; applaud; cry). All these things got to be too much for me. I waited outside alone until the ceremony was over, then with the others took the bus back to Jerusalem.

The next morning, first thing, I called Lou Kaddar, who said, "I'm old, fat, and ugly." I went to see her that afternoon. When she opened the door of her small, tidy apartment, she greeted me by saying, "I would not have recognized you."

I said, "No wonder—I was twelve years old when we last saw each other. I'm fifty-five now."

"I've changed, too," she said. "I'm old, fat, and ugly, as you can see."

She had changed, but there was something about her that was the same. At sixty-seven, she was at heart the same person I had known in 1938, the same marvelous, sweet, out-spoken woman I remembered from my youth. After that afternoon we saw each other every day.

I called Hélène Lefkowitz, with whom I had grown up in the same apartment building in Paris. She had been living in Israel for many years, had married an Israeli, Baruch Avidor, and lived in a *moshav*, which is run like a kibbutz, except that people in a *moshav* have their own houses. She was thrilled to hear from me. I begged her to come to Jerusalem. I told her we had to see each other, that I couldn't leave Israel without seeing her.

Hélène came that evening without her husband. One of her sons brought her to Jerusalem, a three-quarter-hour trip from her *moshav*. We went to a restaurant with Lou, my friend Bernard Fogiel and his wife Ada, and had a fantastic time, reliving our youth. When I saw Hélène, I recognized her at once, even after thirty-nine years. She gave me the same line Lou gave me, saying she wouldn't have recognized me. And to think that people always say to me, "You don't change."

The funniest part of it is, another childhood friend, from the same house in Paris, Milo Adoner, whom we used to call "Schmil," who was also deported and survived, was at the World Gathering. He was fat and bald. When Hélène met him, she said, "I would have known you right away."

I was shocked. I said, "How can you say that to him, who's changed so drastically, and tell me that you would not have known me if you saw me on the street?"

"Because Milo looks exactly like his father!" she said.

The formal opening was held at the Holocaust memorial site Yad Vashem. Once you have seen Yad Vashem, it haunts you for the rest of your life. It contains the most complete archives about the Holocaust in the entire world. It's a devastatingly sad and moving place. That day I didn't want to go on the bus with everybody. I took a taxi, arriving hours earlier than the others, because I wanted time to visit the place thoroughly. At the memorial building, on the second floor, there are rows and rows of archives, with files of names of people who were deported from all over Europe. If the names of family members who didn't come back are not there, you can fill out a form, which I did, for the twelve members of my immediate family.

Emotionally devastating to me, there was a stark building, the Hall of Remembrance. Before entering, you were given a rose to place on the name of the camp you were in. The names of the largest camps, perhaps twenty or thirty, were engraved on the stone floor. There is nothing else in the Hall, except for an eternal flame. I found three of my camps—Drancy, Gross-Rosen, and Buchenwald. I put the rose on the Buchenwald name. I saw people kneeling, praying, and crying. Like most of the others, I was overwhelmed by a deep sadness, and went into a corner of the building and wept. I tried to control my emotions but couldn't do it. Finally, I left the Hall, feeling terribly sorry for myself and grieving for the missing people. Outside, a few survivors came to me and cried on my shoulder. I comforted them, saying that it was all right to cry, while my tears were flowing, too.

On the evening of the opening ceremony, I looked at the crowd, and there was my friend Milo, looking just like his father, with his pals from Paris, all of whom had been in Blechhammer. I joined them, and from then on the Gathering for me was happier. We laughed and had a good time.

The next day I was supposed to go to the kibbutz Netzer-Serini, where some of the people liberated from Buchenwald lived. I had wanted to go there to see if I could find somebody I knew. But my crazy French friends decided not to go, and instead we spent the whole day together. We had lunch at my hotel, then visited the Western Wall and Old Jerusalem. Maybe I should have gone to the kibbutz, but I couldn't do it. I needed a boost, and my friends were that.

I had been seeing a lot of Martine and Louis Fogiel, who showed me their Jerusalem. The Fogiel brothers are tough guys who have made a very good life for themselves. They fought the Six Day War in Israel. They believe in their country. They didn't like to talk about the camps, and didn't want to attend the Gathering. They came only once, for the dedication of a French memorial in Roglit, twenty-five miles south of Jerusalem, a beautiful memorial for the eighty thousand Jews who had been deported from France. All our names were engraved on a semicircular marble wall. It was a deeply moving ceremony, because so many names on that wall were of our relatives and friends who did not return. For all their wanting to forget the past, the Fogiels' memories were much better than mine. They remembered people and events I had forgotten.

The closing ceremony of the Gathering was held on June 18 at the Western Wall, known previously as the Wailing Wall. We were ten thousand people, and the message was loud and clear: "The world must *never* forget the Holocaust." The then Prime Minister Menachem Begin urged us to come and live in Israel, to bring our children. It was a very impassioned speech. We saw the legacy being passed to the second generation in six different languages. Other eloquent speeches were made by Ernest Michel, Benjamin Meed (respectively, chairman and vice-chairman of the Gathering), Elie Wiesel, and Samuel Pisar.

The four days of the Gathering proved to be not only revealing to the world, but to all of us personally. We ran the gamut from sadness to great elation, experiencing profound and meaningful feelings.

The day before I left Israel, Bernard Fogiel picked me up at my hotel in the morning, and with three other Frenchmen, including Milo, we did some sightseeing, making trips to Bethlehem and to Herodion, one of King Herod's palaces which he built on top of a hill in the desert. We saw the Yad Kennedy Memorial and the brilliant Chagall windows at Hadassah Hospital. Then we went to the *moshav* to visit my friend Hélène. She couldn't do enough for us. She served fruit, coffee, ice cream, cookies. She showed me photos of us when we were children, and gave me snapshots of me at the age of five to take home.

That evening, Bernard, threw a party at his home for ten couples. All the men were survivors from Blechhammer. One of them was Shimon Shipper, who had been in all the camps with me, from Ottmuth to Buchenwald. I did not recognize him. He kept recalling incidents that had happened in the camps, how we shared food, and how very close we were.

I knew his stories were true because I remembered the details, but I couldn't place him. I kept looking at him to see if his young face would emerge. I know that I had two friends in Ottmuth, and that one was Georges, but the other was a complete blank. For months afterward, back in Los Angeles, Shimon's face kept appearing and tormenting me. I looked at his recent photo often. Who was this fat, middle-aged, bald-headed man? Try as I would, I could not remember what the young Shimon looked like. And then one day, finally it hit me. I could see us, Georges, Shimon, and me. Instantly, I called Shimon in Tel Aviv to tell him that at last it had all come back. What a relief it was. How wonderful to have found him again after all those years, and to know he had survived.

The morning after Bernard's party, I flew to Paris, happy to have gone to Israel, to have discovered that great country, and to have seen my old friends the Fogiel brothers, Shimon, Lou, and Hélène. Before leaving Israel, I phoned Natalie and told her that I was going to stay in Paris for a week. I needed some time to recuperate.

In Paris, I found out about the letter I had sent to my brother

Jacques from the cattle train. As with Shimon, it was a complete blank. I had forgotten writing anything at all. I couldn't believe that the letter had been written with such hope and courage, and that three days later, my parents would go to their deaths along with 698 selected that day. When my brother had wanted to give me the letter quite a few years before, my sister Madeleine had said, "Don't do that. He doesn't talk about his past. Leave him alone. Don't show it to him. Obviously he doesn't want to be reminded." All of my sisters had copies of the letter, and none of them had mentioned it to me until 1981.

Now, reading the Xerox copy of that letter, which Madeleine gave me, I was so emotionally drained from the trip to Israel, my feelings still raw, I could not finish it. Though I tried to control myself, I began to cry. I was crying for the sixteen-year-old kid and his family, seeing that sealed cattle train, hearing the moans of the people, smelling the awful stench.

I would say that 90 percent of survivors did not want to talk about the years they spent in concentration camps. If asked about it, they would simply answer, "Yes, we were in camps." Some individuals may have talked deeply with whom they were intimate. I would read books and see movies on the subject, mostly to check their authenticity, and I would get tearful, but never as emotionally taken as I was when I went to the World Gathering in Israel. Back in the States, my emotions were still fragile. It took me a while to get hold of myself, and return to my normal way of not feeling self pity.

In the early '90s, after the immense worldwide success of the movie *Schindler's List,* Steven Spielberg was asked by many Holocaust survivors to make a film about their lives. That gave him the idea to organize The Shoah Foundation, in order to give the survivors the opportunity to tell their testimonies on video tape for posterity. My friend Renée Firestone, a survivor from Hungary, who, since 1977 joined The Simon Wiesenthal Center as a volunteer and never stops giving lectures on the subject, urged me to join The Shoah Foundation, which I did. First of all, I gave my own testimony, then I became an interviewer and went all over California to tape other survivors' stories. Also, a few of us, including my friend Renée, got involved with "quality assurance." We watched testimonies from all over the world and made sure that interviewers were doing the proper job guiding the survivors to tell their sad and horrendous stories. It was emotionally exhausting but extremely important. The Shoah Foundation now has these tremendous archives that will help, I hope, to make the world a better one. I take off my hat to Steven Spielberg for having started this gigantic project, and to everybody associated with The Shoah Foundation.

I am very proud to be Jewish. It really makes me want to teach people about the Holocaust, so that history will not be repeated. The letters I receive from students, teachers, and school principals are gratifying. They let me know that I'm not wasting my time or energy.

December 19, 1983
Skokie, Illinois

Dear Mr. Clary:

On Monday, December 12 you spoke at Niles North in Skokie. The day after your visit I instructed my Spanish students to reflect on your presentation and to put their thoughts down on paper. Enclosed herein are the results. I'm certain that you will find them as moving as I did.

You touched a sensitive note in these children and raised their consciousness. Your visit provoked an animated discussion on hatred, racism, genocide and war. It was like a torrent unleashed. You would have been gratified to know what you have accomplished. It is for that reason that I am sharing their intimate thoughts with you. I have asked their permission to do so and they unhesitatingly gave it. You should also know that I count among my students Jews, Gentiles, Indians, Blacks, Koreans, and Hispanics. It mattered not. They all understood your meaning.

Yours is such an important mission. Like a teacher, you can influence hundreds of children in your life. There is no greater reward. C'est pour ça que vous avez survécu, Monsieur Clary. (It is for that that you have survived, Mr. Clary).

Yours most respectfully,

Marla Cowan

POSTSCRIPT

Today, in the year 2000, I enjoy my semiretired life, being with friends; my granddaughters Kimberly and Stephanie and their husbands; my granddaughter Jesse; and my great-grandchildren, Ryan and Gillian. It also gives me tremendous satisfaction to paint and put out new CDs every single year.

The only very sad thing is that on December 11, 1997, my wife Natalie died. She was, for forty-seven years, my best friend, companion, and lover—my pillar of strength. I miss her.

FILMOGRAPHY

1951 *Ten Tall Men*
      The Thief of Damascus
1954 *New Faces of 1952*
1963 *A New Kind of Love*
1975 *The Hindenburg*
1982 *Remembrance of Love*

STAGE CREDITS

1952	*New Faces of 1952*
1955	*Seventh Heaven*
1959	*Monsieur Lautrec*
1961	*La Plume de ma Tante*
1963–64	*Around the World in Eighty Days*
1974	*Sugar*
1984	*Cabaret*
1986	*Irma La Douce*
circa 1990	*Around the World in Eighty Days*

Television Performances

Ed Wynn (1950)
Al Jarvis (circa 1950)
Colgate Comedy Hour (1952)
Patti Page
This Is Show Business
Pantomime Quiz (1954–57)
New Faces (Play of the Week) (1960)
Stump the Stars (1963)
Hogan's Heroes (1965–71)
What's My Line (1971/1973)
Days of Our Lives (1972–87)
The Young and the Restless (1973–74)
The Bold and the Beautiful (1989–91)
Masquerade (1984)
A Conversation with Robert Clary (1989–92)

DISCOGRAPHY

Bluechip 102 (78)
Hollywood Bowl/Slip Around and Do it In My Dreams Tonight

King 4262 (78)
Johnny Get Your Girl/Put Your Shoes on, Lucy

Capitol 702 (78)
Cecilia/Give Me a Little Kiss

Capitol 803 (78)
C'est si Bon/Do It Again

Capitol 891 (78)
Alouette/You Must Have Been a Beautiful Baby

Capitol 972 (78)
Put on an Old Pair of Shoes/Louise

RCA Victor (LP)
New Faces of 1952 (cast album) LOC 1008

Epic (LP)
Meet Robert Clary LN 3171
Hooray for Love LN 3281

Epic (45s)
I'm in Love with Me/Bring Me a Bluebird 5-9128
There Is No Cure for L'amour/Hotter 'n' a Pistol 5-9142
Merry-Go-Round/Heart of Paris 5-9157

Decca (LP)
Seventh Heaven (cast album) DL 9001

Mercury (LP)
Gigi SR 60042
The Night They Invented Champagne/She Is Not Thinking of Me
71260

Atlantic (LP)
Lives It Up at the Playboy Club SD 8053

Sunset (LP)
Hogan's Heroes SUS 5137

MCA (LP)
The Hindenburg 2090

OC (CD) OriginalCastRecords.com (1-888-627-3993)
Sings at the Jazz Bakery 9799
Sings Rodgers & Hart, Johnny Mercer 9770
Sings Irving Berlin & Yip Harburg 8806
Sings Ira Gershwin & Jerome Kern 8714
Louis Lebeau Remembers Cole Porter Not Stephen Sondheim 2101
Sings Alan Jay Lerner & Frank Loesser 6006

COLLECTABLES (CD) (1-800-446-8426)
Meet Robert Clary/Hooray for Love 7408

Researched by Brian Gari

website: www.RobertClary.com

OTHER TITLES OF INTEREST

BETTY GARRETT AND OTHER SONGS
A Life on Stage and Screen
Betty Garrett with Ron Rapoport
306 pp., 52 b/w photos
1-56833-098-7 (cloth); 1-56833-133-9 (paperback)
$23.95 (cloth); $18.95 (paperback)
Madison Books

LON CHANEY
The Man behind the Thousand Faces
Michael F. Blake
408 pp., 110 b/w photos
1-879511-09-6
$19.95
Madison Books

CLARA BOW
Runnin' Wild
David Stenn
with a new filmography
368 pp., 27 b/w photos
0-8154-1025-5
$19.95
Cooper Square Press

MY STORY
Marilyn Monroe
Coauthored by Ben Hecht
New introduction by Andrea Dworkin
176 pp., 14 b/w & 4 color photos
0-8154-1102-2
$22.95 cloth
Cooper Square Press

MY LIFE IS IN YOUR HANDS & TAKE MY LIFE
The Autobiographies of Eddie Cantor
Eddie Cantor with David Freedman / Jane Kesner Ardmore
Foreword by Will Rogers
New introduction by Leonard Maltin
650 pp., 63 b/w photos
0-8154-1057-3
$25.95
Cooper Square Press

A SILENT SIREN SONG
The Aitken Brothers' Hollywood Odyssey, 1905–1926
Al P. Nelson and Mel R. Jones
288 pp., 42 b/w photos
0-8154-1069-7
$25.95 cloth
Cooper Square Press

FRANCOIS TRUFFAUT
Correspondence, 1945–1984
Edited by Gilles Jacob and Claude de Givray
Foreword by Jean-Luc Godard
608 pp., 81 b/w photos, drawings, and facsimiles
0-8154-1024-7
$24.95
Cooper Square Press

LOU'S ON FIRST
A Biography of Lou Costello
Chris Costello with Raymond Strait
288 pp., 31 b/w photos
0-8154-1073-2
$17.95
Cooper Square Press

BLUE ANGEL
The Life of Marlene Dietrich
Donald Spoto
376 pp., 57 b/w photos
0-8154-1061-1
$18.95
Cooper Square Press

LAURENCE OLIVIER
A Biography
Donald Spoto
528 pp., 110 b/w photos
0-8154-1146-4
$21.95
Cooper Square Press

REBEL
The Life and Legend of James Dean
Donald Spoto
352 pp., 41 b/w illustrations
0-8154-1071-9
$18.95
Cooper Square Press

GARY COOPER
American Hero
Jeffrey Meyers
404 pp., 32 b/w photos
0-8154-1140-5
$18.95
Cooper Square Press

CONVERSATIONS WITH BRANDO
Lawrence Grobel
With a new afterword
238 pp., 17 b/w photos
0-8154-1014-X
$15.95
Cooper Square Press

THE HUSTONS
The Life and Times of a Hollywood Dynasty
Lawrence Grobel
Updated Edition
872 pp., 61 b/w photos
0-8154-1026-3
$29.95
Cooper Square Press

FILM CULTURE READER
Edited by P. Adams Sitney
464 pp., 80 b/w photos
0-8154-1101-4
$19.95
Cooper Square Press

Available at bookstores; or call 1-800-462-6420

MADISON BOOKS / COOPER SQUARE PRESS /
MADISON BOOKS / VESTAL PRESS
150 Fifth Avenue
Suite 817
New York, NY 10011